Religious Language, Meaning, and Use

Also available from Bloomsbury

Free Will and God's Universal Causality, by W. Matthews Grant
Gesturing toward Reality, edited by Robert K. Bolger and Scott Korb
God, Existence, and Fictional Objects, by John-Mark L. Miravalle
The Maturing of Monotheism, by Garth Hallett

Religious Language, Meaning, and Use

The God Who Is Not There

Robert K. Bolger and Robert C. Coburn

BLOOMSBURY ACADEMIC
LONDON • NEW YORK • OXFORD • NEW DELHI • SYDNEY

BLOOMSBURY ACADEMIC
Bloomsbury Publishing Plc
50 Bedford Square, London, WC1B 3DP, UK
1385 Broadway, New York, NY 10018, USA
29 Earlsfort Terrace, Dublin 2, Ireland

BLOOMSBURY, BLOOMSBURY ACADEMIC and the Diana logo
are trademarks of Bloomsbury Publishing Plc

First published in Great Britain 2019
This paperback edition published in 2021

Copyright © Robert K. Bolger and Robert C. Coburn, 2019

Robert K. Bolger and Robert C. Coburn have asserted their right under the
Copyright, Designs and Patents Act, 1988, to be identified as Authors of this work.

For legal purposes the Acknowledgments on p. xiii constitute an
extension of this copyright page.

Cover design by Irene Martinez Costa
Cover image © David Jorre/Unsplash

All rights reserved. No part of this publication may be reproduced or transmitted
in any form or by any means, electronic or mechanical, including photocopying,
recording, or any information storage or retrieval system, without prior
permission in writing from the publishers.

Bloomsbury Publishing Plc does not have any control over, or responsibility for,
any third-party websites referred to or in this book. All internet addresses given
in this book were correct at the time of going to press. The author and publisher
regret any inconvenience caused if addresses have changed or sites have ceased
to exist, but can accept no responsibility for any such changes.

A catalogue record for this book is available from the British Library.

A catalog record for this book is available from the Library of Congress.

ISBN:		
	HB:	978-1-3500-5968-9
	PB:	978-1-3502-4451-1
	ePDF:	978-1-3500-5969-6
	eBook:	978-1-3500-5970-2

Typeset by Integra Software Services Pvt. Ltd.

To find out more about our authors and books visit www.bloomsbury.com
and sign up for our newsletters.

For Ron and Bonnie Bruce, empirical proof for the existence of wonderful in-laws.
In memory of
Lynne Rudder Baker (1944–2017) and Robert C. Coburn (1930–2018)

Contents

Preface	viii
Acknowledgments	xiii
Part One Idolatry, Faith, and Agape	1
Introduction to Part One	3
1 Dawkins, Idolatry, and the God Who Is Not There	7
2 Transcendence, Faith, and Fideism	29
3 Picturing a Religious Form of Life	65
4 Truth Pluralism: On Criteria and Religious Belief	99
5 It's All about the Neighbor: Agape and the Religious Life	133
Part Two "There—Like Our Life": Religious Practice without Metaphysics	165
Introduction to Part Two	167
6 The Church from without and from Within	169
7 The Turning World	177
8 Markel's Paradoxes	185
9 Laughter, Love, and Christian Living	191
10 Blind as a Bat	201
11 Models and Mentors	207
Notes	214
Bibliography	237
Index	247

Preface

This book was born out of a friendship between myself (Robert Bolger) and my one-time philosophy professor Robert Coburn. While, in some philosophical sense, its genesis could be traced back to the day we met, it actually developed over many years of discussion on numerous topics, discussion which, while crossing many academic fields and involving many literary genres, in some way or another, always swung back around to religion. As much as anything, though, this work is the product of old-fashioned philosophical dialogue. It displays the contemporary role that philosophy still plays in helping us nurture deep friendship while discussing issues about how to best live life. While it is often thought that the philosopher sits alone, thinks really hard, and then publishes something nominally interesting (something only the chosen few will ever read), it may just be that philosophy is best seen as a team sport, a way of life, something that cannot be successfully done alone but which requires the presence of others, hopefully friends.

Professor Robert Coburn ("Bob") had a long and illustrious philosophical career at several colleges and universities but spent more than thirty years teaching at the University of Washington in Seattle (where he began teaching in 1971). His publications span a wide variety of areas in philosophy, including metaphysics, ethics, philosophy of religion, and epistemology. His book on metaphysics (*The Strangeness of the Ordinary*) was well received and contains one of the best chapters on the relationship between the life of faith and metaphysics that I have ever read. Due to some of his early papers on Wittgenstein and religion, Kai Nielson labeled Coburn as one of the infamous "Wittgensteinian Fideists" (a label that Coburn consistently rejected). Coburn's thinking and writing ultimately proved far too broad, subtle, and complex to fit into any such label.

While I have never read *Tuesdays with Morrie*, I always had the feeling that the friendship I had with Robert Coburn had a quality that I imagined must have existed between Mitch Albom and Morrie (with philosophy rather than journalism being the academic field that bring the two individuals together). As an older undergraduate philosophy student at the University of Washington, I found in Coburn a philosophical mentor and a kindred spirit. Bob not only understood my interest in and struggles with religious belief (Coburn was an ordained Methodist minister, as is my wife) but also understood and accepted my semi-neurotic fear of death that I developed in childhood and carry with me, in varying degrees, to this day. (Coburn once told me that he thought my philosophical brother was Miguel de Unamuno.) I took as many classes from Bob as possible, including an independent study on Wittgenstein that he taught to a class of two (the other member of that class is today a wonderful philosopher working at a major university). Many of our discussions after class took place at the campus museum's coffee shop—a charming little room with wood-paneled walls—where we would drink tea, discuss class, and talk about various aspects of life. I left the University of Washington for graduate school at Umass/Amherst before transferring to Union Theological Seminary and then heading to Claremont Graduate University to get a Ph.D. in Philosophy of Religion and Theology, studying Wittgenstein and Religion with D.Z. Phillips.

In 2005, Lara (who is now my wife) and I moved to Seattle. It was at this time that I reconnected with Bob and sat in on some of the last classes that he taught at the University of Washington before he retired. After a year, Lara and I moved to San Diego for two years, planned our wedding, and invited Bob and his wife to Claremont to celebrate with us (at the reception we sat Bob and his wife with David Foster Wallace).

In 2008, we moved back to Seattle, and it was at this time that Bob and I made Saturdays our day to meet at the same coffee house where we spent so many days during my time as one of his students (this was my *Saturdays with Bob*). For several years, we would separately read the same book during the week and then get together on Saturday to have our own two-person book club. Initially, we discussed contextualism in epistemology and read Paul Tillich's *Systematic Theology Volume I*. Our reading was never systematic, but rather usually involved one of us suggesting something and the other either agreeing with or vetoing the suggestion. We also read such things as Brian Greene's popular books on physics, Frederick Buechner's fiction, David Foster Wallace's nonfiction, Lynne Rudder Baker on the first-person perspective, Rudolf Otto's *The Idea of the Holy*, and Bill Bryson's *A Short History of Nearly Everything*. Coburn, who loved reading popular psychology, introduced me to David Eagleman's *Incognito*. Among many other books and topics that I cannot even recall, we also spent almost two years reading and re-reading Mark Johnston's books *Saving God* and *Surviving Death*. It was the Johnston books that spawned a study of J.J. Valberg's book *Dream, Death and the Self*, a book I found incredibly difficult but which Bob found simply wonderful.

As the years went on, Bob quit driving, so we met at his house. After a while, Bob, who had learned watercolor painting from his wife, began to teach me to paint, and our visits would alternate between Saturdays spent chatting and Saturdays reserved for painting. One of Coburn's many paintings was used as the cover of the book I edited with Scott Korb on David Foster Wallace and philosophy (*Gesturing toward Reality*).

Over the years of discussion, common philosophical themes and interests began to appear between Bob and I, mainly centering on Wittgenstein's later philosophy, Paul Tillich's theology, a belief in the importance of apophatic theology and the utter mystery of God, and an agreement that Mark Johnston had some really important things to say about religion. I had asked Bob on several occasions if he ever thought about publishing anything new or if he wanted to publish a collection of some of his previously published writings on religion; however, it seemed that the days of Bob writing anything new were probably in the past and the topic didn't really come up again. On the ensuing Saturdays, Bob and I simply spent the time enjoying being around each other; this was so whether we were painting, reading philosophy, or discussing the latest movies or an interesting (often very lengthy) article that Bob inevitably found in *The New Yorker*. One day, Bob reminded me of the time I asked if he had anything on religion that he had not yet published. He then handed me a folder of papers and said that if I wanted to try and get them published, I could. The folder contained numerous previously published academic papers on a variety of topics in the philosophy of religion, but also many essays (really more like sermons) that had never been published but which I found incredibly interesting.

Part Two of this present book is composed of the unpublished essays that Bob gave me that day. All of Coburn's contributions to this book are written in the style of a sermon or as a sort of expository lesson on various topics pertinent to the Christian faith. These chapters, in both style and content, are unlike anything he has ever published before, given that he was committed mainly to publishing works that subscribed to the style of the modern-day analytic philosopher (although his interests extended far beyond the narrow scope of this branch of philosophy). Some may see these essays as simply charming little tales about certain aspects of the Christian life, but, to me, they represent an opportunity to show how faith enters our lives once philosophy has done its grammatical work. What makes Coburn's contributions to this book so interesting (and I believe important) is that they are works that have been developed in the mind of a powerful analytic philosopher who saw that the religious life was not just a matter of thinking the right things, reasoning in a prescribed way or believing the right facts. These chapters are ways of talking about religious faith that, at least for a time, places religious practice at the center forcing metaphysical speculators to join the chorus of background noise.

In publishing these essays, I recognized a unique opportunity to publish a work that represents, in literary form, a philosophical position about the life of faith. As I see it, the great mistake in much of philosophy of religion is its preoccupation with trying to defend a version of faith that need not be saved. There is more concern with the existence of God and God's relationship to science than there is a concern for what the concept "God" means or how that concept enters the believers life, influencing the way they see the world around them. Once philosophy does the grammatical work of sweeping away confused accounts of religious belief, then, and only then, will we be able to see the importance of writing about faith in a way that is philosophically powerful yet void of metaphysical speculation. Coburn and I both had an appreciation for seeing religion as a form of life (or a set of interrelated language games), and this book is an attempt to bring together in one volume, philosophical argumentation about the grammar of religious belief with a description of how religious language might be spoken of if we are freed from metaphysical presuppositions and the desire to turn faith into knowledge. While the chapters that make up Parts One and Two are different in their approach and style, they all seek to present a faith that is more about practice and life and far less about believing propositions about the supernatural. It is my hope that their relative consistency, even across stylistic differences, is obvious to the reader. In his wonderful little book, *With Heart and Mind: A Philosopher Looks at Nature Love and Death*, Richard Taylor writes, "We are continuously assailed by two voices. One gives the testimony of the intellect or reason, the other that of simply seeing; and while one might suppose that the two would coincide, they seldom do."[1] I believe in this volume heart and mind do actually coincide.

I am not exactly sure what David Foster Wallace meant when he used the phrase "every love story is a ghost story" or exactly what D.T. Max had in mind when he titled his wonderful biography of Wallace by the same phrase,[2] but I do know that every friendship (which of course is a form of love story) has an end either with the death of one of the friends or because of circumstances in life that cause such things to cease. In this sense, an ending turns the ever-present friend into a kind of ghost of times past, a visitor who pops in and out of our lives, reminding us of what was and, sometimes, imparting the present with wisdom. My friendship with Bob became an event ever frozen in memory when he passed away in July of 2018 at the age of 88. My last visit with Bob was on the evening he died and at a time when he was no longer consciously aware of his surroundings (in any obvious sense at least). That evening, alone with Bob in his room, I read Paul Tillich's sermon "You Are Accepted," talked about Tolstoy's *The Death of Ivan Ilyich*, and played, on my phone, a recording of Dylan Thomas reading "Do Not Go Gentle into That Good Night" (which Coburn would often recite to me by heart). I also repeated to him the words of Julian of Norwich that he would often quote to me when I spoke of my fear of death: "all shall be well, and all shall be well, and all manner of thing shall be well." I thanked Bob for sharing his wonderful life with me and thanked him for being my friend. Then I left. About an hour later, I got the call that Bob had died shortly after my visit.

In life, Robert C. Coburn taught me how to think, how to laugh, and how to love other people. In death, he showed me that in the end there is some sense to the idea that "All shall be well." What we agreed on philosophically was that the religious life was of enough importance to human existence that it should continue to be handled with care so that it is not presented as mere superstition or simple intellectual twaddle. This book represents an attempt to present the religious life as something that still deserves to be at the center of human existence.

Robert K. Bolger
Bothell, Washington
2019

Acknowledgments

I am grateful to Colleen Coalter, Becky Holland and Helen Saunders at Bloomsbury for seeing this book through from beginning to end. Thanks also to my patient editor Otis Houston, who read every word of this book more than once. Thanks to Patrick Horne, my long-time friend and philosophical discussion partner. Finally, I want to thank my wonderful wife, Lara, for the patience, love, and understanding that, I believe, only she is capable of offering to the degree she does. Without her, life would be a mere continuous string of days dampened by various shades of gray and ending in death. With her, color permeates life (even in Seattle).

Part One

Idolatry, Faith, and Agape

Robert K. Bolger

We have to believe in a God who is like the true God in everything, except that he does not exist, for we have not reached the point where God exists.

Simone Weil

Introduction to Part One

Wittgenstein once wrote, "Philosophy is a battle against the bewitchment of our intelligence by means of language."[1] Language can often get in the way of what it is we mean to say. This is not because what we want to say is something that does not involve using words, but rather because we are often fooled into thinking that our words must mean one thing when in fact, as they are used, they sometimes mean something else. This isn't quite our fault but rather part and parcel of the fact that sometimes language, which on its surface looks quite similar, turns out, on inspection, to be vastly different in meaning. Take for example the following:

1. After Easter, I hope to go to Pittsburgh.
2. After I die I hope to go to heaven.

If we are not careful we may think that something similar is being said in these two statements, but surely the way these two sentences get used is vastly different. Going to Pittsburgh and going to heaven cannot be that similar no matter how much you may love Pittsburgh. Furthermore, the only way to figure out the meaning of these sentences is to pay attention to how they actually get used in the context in which they find their home. The problem is that many of us do not pay enough attention to language use to see exactly what is being said, and this leads to a variety of conceptual confusions about meaning. This is most evident, for better or worse, when it comes to language about religious faith. Since religious language is unique in that it is attempting to both speak about the ineffable and relate the ineffable to the everyday, it is especially susceptible to confusion, as spiritual language gets indiscriminately mixed up with empirical statements that, at least sometimes, share a similar grammatical structure (compare: "The king of France exists" with "God exists"). If the confusion runs deep in religious practice and, if it gets ignored for too long, then the result is a confused version of faith that often loses its meaning upon close inspection.

The only way out of this conundrum is through it; that is, we must look at language use to see what may have gone wrong and then, in the midst of the muck and mire of life, find our way back to the place we thought we inhabited in the first place. In his book *Theology without Metaphysics: God, Language, and the Spirit of Recognition*, Kevin W. Hector states that one way to free ourselves from an unwarranted metaphysical picture is "by setting another alongside it."[2] But not just any picture will do, since, in dismantling one picture, we do not want to commit ourselves to another one that is just as flawed as the first. This is why Hector continues by saying that "it is crucial that the alternative picture treat the homesickness one may feel for that which has been left behind; otherwise, the therapy may not take."

Part One of this book is an attempt to practice philosophical therapy by pointing out a picture of religion that, while quite common, is also quite flawed. Yet in the very act of dismantling one picture of religion, I am attempting to present another one, one that not only avoids the pitfalls of a form of religious practice that I find idolatrous but also one that treats our homesickness by showing us the path from nonsense to faith. Whether this book succeeds in that endeavor will be up to the reader to judge.

Part One is also an attempt to trace the path from religious confusion to religious faith by first convincing the reader that there is a common and popular type of religious belief that they are better off without. However, to leave it there would be to end the therapeutic session before the real breakthrough occurs. That is why once a confused version of religious faith is exposed, there must be a real attempt to try and replace it with something that indeed fills the feeling of homesickness that comes with losing something we felt comfortable with. In the end, by bidding *adieu* to God, we are making room for faith, since the God we are bidding goodbye to was not God at all but rather a projection of who we wanted God to be. Here is how Part One will unfold.

Chapter 1 is an attempt to show how the God presented by Richard Dawkins is actually the God believed in by many religious folks. It then sets out to show how this anthropomorphic supernatural God gets used as part of a religious practice that is best seen as a version of religious idolatry. Yet, this sort of idolatry rests as much on the side of humans as it does on the side of the token God that is being worshipped. This is because at the heart of the practice of religious idolatry stands the human ego and its desire to prefer itself and its existence over others. In this sense, the human condition sets the stage for the very existence of an idolatrous faith. What we need is a different way to interpret the meaning of the religious life, one that takes the death of the ego seriously.

Chapter 2 begins to look at a new way of being religious by looking at various ways that the concept of transcendence shows up in religious faith. It is the beginning of a presentation of faith that seeks to avoid the pitfalls of metaphysics by seeing religion as a way of interpreting or assessing existence. These senses of transcendence lead naturally to questions about meaning, truth, and justification and whether these are the sort of concepts that can be applied to the religious form of life at all. With these questions lingering, the chapter ends with a discussion of fideism in order to show that while some uses of fideism are unwarranted and irrational, some uses are actually justified and natural since they are part and parcel of the grammar of religious language.

Chapter 3 is a discussion of how certain common religious doctrines (like forgiveness of sin, the promise of eternal life, and especially the claim that evil has an ultimate purpose) often get severed from the life of the believer, leading the believer to see faith mainly as a function of believing the right things and less a concern with living the right way. After looking at the various ways that these doctrines can become manifestations of idolatry, the chapter seeks to reframe the way we see religious doctrines by arguing for the shift from propositions to pictures. Chapter 3 then concludes with an account of how the doctrines that began the chapter can be reconceptualized to make room for authentic expressions of religious faith.

Chapter 4 seeks to offer an account of the truth of religious belief by spelling out the relationship between truth and criteria. It argues that one way to make sense of the plurality of truth claims is by accepting what has come to be called the "deflationary theory of truth." The chapter then extends the deflationary theory into the context of Wittgenstein's account of the importance of criteria, arguing that the best way to make sense of truth in religious practice is to link truth with meaning and then try to locate the criteria that represent genuine faith. The chapter then outlines the benefits to theology of certain forms of what I call "theological atheism" (using the work of Tillich, Weil, and Wittgenstein). It concludes with a brief discussion of the importance of agape as the main criterion for genuine religiosity.

Chapter 5 looks to expand on the importance of agape when it comes to faith by looking at this concept through the lens of stories using Tolstoy, Jesus, and Peter Singer as discussion partners. Impediments to agape, in the form of sin as separation, are then analyzed through the work of Paul Tillich. The chapter then seeks to argue, once again, that agape is at the center of any discussion of genuine religion, so much so that we may do well to take the claim that "Love is God" literally without reducing God to a mere emotion.

Although the content of each chapter is different, the lesson is the same; namely, that contemporary religion has lost its way in seeking to make the heart of faith a matter of believing rather than living. Religion, seen as a set of beliefs, creates a situation where faith is manipulated by the natural propensity for human selfishness, which uses faith to preserve the ego and to find an escape from a world that often seems harsh and cruel. In attempting to show that religion is best seen as a way of life committed to actualizing love for the neighbor rather than as a set of beliefs about supernatural facts, faith is freed from an inordinate selfishness that, in the end, bends our wills toward idolatry. Faith thrives only when the idol God is driven from the throne, allowing the believer's affections to be shifted from the skies to the earth. In this way, religion is turned from the God who is not there to the Other who is ever-present.

1

Dawkins, Idolatry, and the God Who Is Not There

In the beginning of his book *Foreskin's Lament: A Memoir*, Shalom Auslander shares a description of the God he met growing up in an orthodox Jewish family. Auslander writes:

> When I was a child, my parents and teachers told me about a man who was very strong. They told me he could destroy the whole world. They told me he could lift mountains. They told me he could part the sea. It was important to keep the man happy. When we obeyed what the man had commanded, the man liked us. He liked us so much that he killed anyone who didn't like us. But when we didn't obey what he had commanded, he didn't like us. He hated us. Some days he hated us so much, he killed us; other days, he let other people kill us. We call these days "holidays." On Purim, we remembered how the Persians tried to kill us. On Passover, we remembered how the Egyptians tried to kill us. On Chanukah, we remembered how the Greeks tried to kill us—Blessed is He, we prayed.[1]

Auslander's God is one that many of us recognize from our own religious upbringing. This God is often the one that we, like Auslander, met during our childhood religious instruction. We colored pictures that portrayed how God's power turned a few paltry fish and a bit of bread into a feast for 5,000 people, and we read quaint picture books illustrating God's mighty power to split the sea to save the Israelites and explaining Noah's daunting task of rescuing all the animals from the impending flood. We were told stories about how God brought Jesus back to life from the dead and took him up into the clouds like a rocket ship so that he could live forever with his Father (who was up there somewhere), and we were told that heaven (also up there somewhere) would be ours if we believed in Jesus.

My childhood God, again, much like Auslander's, was a big, powerful, invisible man (although I'm pretty sure mine was Catholic). He was a God who watched over all I did and who would ultimately sentence me to eternal torture, heavenly bliss, or, in middling circumstances when a clear decision could not be made, to a sort of divine waiting room that we Catholics called purgatory. Much of my young life was spent saying prayers to help my grandma and grandpa gain early release from purgatory as soon as was divinely allowed (I figured that Grandma and Grandpa were well-behaved enough that they probably didn't go straight to hell, but they probably were not quite virtuous enough to go straight to heaven, either). As far as I could tell, purgatory worked like the water balloon clown game at the carnival: once enough water was squirted into the clown's mouth, the balloon would pop. I assumed that some pre-set number of prayers would one day magically spring my grandparents from their purgatorial cell.

As a sort of invisible man, the God of my own childhood possessed human-like properties and the power to control and manipulate the natural world. This God was supernatural and anthropomorphic, a being who was in control of all that happened, lived really far away, and, although invisible, could hear and see everything. Now, since much that happened in the world seemed unfair to me, even as a child (e.g., my grandfather, whose release from purgatory I prayed for nightly, had died in an accidental fall down the steps when I was around eleven years old), and since there was always suffering and pain around, I came to understand that even though God *could* change things in the world, God often refrained from doing so for very good reasons, reasons which we, as mere humans, simply could not understand. God's ways were not our ways, we were taught, and all things worked together for good to those who love him, we were told. We could not control this God's love, so we tried desperately to earn it by being constantly diligent not to piss him off. While this God was quite powerful, he was much like us just imbued with a variety of superlatives. He was, to borrow Nietzsche's words, "human, all too human."

For the most part, as we mature in our religious lives, most of us pass through the anthropomorphic stage of faith and we enter a phase where the anthropomorphic God is either rejected outright, leading to atheism or agnosticism, or transformed into something more metaphorical, pragmatic, and/or mystical. But, culturally speaking, the big man in the sky has not gone quietly; this being resurfaces here and there and sometimes even digs into the cultural landscape, becoming part of the very background of religious faith. In many ways this is the situation today, an anthropomorphic God is often *the* God that many believers worship; this God is their buddy, their friend, and someone who knows them better than they know themselves.

The revived importance of the anthropomorphic God is best seen in the work of a group of individual writers referred to as the "New Atheists." It isn't just that these individuals have become atheistic cultural icons or sold innumerable books, both of which are true and which also speaks to the way they have hit on a cultural nerve; it is also the time and energy that many believers spend responding to the arguments of these individuals. We generally only spend our energy arguing for things we think worth preserving, and many Christian philosophers and theologians have shown, in their varied responses to the New Atheists, that the God that these individuals deny is one that they feel deserves to be protected from the ravages of nonexistence. In what follows, I want to focus on the God of Richard Dawkins in order to show that the anthropomorphic supernatural deity, a God, as I will argue, constructed out of fear and a desire for safety, is also the God that many today worship and revere as The Highest One. In doing so, these worshippers lay the foundation for a revival of religious idolatry with a being called "God" playing the role of the Golden Calf.

Dawkins Contra Religion

In his introduction to *The God Delusion*, Richard Dawkins quotes Einstein's view of religious belief with a sort of distant longing. Einstein writes, "To sense that behind anything that can be experienced there is a something that our mind cannot grasp and whose beauty and sublimity reaches us only indirectly and as a feeble reflection, this is religiousness. In this sense I am religious."[2] This is a nice statement of what belief in a non-anthropomorphic God might look like. There is a mystery to existence that is sublime and beautiful, a mystery which we can grasp, however feebly, upon reflection. Dawkins has two responses to Einstein. First, he writes, "In this sense [the sense that Einstein outlined] I too am religious, with the reservation that 'cannot grasp' does not have to mean *forever ungraspable*."[3] To say that something is "forever ungraspable" would, for Dawkins, be asking too much. It would go against his bent toward scientism, since it would be tantamount to admitting that there is something that science, in practice and in principle, cannot explain. Whatever "God" means for Dawkins, it must be something that can be grasped and explained (or at least be explainable in principle) within the discourse of science. What is needed, if religion is going to make any sense for Dawkins, is a scientific point of contact between God and the world. Of course, if that were the case, whatever it is we have on our hands would cease to be religion (but that is another matter).

Dawkins continues with his second response to Einstein, writing: "But I prefer not to call myself religious because it is misleading. It is destructively misleading because, for the vast majority of people, 'religion' implies 'supernatural.'"[4] Here Dawkins is on to something important, namely, the idea that on many accounts of what it means to be religious, there is an explicit (but sometimes implicit) acceptance of supernaturalism, that is, an acceptance of the idea that God supernaturally interacts in the world, on our behalf, through miracles—the manipulation or suspension of natural laws. Even though Einstein's account of religion was not supernaturalistic *per se*, Dawkins rightly notes that most accounts of religion are indeed committed to some form of supernaturalism, and this, for him, is too much to swallow in an age of science.

Both of the reasons that Dawkins offers for not calling himself religious draw attention to his belief that science is the only way to get at the truth about the nature of reality. Of course, this view is not only not a scientific claim; it is not even based on the practice of science at all. It is, rather, a metaphysical position about the nature of reality and realities ability to be grasped (ultimately) by a scientific description of things. While this topic is philosophically interesting, to focus on it now would get us off on a tangent.[5] Actually, I have little interest here in *why* Dawkins rejects religion and much more interest in *what* it is that Dawkins is rejecting. If we focus our gaze on just what it is that Dawkins rejects, rather than why he rejects it, then we can begin to see his arguments and criticisms in a whole new light. In fact, odd as it seems, Dawkins might just take on the role of something like an Old Testament prophet who is trying to call believers back to their first love and away from the worship of something unworthy of their fealty. But this is to get ahead of ourselves. First, we need to see more clearly what Dawkins has in mind when he says that religious belief entails a commitment to supernaturalism.

Dawkins and the Return of the Invisible Man

In *Saving God*, Mark Johnston writes that "Supernaturalism is belief in invisible spiritual agencies whose putative interventions would violate the laws of nature, at least as those laws are presently understood."[6] Compare this with Dawkins when he writes:

> A theist believes in a supernatural intelligence who, in addition to his main work of creating the universe in the first place, is still around to oversee and influence the subsequent fate of his initial creation. In many theistic belief systems, the

deity is intimately involved in human affairs. He answers prayers; forgives or punishes sins; intervenes in the world by performing miracles; frets about good and bad deeds and knows when we do them (or even *think* of doing them).[7]

This definition of a supernatural God suggests the need for a distinction to be made between "supernatural" and "supernaturalism." Supernatural, in its minimal sense, is the belief that something exists that transcends the natural order (i.e., the stuff described by science). Naturally, any God worth the title will indeed be thought of as "supernatural" in some sense of the word, even if it is thought of in partly immanent terms (such as in panentheism). Supernaturalism, on the other hand, entails (at least) three important points. First, it entails that God initially created and designed the world with a specific purpose and plan. This is why Dawkins defines the God hypothesis as the existence of "a superhuman, supernatural intelligence who deliberately designed and created the universe and everything in it including us."[8] The use of "deliberately" here assumes a divine plan of some sort was in place during (or "before") creation. On this account, Dawkins assumes, rightly I believe, that if God created and designed the world with a plan in mind, then we would expect the world to exhibit signs, within the creation, of this design. Second, supernaturalism is committed to an interactionist God who, through sheer act of will, intermingles with the world to bring about miraculous changes. These miracles happen as part of God's ultimate purpose, even though humans may not understand why they occur when they do. Lastly, supernaturalism entails that God be seen as a being who acts in some ways analogous to the way a person is said to act. That is, God is thought of in anthropomorphic terms and spoken of in anthropomorphic language. God has plans and desires, God acts to bring about certain purposes, God hears the prayers of believers, and God rewards and punishes peoples for the things they do (or fail to do). In all these ways (and more) God is spoken of in anthropomorphic terms.

Supernaturalism about God (as opposed to a supernatural God) amounts to the combination of divine interactionism with anthropomorphism. For brevity's sake, we can refer to this sort of belief in God as *supernatural theism*. This sort of theism can be summarized, following a definition Brian Davies offers, as a commitment to the following three propositions:

1. God is a person without a body [anthropomorphism].
2. God is an invisible agent with a succession of thoughts, beliefs, hopes, desires, and memories [anthropomorphism].
3. God differs from us since he lacks a body. He also differs from us since his knowledge and power are much greater than ours and since he can

intervene in the world so as to produce miracles [anthropomorphism + divine interactionism].⁹

Once we come to see that the God that Dawkins presents in *The God Delusion* is the God of supernatural theism, we also see the logic of his thinking of God as something that might, for all we know, conflict with science. This is because the God of supernatural theism is a God that enters into the scientific mix when believers use this being as a working hypothesis, a hypothesis which is often taken by believers to explain certain aspects of the world (or maybe the existence of the world as a whole). In 1992, long before *The God Delusion* was published, in a debate with the archbishop of York, Dawkins stated, "You can't escape the scientific implications of religion. A universe with a God would look quite different from a universe without one. A physics, a biology where there is a God is bound to look different. So the most basic claims of religion are scientific. Religion is a scientific theory."[10] On this account of things, since God causally created and continually interacts with the world—sometimes through miracles—God's signposts will (or should) be visible in what we observe. These signposts will be the sort of things that are visible in the natural world, things that science can, in principle, investigate. For Dawkins, God is a hypothetical explanation for the way the world is; but, of course, God is not the only hypothesis.

Dawkins, acting as a responsible scientist, posits a competing hypothesis for the explanation of all that we see around us, writing:

> In a universe of electrons and selfish genes, blind physical forces and genetic replication, some people are going to get hurt, other people are going to get lucky, and you won't find any rhyme or reason to it, nor any justice. The universe we observe has precisely the properties we should expect if there is, at bottom, no design, no purpose, no evil, no good, nothing but pointless indifference.[11]

A capricious world, which is the result of chance, time, and matter, is another possible way to explain reality (i.e., it is another hypothesis for why the world is as it is). In fact, on Dawkins's account, if we are honest when we look at the natural world, we will see that a world brought about by purely naturalistic means is a better explanation of the facts than a world brought about by the God of supernatural theism.

With two competing hypotheses in place, we could, in theory at least, turn to the evidence to see which one offers the best explanation for the empirical world. If the evidence of the natural world is what we would expect given supernatural theism, then the God hypothesis is a good one; if not, then God is, as Victor Stenger states, a "failed hypothesis."[12] If, on the other hand, the way the world appears is best explained by a naturalistic scientific explanation, then that would be the better hypothesis and the God hypothesis would be falsified. The point is that God, on this account, while meeting the requirements of supernatural theism, plays the role of an explanatory hypothesis. It is important to see here that Dawkins is not sneaking God into the mix of scientific inquiry, but rather defining God in such a way that God becomes a natural candidate to play the role of hypothetical *explanans*. If God is the sort of being that supernatural theism says God is, then seeking to explain the way the world is, based on God's plans and purposes, is quite natural and understandable.

Some have argued that Dawkins simply doesn't think deeply enough about theology and philosophy of religion. This has been where much of the criticism of Dawkins has been leveled. For example, in his review of *The God Delusion*, Terry Eagleton writes, "Imagine someone holding forth on biology whose only knowledge of the subject is the *Book of British Birds*, and you have a rough idea of what it feels like to read Richard Dawkins on theology."[13] Or, take Alvin Plantinga's scathing criticism:

> Now despite the fact that this book is mainly philosophy, Dawkins is not a philosopher (he's a biologist). Even taking this into account, however, much of the philosophy he purveys is at best jejune. You might say that some of his forays into philosophy are at best sophomoric, but that would be unfair to sophomores; the fact is (grade inflation aside), many of his arguments would receive a failing grade in a sophomore philosophy class.[14]

Of course, we could go on in this way for quite some time if we desired, but the arguments are usually quite similar. Generally, they point to the fact that Dawkins and his New Atheist pals are lacking in knowledge when it comes to the history of theology and philosophy of religion. Such ignorance on their part, so the argument continues, leads them to create spurious claims about religion that are either born out of their lack of theological knowledge or, worse, spun in a web of intellectual sloppiness. The gist of these criticisms is that Dawkins, by bringing God into the debate as a sort of scientific hypothesis, misses the *real* meaning of belief in God.

I think these arguments against Dawkins are all on the right track; Dawkins and his pals are certainly light on knowledge when it comes to theology and philosophy of religion, and, furthermore, to think of God as an explanatory hypothesis is indeed to ignore the way the concept gets used by many religious believers. The mistake made by those who criticize Dawkins, however, is that they want to act as if Dawkins does not have an audience at all; they talk of Dawkins as if he were preaching to a nonexistent choir or whistling in the dark of an empty church. But this is tragically not so. Dawkins has an audience and, for better or worse, the choir that he is preaching to (and debating with) is filled with his religiously oriented critics. They argue with Dawkins because his nonexistent God is their Savior and his supernatural man in the sky is their hope.

Dawkins's atheism receives the attention it does because supernatural theism is alive and well in both the pews and the lecture halls. Dawkins is atheistic about a concept of God that many, in the church and the academy, love and cherish. There are innumerable religious folk who believe that God is indeed the God described by supernatural theism. They take it as an obvious platitude that God is a being who created and designed the world and that this being, sometimes at least, supernaturally intervenes in the world to bring about certain changes. God, for them, is a "something" with supernatural powers who wipes away their sins when they "truly" believe, who allows suffering to exist in order to bring about a greater good, and who, someday, will usher them off to a wonderful place called heaven. This God hears their prayers and, sometimes, acts to intervene in order to make the miraculous occur as an answer to those prayers. Sometimes, though, the prayers go unanswered because God has a greater purpose. However the details are spelled out, there can be little doubt that many believers, generally (but not always) those of a more conservative bent, accept supernatural theism and live a religious life where their God is taken to be a powerful, loving person (without a body). It does no good to try and argue that Dawkins's arguments are irrelevant or miss the point since his detractors reveal their commitments by what they write. Furthermore, the general disdain for Dawkins among the "religious" shows that the God Dawkins attacks is one that holds some important place in their hearts and minds.

So Dawkins has his religious audience, and his atheism tends to mirror their theism. In his little essay "How to Be an Atheist," Denys Turner points out that "historically … atheisms have … been mirror-images of a theism; that they are recognizable from one another, because atheisms fall roughly into the same categories as the theisms they deny."[15] Pointing out Dawkins's philosophical audience is simply a matter of pointing out the way that some contemporary philosophers tend to define God. In order for Dawkins's atheism to be relevant, he must have something in common with his opponents. If his concept of God and his opponents' concept of God were radically different, then the best way to deal with Dawkins would be silence, ignoring him the way most of us ignore those who believe in a flat earth or astrology. Why respond to someone who is not addressing you? But, as I have been arguing, silence cannot be the response of many believers because, despite their denials, Dawkins's concept of God is their deity of choice.

Some of the biggest (or at least the most influential) names writing in philosophy of religion today tend to think of God as a sort of big man in the sky, albeit one who (necessarily) lacks a body. Richard Swinburne writes, "I take the proposition 'God exists' ... to be logically equivalent to 'there exists a person without a body (i.e. a spirit) who is eternal, is perfectly free, omnipotent, omniscient, perfectly good, and the creator of all things.'"[16] Compare this with Alvin Plantinga who states that "God is a person. But ..., unlike human persons, God is a person without a body. He acts, and acts in the world, as human beings do, but, unlike human beings, not by way of a body. Rather, God acts just by willing: he wills that things be a certain way, and they are that way."[17] John Hick even takes it as a test of ontological correctness whether or not one can admit that "in addition to all the many human consciousnesses there is another consciousness which is God."[18]

The God defended and believed in by the likes of Swinburne, Plantinga, and Hick represents a deification of human consciousness. Their God is pure consciousness with attributes, powers, and the ability to bring about change by the sheer act of thinking. Their God is a person purged of the restrictions of the body and imbued with infinite power. Ludwig Feuerbach noticed this theological trend long ago, writing, "The task of the modern era was the realization and humanization of God—the transformation and dissolution of theology into anthropology."[19] All of this is reminiscent of the God that William Watson describes in his poem "The Unknown God," writing, "A God of kindred seed and line; Man's giant shadow, hailed divine."[20]

It should be clear by now that Dawkins is surely not whistling in the dark; he is rather engaging a cultural religious obsession with supernatural theism, an obsession that is alive and well. If part of the job of the Hebrew prophet was to call people away from idol worship and back to the worship of the Highest One, then, as I stated above, it may just be that Dawkins should be praised as a sort of modern-day prophet. If a prophet is without honor in his own town, how much less will an atheist biologist be welcomed in by the church? Just like the prophets of old, Dawkins comes to let the supernatural theist know that his or her god is not God.

At this point, someone may well wonder what exactly is wrong with supernatural theism. Maybe the way forward is indeed to fight it out with Dawkins, defending supernatural theism through debates, publications, and intellectual discourse. It isn't, however, that there is anything wrong with supernatural theism *per se*, but religious beliefs do not exist *per se*. Religious beliefs garner meaning as they are incorporated and woven into the life of the believer. The believer's language about God gets intertwined with their life: their prayers, their acts of charity, their religious practices, and their interactions with others. The only path that will reveal conceptual confusion when it comes to supernatural theism is the path of grammatical investigation. That is, we must look at how supernatural theism gets used, how it shows up in religious life as a variety of beliefs and practices; only then can we make conceptual headway into exactly what is going on. My claim is that when we do look at some of the ways that the God of supernatural theism shows up in religious life, we will see that the result is a form of life that is more idolatrous than it is religious. It is idolatrous (and thus anti-religious) because it promotes a form of "religious" faith that turns the believer away from the Highest One and toward an Idol-God (or toward a version of our self that gets projected outward as "God"), a God who can be manipulated as a way of helping the believer turn away from the contingencies of life and turn toward a fantasy world created to help them avoid the "slings and arrows" of finitude. Religious faith, with supernatural theism at the center, tends to show up as a means of assuaging our fears and satisfying our own egos as we seek to escape the world that is and replace it with a world we wished were so. Supernatural theism creates an escape from reality by creating a faith where God exists in order to cater to our needs, it seeks to explain away evil and suffering so that life is not so damn painful, to offer us easy forgiveness from our sins so we can avoid the work of dealing with guilt, and to grant *us* life eternal. As Abraham Joshua Heschel writes:

> We often assume it is God we believe in, but in reality, it may be a symbol of personal interests that we dwell upon. We may assume that we feel drawn to God, but in reality, it may be a power within the world that is the object of our adoration. We may assume it is God we care for, but it may be our own ego we are concerned with. To examine our religious existence is, therefore, a task to be performed constantly.[21]

The God of Dawkins is simply a starting point, a hint or a clue to us that something has gone wrong in religion today. But it is only by offering a perspicuous representation of some of the uses of supernatural theism, and then showing how such uses perpetuate an idolatrous faith, that the full importance of Dawkins's arguments can be seen. The rest of this chapter will be an attempt to explain this sort of religious idolatry, pointing out its relationship to a life that is constantly turned inward and engrossed with a concern for self-preservation.

Idolatry and Religious Practice

In *Saving God*, Mark Johnston writes that idolatry, in the context of religion, is either "worshipping the wrong god, or worshipping the right God in the wrong way."[22] This two-pronged definition of idolatry is important since it points out that idolatry necessarily has a subject (i.e., the idolater) and an object (i.e., the idol). The problem is that this definition presents the idol and the idolater as if they are logically separable. That is, it appears that there are worshippers, and something called the "right God" and the "wrong God" to which worship is directed. What Johnston's definition lacks is the idea that, in fact, the rightness or wrongness of the *object* of worship (the "right" or the "wrong" God) is actually determined by the life of the worshipper and the way that the concept of God gets used in their religious practice. While God (or god) and worship can be separated linguistically, they are actually logically inseparable. Because of the importance this idea plays in our overall discussion of idolatry, this should be explained further.

When we think of idols as physical artifacts or objects in nature like a golden calf, the sun, or some other natural or graven image, it seems pretty easy to make sense of idolatry as "worshipping the wrong God." In these sorts of examples, we have the requisite subject who is the worshipper and an object that is worshipped, and we want to say that the idols are clearly unworthy of being worshipped since, as physical things, they localize (or locate) the infinite to a particular place. Johnston writes that "graven images or idols are human creations, and if they were embodiments of the god, then human craftsmen would have influence over when and where the god is embodied. So, the god embodied in the idol cannot be the Highest One, for no human being … could have influence over when and where the Highest One is embodied."[23] This sort of idolatry denies the absolute transcendence of God, trading transcendence for divine domestication. The worshipers may not believe that the idol itself *is* God, but they do believe that the idol embodies God such that God is compelled to "show up" when the idol is worshipped. Johnston writes, "The god is HERE, somehow contained where the idol is, and so can appreciate the proffered act of fealty made before the idol."[24]

The claim of idolatry, however, is not quite so simple, and this is the important logical point that needs to be made. There is nothing, no sticks, no stones, no sun or moon, no golden calf, and no god (or God), that is an idol *in and of itself.* Idols, like money, or flags, only come into existence when they are used in a certain way. Flags are only bits of material and money only bits of paper, but both take on new meaning (and a new identity) when they are used in specified ways by a community of individuals. Idols are the same way.

An object becomes an idol when a community of worshippers incorporate it (whatever *it* is) into a certain form of life, a form of life in which we are then (after the fact) able to identify the object of worship as an idol. This is important since it shows that idols only exist in relation to idol worshipers. They come to life when worshippers, by the way they live in light of their god, show that whatever it is they are worshipping, cannot be God. The meaning of "God" is seen in the life that the believer lives, and some lives negate the claim that it is God that is being worshipped. This negation, however, is tied to the kind of life the individual (or the community) lives; it is not simply a matter of looking to see what it is that is being worshipped. If someone is said to be worshipping the right God in the wrong way, what we are really saying is that they are not worshipping God at all. It makes no sense to think that we can separate the idea of the right object of worship from the act of worship itself. If someone's worship is deemed religiously acceptable (in some way), then what we are really saying is that they are worshipping the right God. There is no sense to be made of their having right worship aimed at the wrong God since the very concept of God is tied logically to the religious life, including the life of worship and praise (among other things). The religious life and the object of worship are logically inseparable. Peter Rollins recognizes this same point, writing that "Idolatry does not rest on the idea of the object itself but rather in the eye of the beholder. In other words, it is the way one engages with an object or idea that makes an idol an idol rather than some kind of property within it."[25] And, similarly, Simone Weil writes, "The value of a religious or, more generally, a spiritual way of life is appreciated by the amount of illumination thrown upon the things of this world. Earthly things are the criterion of spiritual things."[26] Our religious language, including our language about who God is, only has a sense in relation to the sort of life the believer lives under the gaze of his or her God.

Recognizing this point means that identifying idolatry may not be as easy as simply looking to see what object is being worshipped, even if the object is a golden calf, the sun, or a statue of an ancestor. It may be that the worshippers are only using these physical objects as a representation of the transcendent. Maybe the object is something to focus their minds on, something like a meditation mantra, or maybe the physical object is playing the role of an icon, such as those used in the Orthodox Church. In this case, the worshipper's thoughts and attention are carried past the object and directed to something ineffable and mysterious.[27] The point is that whether an object of worship is an idol or not depends on the worshipper's life and actions; it depends on how the concept of "idol" is used.

This logical point about idols applies not only to objects that are visible but to concepts as well. If a concept of God is constructed, but somehow misses the mark of capturing true divinity, then, again, what we get is a sort of linguistic golden calf, or what Peter Rollins calls a "conceptual idol."[28] Even in these sorts of cases, however, the only way to determine if the concept is being used in an idolatrous way is to look to the life of the worshippers and see the role the concept plays in their religious practice. A concept of "God" "missing the mark" simply means that the concept is incorporated into a "religious" form of life in such a way that the fruits of such a life are—in certain ways that will be spelled out shortly—irreligious. This point will be of utmost importance when we look, in the chapters that follow, at how religious doctrines can take on an idolatrous tone.

Even though Johnston's initial definition of idolatry that we saw above doesn't seem to capture the necessary connection between religious practice and idolatry, Johnston does pick up on it in other places in *Saving God*. In fact, as we will see, Johnston gives us just what we need; that is, he offers a way of showing just when the use of the concept of God reveals a sort of religious idolatry. This can be seen most clearly when Johnston discusses the distinction between salvation and spiritual materialism.

Salvation and Selfishness

Spiritual materialism, as Johnston defines it, is a means of turning the spiritual life into a self-seeking commodity. The "religious seeker" uses a simulacrum of religious practice as a way of achieving some sort of personal gain. Johnston writes that "'Spiritual Materialism' is a term from the sixties, used then to denote the consumerist attitude of self-described 'seekers' who were always on the lookout for the latest, most fashionable guru or meditation technique or method of self-transformation."[29] As Johnston sees it, the main problem with those who participate in spiritual materialism is the lack of any sort of inner transformation (other than a need to fulfill their own egoistic desires). They remain selfish, even in the midst of their spiritual seeking. "The implied criticism," Johnston writes, "was that the spiritual 'materialistic' seekers had undergone no fundamental change in their orientation to life but had simply taken up the hobby of self-improvement, with its endless opportunities for self-worship."[30]

The spiritual materialist remains one who thinks primarily of themselves—how they might, through spiritual practices of various sorts, attain more success, more power, more money. The sinister aspect of spiritual materialism is that all of this self-seeking behavior is disguised and shrouded in the cloak of spiritual language, making the whole charade a sort of theological ruse. The link between spiritual materialism and idolatry is seen in the fact that the God worshipped by the spiritual materialist is a God whose will can be swayed for self-gain. In other words, spiritual practice is directed toward a supernatural God who can be manipulated to serve the worshipper rather than the worshipper being transformed to serve God by serving others. God, in this sense, becomes an idol. The divine idol is identified as such by being the object of worship of those whose goal is to fulfill their own desires, even though this goal is cloaked in religious language. Johnston writes that "The spiritual materialist is inauthentic in his engagement with religion, and with his spiritual quest or search precisely because he simply turns his ordinary unredeemed desires toward some supposedly spiritual realm. However intense his experiences, they do not deepen in him the theological virtues that constitute the change of orientation that makes for a new life."[31]

Spiritual materialism is the flip-side of salvation, but in order to understand Johnston's account of salvation, it is important to understand what he takes the purpose of religion to be. Johnston writes:

> Genuine or true religion must be genuinely directed upon what religion is for. There are certain large-scale structural defects in human life that no amount of psychological adjustment or practical success can free us from. These include arbitrary suffering, aging (once it has reached the corrosive stage), our profound ignorance of our condition, the isolation of ordinary self-involvement, the vulnerability of everything we cherish to time and chance, and, finally, to untimely death ... The religious or redeemed life is a form of life in which we are reconciled to the large-scale defects of ordinary life.[32]

Being reconciled to the facts entailed by human finitude does not mean that the vicissitudes of life disappear; rather, to be reconciled to these large-scale structural defects is to find "a way to go on, keeping faith in the importance of goodness, and an openness to love."[33]

It is important here to understand that Johnston does not believe we can be released from the effects of these "large-scale structural defects" simply by making some sort of "psychological adjustment" to our current, unredeemed, way of living. The reconciliation (or salvation) occurs *not* when we believe the right things, but when our view of life is transformed in such a way that the structural defects are not just something we tolerate but rather something we accept as part of a world where love and goodness endure.

The transformation necessary for salvation to occur involves, *contra* spiritual materialism, overcoming our natural tendency to preference ourselves and our own needs over the needs of others. Salvation involves a decentering that occurs when we realize our wants do not stand alone at the moral center of the universe. Spiritual materialists constantly place themselves in the center of existence, so the large-scale structural defects, which threaten all of us in one way or another, become, for them, a threat to their very world. This is because the world of the egotistical individual begins and ends at the borders of their own flesh. On Johnston's account of salvation, an authentic religious form of life allows for the development of a transformed perspective where we are not situated at the center but content to take our place as one among many. As we become less important (at least in our own eyes), the importance of the world expands. When the transformation from self-centered to other-centered occurs, there is a sense of gratitude for life as a whole, a caring for others, and a belief that goodness and love can endure the travails that come with finite existence. D.Z. Phillips summarizes the sort of religious perspective I have in mind, writing:

> in recognizing that life itself is a gift, and that the ways things go in it are a grace, the believer dies to the "I" that sees itself at the centre of the universe. In fatalism, there is acceptance of the inevitable, but no love of it. In the religious response I am talking of, there is a requirement to love the fact that God has given life with its contingencies to human beings. This love is gratitude for existence.[34]

In religious terms, we might call this "dying to self" and seeking to "love our neighbor as ourselves." We develop an agapistic love for others that was impossible when self-concern ruled our life. Johnston describes the situation in the following manner: "There is a massive consensus, across the major religions, that salvation crucially requires overcoming the centripetal force of self-involvement, in order to orient one's life around reality and the real needs of human beings as such."[35] Salvation comes into view as the believers' life is oriented away from themselves and toward their neighbor.

Naturally, the notion of the selfless love of others (*agape*) combined with a form of egoless humility has always been a theme at the center of genuine religious faith. In his book *The Strangeness of the Ordinary*, Robert Coburn writes, "In short, their [the believers] behavior exhibits the kind of orientation depicted by the picture of Christ in the Gospels, the orientation of the self-sacrificing healer of the physical and spiritual ailments of others."[36] Abraham Joshua Heschel writes, "For the essence and greatness of man do not lie in his ability to please his ego, to satisfy his needs, but rather in his ability to stand above his ego, to ignore his own needs; to sacrifice his own interests for the sake of the holy."[37] Finally, D.Z. Phillips adds:

> To follow Christ is to follow him in his Passion. In worship, this means following Christ in the Eucharist. It means wanting to love God in the sense of wanting to be a vehicle for his self-less compassion but realizing that whether this wish is granted itself depends on grace. It is important to recognize that for much of our lives we do not want this. Instead, the "I" intrudes or dominates us in such a way that it makes love of God impossible.[38]

This discussion allows us to expand the concept of idolatry to include the fact that an idolatrous life is a life that is habitually lived with our ego at the center. By serving our own self-interests, we displace the divine as we refuse to turn from our own egos to serve those in need. Consider Johnston again: "Idolatry is, then, invariably the attempt to evade or ignore the demanding core of true religion: radical self-abandonment to the Divine as manifested in the turn toward others and toward objective reality."[39] Contemporary idolatry is intimately involved with a selfish and self-centered attitude toward life. The divine idol shows up when the concerns of the so-called religious individual are turned inward toward the self. The divine gets manipulated and used for selfish (often psychological) gain; God is a way of avoiding the ills of life. However, not just any idol will do when it comes to the practice of spiritual materialism, for in order for the practice of religion to satisfy the fancies of the ego, the divine idol must be a being whose will can be twisted and bent so as to match the desires of the worshipper. If life's vicissitudes, seen as its "structural defects," must be managed and controlled, then what better way is there to control them than by avoiding their sting altogether? God, as an idol, gets used, as a sort of commodity, in order to purchase peace of mind on the cheap. This is similar to something Jeffery Pugh writes about Bonhoeffer's later theology. Pugh writes, "Bonhoeffer's analysis of religion addressed the fact that those anxious souls who used the religion of Christianity in its transcendental clothing to answer questions about the unknown dimensions of life and death constructed a religious idol."[40]

In some ways we are back where we started in that the idol is linked, logically, to the life of the "worshipper" who preferences his or her own anxious desires over the needs of others. The divine idol that is revealed, however, is one that, of necessity, must be malleable so our ways can become its ways and our desires its desires. This sort of deity is the God of Dawkins and the God of supernatural theists, since that God is utterly anthropomorphic. An anthropomorphic God is a God who can, and does, easily take on the character of the humans who are doing the worshipping. To quote Ludwig Feuerbach, "The divine being is nothing else than the human being, or, rather, the human nature purified, freed from the limits of the individual man, made objective—i.e., contemplated and revered as another, a distinct being."[41] It is the anthropomorphic God of Dawkins (and his religious kin folk) that is best suited to be the token God of the idolatrous life since this God is close at hand, powerful, and always there to help in our time of need—or at least explain why help is not immediately forthcoming.

In the next two chapters we will look at how specific Christian doctrines can be manipulated and used as part of the practice of spiritual materialism, and then we will discuss possible ways of overcoming the natural tendency to live an idolatrous life. However, before ending our discussion here, it is important to show more clearly how spiritual materialism rests on a certain cognitive domestication of the divine.

Idolatry and Supernatural Theism: Domesticating the Divine

In his little essay, entitled "The Religious Significance of Atheism," Paul Ricoeur claims that the two poles of religious feeling, poles which we must overcome if we are to move from the mere practice of religion to something more akin to faith or trust, are "the fear of punishment and the desire for protection."[42] No one likes to be punished, especially eternally, and being protected from harm also seems quite natural. But, when these sorts of human concerns compel one to participate in a religious form of life where God can be manipulated and molded in a way that helps us escape reality and serve our own egos, idolatry quickly ensues. Humans attempt to construct—or participate in—an idolatrous religious belief system where God is chiefly seen as our helper—a sort of buddy, or divine protector, created to keep us from harm, help us make utilitarian sense of suffering, and save us from the possibility of ultimate nonexistence. It isn't that existential concerns are not valid reasons to believe in God (I will argue later that these concerns are at the heart of authentic religious practice); it is just that when supernatural theism is used as an escape route from these existentially traumatic aspects of existence, we are a long way from true religion.

As we have already seen, the common theme that runs through an idolatrous faith is the idea that religion is primarily about and for us. It is our skin we desire to save, so we participate in a religious belief system that serves to assuage our fears by means of an escape from the nastiness of life. Religion, on this account, is mere wish fulfillment, to use Freud's language, or inauthenticity, to borrow from

Sartre, or maybe it is anthropology sent heavenward, as Feuerbach thought. We do not just construct a God in our image, but one much more powerful than us, one who is able to help us by supernaturally intervening on *our* behalf. We come to believe in the existence of a God who can protect us and, if we believe the right things, will save us from ultimate punishment. Of course, if we are going to believe in a God who is there for us, we must have some pretty clear ideas about who this God is and what this God desires. Yet, if the concept of God is constructed out of a fear of life, the result will be a trading of transcendence and mystery in favor of a God who is predictable, knowable, and domesticated.

To domesticate something is to tame it in such a way that it becomes something safe to have around. But more than that, it means to tame something so that it becomes your ally and friend, one who prefers you and your ways over other possibilities. Therefore, in some way, idolatry requires that we domesticate God so that our ways become God's ways, or, at least, so that God's ways become the sort of things that are knowable to us so that we can have confidence that God's ways favor us. Johnston describes the domestication of God as follows: "Instead of God's appearing as the wholly other, the numinous One who transcends anything that we can master by way of our own efforts, he appears as a potential patron, a powerful ally whom we might win over to our side."[43]

If the idolater does not domesticate God, then there is the risk God may have different plans than us or that God's ways may be shrouded in mystery. This may mean that God's greatest desire is not to simply save our ass from harm or our souls from hell. Too much mystery and our attempts at domestication can be disastrous (as those who have been attacked by their wild animal "pets," such as tigers and monkeys, can attest).

To domesticate God, then, is to claim that we have knowledge about who God is and what God desires. Furthermore, it is to claim that we have discovered that God's ways favor us in some important manner. But there seems to be a certain amount of epistemological hubris in thinking we can know the mind of God. While humans are pretty good at describing the middle-sized empirical objects that pepper our world, or describing the sort of things discovered by the use of scientific instruments, what confidence can we have that we are getting it right when we speak about God? One way to begin to discuss divine domestication is to look at some of the ways that theology moved from a commitment to divine transcendence and mystery to the belief that God's essence and plans were ultimately knowable by finite creatures like us. One thing we will find is that when divine mystery is not taken seriously, various sorts of divine domestication shortly follow.

One of Thomas Aquinas's main insights was the idea that there was a definitional convergence between God's essence and God's existence. William Placher, paraphrasing Aquinas, writes that "Creatures *have* being, a being they derive from God, but God just *is* being."[44] In this case, the way "being" is used in relation to finite creatures and the way it is used when referring to God is vastly different. Therefore, Placher continues (again paraphrasing Aquinas), "God's relation to being is just totally different from anything else's relation to being, and we cannot imagine what 'being' means as applied to God."[45] While Aquinas did feel there were reasons to believe that God existed (this was the conclusion of the famous Five Ways), he also believed that it was necessary to maintain humility about just what it was that we could know about God. Karen Armstrong explains:

> All the "proofs" have achieved is to show us that there is nothing in our experience that can tell us what "God" means. Because of something that we cannot define, there is a universe where there could have been nothing, but we do not know what we have proved the existence of. We have simply demonstrated the existence of a mystery.[46]

The idea of an inexplicable mystery when it comes to the divine did not go over well with everyone. John Duns Scotus (1266–1308) thought that a commitment to the Thomistic idea of divine mystery made it difficult to say much at all about God. Scotus was rather more optimistic than Aquinas about our ability to think about God using the language we use to speak about finite creatures (the difference being one of degree). This unique use of reason led him to conclude, as Armstrong writes, paraphrasing Scotus: "that the word 'existence' was *univocal*; that is, it 'had the same basic meaning,' whether it applied to God or to men, women, mountains, animals, or trees."[47] Francisco Suárez (1548-1617), siding with Scotus against Aquinas, used the concept of "internal attribution" to argue that "Both God and creatures have being, and therefore, understanding what 'being' means in reference to creatures, we can extend the usage to God by analogy of internal attribution."[48] We can compare this to Descartes (who was intimately aware of the work of Suárez), who writes:

> So there remains only the idea of God; and I must consider whether there is anything in the idea which could not have originated in myself. By the word "God" I understand a substance that is infinite, independent, supremely intelligent, supremely powerful, and which created both myself and everything else (if anything else there be) that exists. All these attributes are such that, the more carefully I concentrate on them, the less possible that they could have originated from me alone. So from what has been said it must be concluded that God necessarily exists.[49]

All of this talk of univocal language when it comes to speaking about God has its contemporary representatives in analytic philosophy of religion. Take, as an example, the late William Alston, who writes:

> We can say of a human being that she will tend to do what she can to bring about what she recognizes to be best in a given situation, and we can take this tendency to be partly constitutive of the concept of recognizing something to be best. We can then formulate the divine regularities in tendency terms also. Thus it will be true of God also that if He recognizes that it is good that *p* He will tend to bring about *p* insofar as He can unless He recognizes something incompatible with *p* to be a greater good.[50]

The gist of all of this leads to a sort of *semantic domestication* of God, the claim being that we can know who God is because some aspects of the language we use regularly in daily life also can be applied to God univocally (with some minor adjustments here and there). Of course, we cannot domesticate a divine being who is essentially shrouded in mystery, so this sort of linguistic turn toward the concept of "univocal being" was a necessary first step on the road to domesticating God. Here is how Placher sums up the situation: "We can understand God, many seventeenth-century philosophers and theologians believed, because God is not utterly different from us. God's omniscience, omnipotence, and infinite goodness are the same sorts of qualities we have, differing only in degree."[51]

The domestication of God is not just an attempt to get it right when speaking about God; it is also partly an epistemological attempt to make the ways and purposes of God understandable to the human mind. This sort of thing has happened at various times and in various ways, but some have tried to pinpoint the tendency with some precision. For example, the Irish philosopher Peter Rollins has located part of the problem occurring around the time of the Enlightenment, when some began to think that revelation offered a clear-cut grasp of God's inner thoughts. The problem was not that revelation revealed something *theologically* significant about what God desired, but that revelation was, like a sort of *science*, offering us access to God by means of the correct use of human reason. Rollins writes, "It is argued that if God's communication to humanity is to mean anything at all, it must mean precisely what it infers: that God has graciously disclosed something of God's nature to us. In this rendering, theology … is understood as the science that places God within the realm of reason."[52] Revelation, on this account, gets co-opted by the cultural obsession with reason and takes on the look of its surroundings. In this way, revelation, filtered through reason, is able to grasp *the* meaning of who God is and what God wants of us. This led to the situation where, as Rollins writes:

The dominant thinking within both the university and the Church accepted that humans had a capacity to grasp objective, universal truth. Whether it was the painstaking empirical work of the natural scientist, the positivist research of the social scientist or the hermeneutic approach to scripture engaged in by the theologian, it was believed that, by employing pure reason … one could decipher the *singular* meaning of what was being studied (whether it be the natural world or a supernatural revelation).[53]

This is a form of *epistemological domestication*, whereby the divine gets boxed in by the rationality of the time. The use of reason becomes the means of answering many "why" questions about God and God's revelation, but this use of reason was not necessarily the reasoning offered in a religious context by believers (which would be too loose and subjective for scientific sensibilities), but rather reason which was imported from other contexts (such as science) into religion. The Enlightenment concept of revelation became a pseudo-science seeking to replace transcendence with human reason. This sort of thinking about revelation had, and continues to have, repercussions for how we think about God's existence, repercussions that lead to a final form of divine domestication.

Evidence for God's existence treats God as a being, a thing, a fact which stands in need of some sort of proof for its existence. In this way, God's very existence becomes contingent on the rational reasons that one could give for why they believe God exists. D.Z. Phillips describes this situation when he writes:

> Once this assimilation of belief in God to other kinds of belief takes place, asking whether belief in God is rational quickly becomes a matter of seeking evidence for the existence of God. Such evidence, if it can be found, will constitute the foundation of the belief. If it cannot be found, it will have been shown that there is no good reason for believing in God.[54]

To make the existence of God dependent on a certain contingent way of reasoning about God strips the divine of any sort of freedom to be revealed in surprising ways. Much like revelation, when God's existence becomes dependent on human reason, God becomes subject to the parameters and boundaries of reason, which is imported into religion from outside the practice of faith. God becomes a conclusion in a logical proof with no reference to who God is within the practice of religion itself. Phillips asserts, "Because the question of divine reality can be construed as 'Is God real or not?' it has been assumed that the dispute between the believer and unbeliever is over a *matter of fact*. The philosophical investigation of the reality of God then becomes the philosophical investigation appropriate to an assertion of a matter of fact."[55] This, of course, is what Dawkins suggests when he portrays God as a hypothesis. When we make God's very existence dependent on human categories, we create a being that is under our intellectual control. We can call this sort of domestication *ontological domestication* since God's very existence is made to fit human categories of thought and reason.

Simone Weil once wrote, "We have to be careful about the level on which we place the infinite. If we put it on the level which is only suitable for the finite, it does not much matter what name we give it."[56] Richard Bell comments on this quote by saying, "The reason we have to be careful is because we make 'God' the mere product of imaginary consolations. Such a god is man writ large, conceived as an extension of human powers."[57] Weil and Bell sum up the lesson of this chapter and the lesson that I believe Richard Dawkins, unwittingly, offers to the church. If the God we worship leads us to ourselves and away from others, then we become idolaters and our religious practice a form of idol worship. Dawkins offers us an atheism that removes obstacles to salvation by dismantling a domesticated anthropomorphic God. But our conclusion here is just the beginning of the path to a non-idolatrous faith. In order to continue to traverse this path, we still need to take a look at how some particular religious doctrines become a means of support for an idolatrous faith. In the process, we will also need to forge a pathway forward that will show us how religious language can take on meaning that both preserves its indispensability as the language of faith and leads us away from ourselves and toward those in need.

2

Transcendence, Faith, and Fideism

In the beginning of his book *Saving the Appearances*, Owen Barfield, a friend of C.S. Lewis and a member of the Oxford literary group *The Inklings*, writes, "There may be times when what is needed most is, not so much a new discovery or a new idea as a different 'slant'; I mean a comparatively slight readjustment in *our* way of looking at the things and ideas on which attention is already fixed."[1] If Barfield's suggestion makes sense, and I believe it does, then we must actually possess the ability to shift our interpretive gaze away from old ways of seeing things—things which we may have been focusing on with fixated certainty for some time—and begin to see reality imbued with new (and maybe even unforeseen) meaning. This is the point of the famous duck/rabbit drawing where, if we look at the image in one way, we see the image of a duck, but, when instructed to see the duck's bill as if it were actually rabbit ears, we begin to see the image of a rabbit. A slight shift in perspective and our world (ever so slightly) changes. Barfield's assertion and the example of the duck/rabbit drawing point to the possibility that the meaning of the things we have tended to fix our gaze on is malleable and open to semantic revision simply by shifting our perspective. Reality, it turns out, may be more pliable and pluralistic than we often tend to think.

Barfield's suggestion seems especially pertinent and instructive when it comes to religious belief. What is needed, or so it seems, is not another hackneyed philosophical argument for the existence of God or more reasons why religious belief is just as rational as science, but, rather, a shift in how we gaze on the meaning of religious belief and practice as a whole. We do not need to revamp or reconstruct religion out of whole cloth; rather, we simply need a reminder to look in a new way on what is already in plain view. Religion in particular (much like reality more generally) seems open to just this sort of semantic overdetermination; looked at in one way, and our religious gaze produces idolatry, a shift in perspective, and our idolatry is reconfigured as love.

One way to begin to see how this sort of gaze shifting might open up new options for the meaning of religious belief is to begin to see religion as a sort of lens or filter through which we interpret life. This lens, being that it is religious, should be motivated by love and selflessness rather than ego and constant self-concern. In this case religion is best seen as a world-picture (or worldview) rather than a simple set of beliefs about the existence of supernatural entities. Religious belief, on this construal, is best taken as a non-metaphysical way of assessing life, especially our life in relation to those in need. By calling this sort of religious commitment non-metaphysical, I do not mean to imply that the religious way of life lacks cognitive content, or that it cannot be justified, or that religious belief lacks truth value. Rather, I claim that all these evaluative terms ("cognitive content," "justification," "truth") need to be defined in terms of their religious use before we can see how they gain purchase within a religious context. The meaning of concepts like "cognitive content," "justification," and "truth" may indeed have a perfectly natural use in religious discourse, but in order to see this, we must let religious language (and not metaphysics) have the last word.

All of this presupposes that we can give an actual account of religious belief and practice that avoids the pitfalls of idolatry and supernaturalism that were outlined in the last chapter. It may be that all we really need is to be reminded of what a non-idolatrous account of religion looks like since this sort of faith has probably always existed even when the dominate form of faith was idolatrous. In what follows I want to look at Robert Coburn's suggestion that religious belief is best seen as an answer to what he calls religious limiting questions. I then want to see how the concept (or doctrine) of transcendence can serve as a paradigmatic instance of what it means to see things religiously. I will then conclude with a discussion of the various senses of fideism (or the idea that religion is in some way insular and protected from criticism), arguing that some forms of fideism are an essential part of the practice of religion, a part that should not be shunned but accepted as a necessary entailment of the grammar of religious belief.

Religious Limiting Questions

I take it to be uncontroversial that, in some important way, religious language receives its meaning from the lives of the people who speak it fluently and use it regularly. Religious language is intricately intertwined with the lives of the individuals who find a way to live a genuinely religious life. These people are, so to speak, native speakers. This should not be taken to mean that any and all uses of religious language are of equal value, for, as we have already seen and as I will mention again, religious language sometimes gets derailed, leading to concepts that are confused or idolatrous. But surely not all religious language is idolatrous; in fact, recognizing idolatry requires that we are able to make sense of a religious use of language that is not idolatrous. An idolatrous use of religious belief is parasitic on being able to formulate a non-idolatrous account of religion. The criteria of religious meaning (be it orthodox or heterodox) are found within religion's own talk about itself, and it is these criteria that allow us to see why some forms of religious practice are deficient while others are religiously viable.

Since religious belief is a way of interpreting the meaning of our existence, it would appear natural to want to know what role these beliefs play in our lives, especially if we take it as given that not all religious belief is belief in supernatural beings or simply ways to feed our egos or assuage our fear of meaninglessness and death. There appear to be at least two ways of making sense of religious belief that will allow us to see how religion can be more than mere idolatry.

First, religious language often arises out of a felt need on the part of certain individuals to make sense of existence in a way that avoids the pitfalls of idolatry. Religious faith is a way to unify all the disparate aspects of one's life, a way to find significance and meaning in one's daily mundane existence, and a way to take seriously the importance of community and service to others. In this way, religious language is more than just a set of believed propositions about supernatural existence—it is a commitment to a worldview in which we "live and move and have our being" (Acts 17:28 RSV). Second, religious language, at least from time to time, functions as a guide or a model or a signpost, which points the believer toward a life that is transformed by its encounter with others, especially those in need. It propels the believer to a life of radical *agape*, whereby those in need become the face of the divine, and active love toward others becomes the main goal of manifesting the love of God on earth. The sacred stories and religious pictures that are part of the faith serve as a constant reminder of the religious mandate to live for others, to die to self, and to love our neighbors. Religion, in this case, is a constant reminder to stay the ethical course, a course of love and service that was modeled in the sacrificial life of Jesus.

If religion is both part and parcel of helping believers make sense of their life and helping to give them the courage and fortitude needed to stay the ethical course of loving their neighbor as themselves, then it makes sense to say that religion has both an existential component and a regulative component. Religion, at least sometimes, serves as an impetus for making meaning out of existence and for regulating, motivating, and guiding believers as they actualize the call to live agapeistically. With the existential/regulative distinction in mind, I want to begin here by looking at the existential function of religious belief. We will look at the regulative aspect of religious belief later in this chapter and in the next.

In his essay titled "A Neglected Use of Theological Language," Robert Coburn presents a still-neglected, but nonetheless important, way to account for the function of some aspects of religious language. Coburn's argument relies on what he calls "religious limiting questions," a concept borrowed from Stephen Toulmin's idea of limiting questions in general. Coburn writes, "By a limiting question I shall mean a form of words which has the grammatical structure of a question, but which is such that a typical utterance of the form of words does not amount to asking a straightforward question of either a theoretical or practical sort."[2] These sorts of questions, when uttered, are not actually seeking a substantive answer (like when we ask, "What sort of cat is that?" or "What can I do to be a better employee?") but rather express a certain inner state or condition of the one asking the question. When we hear a limiting question expressed, we gain insight into the internal state of the one asking the question, similarly to the way we gain insight into a person's inner feelings when we witness him or her exhibiting pain behavior (which, of course, includes using pain language).

Examples of the sort of questions that count as limiting questions are, "Why should I do the right thing?" and "Why must I tell Joe of Sarah's infidelity?" These types of questions, at least sometimes, are not ones that seek a simple, factual answer. Rather than thinking that the person asking such a question is in need of an ethics lesson, it is possible to see their questions as, what Coburn calls, "a species of learned moral-conflict behavior."[3] In these sorts of situations, the one asking the question may have arrived at a point where they are simply at a loss in deciding between doing what is right and doing what is profitable (or expedient). They may be expressing an inner-conflict or simply revealing the fact that they do not know how to go on. The limiting question is an outward expression of an inner conflict. So, again, while a limiting question has the grammatical look and feel of a "normal" question, it is actually indicative of the individual expressing what amounts to a conflicted state of mind.

Even though, in these sorts of examples, the individual was in a moral quandary, similar things could be said about other limiting questions that are not overtly moral. Questions like, "Why did this have to occur to me at this time in my life?" "Is there any real meaning to life?" or "Why is there something rather than nothing at all?" These questions, all based on Coburn-type examples, can also be seen as a verbal expression of an inner existential conflict. Of these types of limiting questions (ones that are not overtly moral), Coburn writes, "it appears at least sometimes to be the case that the occasions upon which these questions are raised are occasions in which the questioner is in a 'spiritual' condition of some kind ... or is engaging in a spiritual activity of some kind, a condition such as grief or despair."[4] These limiting questions, like their moral counterparts, represent the fact that, as Wittgenstein writes, "An 'inner process' stands in need of outward criteria."[5] The oddity here is that the question itself serves as the outward criteria for an inner state of turmoil, discontentedness, or upheaval of some form or another.

It is a pretty short move from a limiting question in general to what Coburn refers to as a *religious limiting question*, especially since the latter is simply a species of the former. Coburn categorizes the religious limiting question as being expressions of the following three types of problems: problems focused on morals, problems of morale, and problems focused on the ultimate significance of things. Moral problems typically involve conflict between what we feel we should do (our duty) and what we actually do (or feel we want to do). They are the sort of questions we looked at above. Problems of morale, on the other hand, involve problems that, as Coburn writes, "arise out of our inability to reconcile ourselves to the various ills that flesh is heir to—sickness, failure, missed opportunities and the final ineluctable frustration of death—death of friends and family, and ultimately our own death."[6] Problems about the ultimate significance of life involve, among other things, a desire to reconcile disparate aspects of life or to find some sort of overarching principle that can unify our existence. It is an attempt to make sense out of life *as a whole*.

Utilizing these three categories (morals, morale, and ultimate significance), Coburn writes that "religious limiting questions can be characterized as that class of limiting questions the asking of which constitutes behavior which expresses and is criteriologically connected with the condition of having or feeling a problem of one or more of the kinds just noted."[7] William Brenner, commenting on the philosophy of D.Z. Phillips, seems to have something akin to Coburn's religious limiting questions in mind when he writes that:

> Many of the questions we ask and things we say are expressive of our attitudes, and thus of our state of soul. Asking questions like, "Why did this happen to *me*?" or "Why wasn't I born with more talents and opportunities?" may be symptomatic of what William James called "a sick soul." Spiritual health—what believers might call "the peace of God which passeth all understanding"— requires restraining or limiting the natural and culturally reinforced drive to

press such questions. It requires, not the acquisition of more factual knowledge or theoretical understanding, but a profound change in attitude towards the vicissitudes of life and our vulnerabilities.[8]

Of course, given the interrelatedness of life, it should be clear that there will inevitably be some overlap between the general set of limiting questions and those that we refer to as religious limiting questions. This will be especially so given the close relationship between religious faith and ethics.

Now even though the religious limiting questions, as with limiting questions generally, are not after a factual (or better, an empirical) answer, there is a certain type of "answer" that can serve to satisfy the questioner, not simply by offering more facts, but rather by dissipating the need to continue expressing the question. Coburn refers to these type of answers as "logically complete" answers, where a theological answer to a religious limiting question is considered "logically complete" when accepting the "answer" means that the questioner ceases asking the question unless he or she (a) does not understand what the answer is saying or, (b) simply does not accept the answer at all. The logic of the relationship between the religious limiting question and the "answer" is such that to understand and accept the answer necessarily means to cease asking the question. The religious limiting question is answered by eliminating the need to express the question at all, which is also indicative of having received relief from the existential/spiritual state that gave rise to the question in the first place. This is not any different from the way most answers function. When we receive an answer to a question, we generally stop asking the question. The difference here is that the answer calms an inner existential state of which the question was an expression, rather than making the question irrelevant by means of an accumulation of pertinent facts. The logically complete answer is therapeutic in that it shows the illogic of continuing on in the same way once an "answer" is accepted, but it is also cognitive in that it delineates the logical relationship between question and answer such that the answer is seen as having the ability to dissipate the sting of the question. In the process of accepting the answer as an answer, we learn something cognitively (and therapeutically) significant.

In the course of his discussion, Coburn deals with a variety of issues regarding the nature of religious limiting questions and the sort of things that serve as answers to such questions. I just want to mention, briefly, two points Coburn brings up regarding the function of the logically complete answer to religious limiting questions. First, Coburn notes that the nature of theological language is such that the acceptance of one statement might very well serve as an answer to a variety of different religious limiting questions. For example, the acceptance of a single theological "answer" may end up serving as a logically complete answer to a variety of religious limiting questions. Coburn writes:

> Thus the assertion of a sentence like "Jesus is the Christ," because of the logical connection of the notion of the Christ with the entire Judeo-Christian framework of ideas concerning God, Creation, the Fall, etc., might very well be an appropriate "answer" to such ostensibly different limiting questions as: (a) "why ought I do what is right?", (b) "why do men have such hard hearts", (c) "What is the ultimate end of life?", and, (d) "Why is there anything at all?"[9]

The point is that there is not necessarily a one-to-one correspondence between religious limiting questions and theological answers. I think this is especially important if we take Christian belief as the commitment to a story or a meta-narrative, and not just a set of loosely related propositions. The story will involve an interweaving of various religious ideas such that it might be difficult (if not impossible) to cite one belief as being *the* answer to any specific religious limiting question.

Second, and most importantly I think, Coburn notes that answers to religious limiting questions are not simply the acceptance of a proposition (or even a set of propositions) but rather a commitment to a way of living or a way of interpreting (or assessing) our lives. This does not negate religious belief as much as it insists that such belief must be explained in relation to the religious life in which it is embedded. Coburn writes that "one of the matters of which any analysis of theological discourse must provide some account is just this tendency for religiosity [i.e., a religious way of living] and religious belief to coalesce."[10] That is, belief and practice will merge in such a way that to give an account of one without reference to the other will result in an inadequate explanation of both. Coburn puts this point in the following way:

> If we understand the notion of "responding to life, or the world, religiously," or simply "being religious," by reference to such things as the disposition to live agapeistically, to exhibit hope in the time of tragedy, to take the deep things of life seriously, to engage in worshipful practices ..., and periodically to entertain or have in mind various of the pictures, parables, sayings, etc., of some religious tradition, then it can be argued, I believe, that responding to life religiously is a criterion for saying of a person that he has religious belief.[11]

If accepting a theological answer to a religious limiting question means living in the way Coburn describes, then it makes sense that this sort of belief (with the corresponding religious way of life) would be incompatible with continuing to express religious limiting questions. The question is answered by our changed outlook on life, an outlook that leads to a dissipation of the original question. This view of the relation between religious language and religiosity is reminiscent of what Wittgenstein says in *Culture and Value*: "a religious belief could only be something like a passionate commitment to a system of reference. Hence, although it's a belief, it's really a way of living, or a way of assessing life. It's passionately seizing hold of this interpretation."[12] Accepting a logically complete answer to a religious limiting question is tantamount to seeing life through a new lens; it is nothing less than an acceptance of a new form of life.

By showing how it is that religious limiting questions are correlated with religious language, Coburn has provided a reminder of the intimate logical relationship between religious belief and religious practice. In fact, he has linked belief and practice in such a way that a religious belief that is not surrounded by a religious way of living would make no sense. But what does it mean to say that a religious belief is a way of assessing life? What might that look like in practice? In what follows, I want to look at a variety of ways that the concept of "transcendence" might show up in religious life, not as a way of contradicting the claims of science or as a means of adding extra objects to our ontology, but rather as a way of seeing life from a religious point of view.

Senses of Transcendence

Religious belief generally entails some use of the concept of the transcendent. A religion without any use for transcendence would be better off being called a philosophy of life rather than a religion (in fact, religion may be seen as something like a philosophy of life plus transcendence). Of course, the meaning of transcendence will vary depending on exactly how the concept gets used and based on just what it is that is being transcended. In general, to speak of x transcending y is to think of the explanation for x not being contained in any description of the facts and/or relations contained in the description of y. This does not mean that transcendence has no relationship at all to the immanent; it is just that the description of the immanent will not fully explain all aspects of the transcendent. Transcendence is not simply a commitment to free-floating things that are supposed to exist utterly separate from the stuff that concerns us in our day-to-day lives; rather, transcendence is a way of looking on our mundane experiences and seeing them as being more than just the conglomeration of facts. Transcendence allows us to see through the world (as if the world were a sacred icon) and experience it as more than meets the eye.

Within religion, the paradigm example of transcendence is the transcendence ascribed to God. Of course, even the meaning of a transcendent God would have to be spelled out depending on how it is used. All too often, I'm afraid, the transcendence of God is treated like a transcendent object floating around in the sky with little effect on our lives (unless we are in a pinch or on our death beds). However, generally speaking, a transcendent God is seen, minimally, to entail that while God can be experienced through our encounter with the natural world, God's essence is not fully explicable in terms of facts about the natural world. While speaking of the transcendence of God in this minimal way is a starting point for understanding the meaning and use of the concept in religious language, it is only a starting point. To limit transcendence to simply speaking about God is far too narrow a use to cover the variety of ways that the concept gets used in religious practice. If religious belief is a way of assessing life as a whole, we would expect transcendence to have a broader use than just referring to a transcendent God. An expanded use for transcendence, however, should not be taken to mean that there are more transcendent things out there waiting to be discovered, but rather that the concept of God, which is more a filter through which we view life than an object that exists, is much more expansive and all-encompassing than usually thought. Transcendence, as a theological philosophy of life, must be expanded to include all aspects of life and reality if religious belief is going to be taken as more than just a simple set of beliefs. Transcendence, on this account, is not a commitment to a transcendent ontology *per se*, but rather a way of transcendently interpreting (or seeing) reality religiously. To say this in another way, we might say that transcendence is a stance taken toward the immanent. Here is how John Cottingham describes things:

> Now all the cases just mentioned, our vivid awareness of natural beauty, our responses to the mysterious power of great art and music, and our sense of awe before the authoritative demands of morality—all these may be described by the believer as revelations of the sacred, as intimations of the divine reality that is the source of all truth, beauty, and goodness.[13]

In his book *A Secular Age*, Charles Taylor writes about three senses (or uses) of transcendence that he finds at play in the religious life. First, Taylor writes of "the sense that there is some good higher than, beyond human flourishing. In the Christian case, we could think of this as agape, … In other words, a possibility of transformation offered, which takes us beyond merely human perfection."[14] We can refer to this as the "transcendence of the self." Next, Taylor writes that "this notion of a higher good as attainable by us could only make sense in the context of belief in a higher power, the transcendent God of faith which appears in most definitions of religion."[15] From what Taylor writes, it appears that he is concerned with the general concept of a transcendent God; I, however, think that what is needed is not simply a transcendent God—which begins to smack of the sort of supernatural theism that was criticized in the last chapter—but the transcendence of (a certain concept of) "God." We can call this the "transcendence of God" (think of Meister Eckart praying that "God rid him of God"). Lastly, Taylor writes, "the Christian story of our potential transformation by agape requires that we see our life as going beyond the bounds of its 'natural' scope between birth and death."[16] On a certain reading of "beyond," this last quote could be seen as possessing a whiff of a sort of Kantian need for an afterlife in order to balance the scales of justice that are lacking in this life. I would prefer to think of "beyond" (as in our life going beyond the "scope of birth and death") in a different way, namely as the uniquely human ability to transcend the feeling that we are ontologically separate from other things and other people in the world. What is transcended is our feeling of separateness, the feeling that we are the center of the world rather than something that is essentially interrelated to other things and people. It is the feeling that the reality of separate and discrete individuals, the world described by much of the natural sciences, is not the only way to see things. It is this world of compartmentalized discrete individuals that we must, in some sense, transcend (or move beyond). I call this sense of transcendence the "transcendence of nature."

What Taylor offers is a really useful typology for the possible ways that transcendence shows up in religious life. It is a vast improvement over the narrow and myopic view that sees transcendence applying only to a being called "God" (or, by extension, to humans through some sort of immaterial soul). In what follows, I want to expand on Taylor's various uses of transcendence, not as a correction or addition to what Taylor has written in *A Secular Age*, but simply as a way of expanding on the content of his helpful typology.

Transcending God

As I mentioned above, to speak of a transcendent God is not the same as speaking of the need to transcend god. Taylor is, I believe, correct when he states that religious belief is committed to a transcendent deity, but that alone does not get us very far, especially if the transcendent God is a being with human-like properties, the sort of invisible man we met in Chapter 1. This sort of being has been given, by *fiat*, the moniker of transcendence. Yet simply attaching the word to a being does not automatically transform that thing into something worthy of devotion. This is especially true if fealty to, and worship of, this being becomes a thinly veiled instance of self-worship. Atheism is the correct attitude toward any entity who poses as a god but lacks the transformative power to pull of the job. This is what Wittgenstein captures when he writes, "If I thought of God as another being like myself, outside myself, only infinitely more powerful, then I would regard it as my duty to defy him."[17] In order to take the idea of a transcendent God seriously, we need to first learn to transcend God and defy any idol that we have created in our own image even if we have gotten used to calling that idol our "God."

By joining Dawkins in being atheistic about the anthropomorphic God of supernatural theism, we are once again actualizing a sort of purifying atheism. Simone Weil writes, "Religion in so far as it is a source of consolation is a hindrance to true faith; and in this sense atheism is a purification."[18] This atheism is purifying because it rids us of an idol while simultaneously opening the door for the entrance of a God who is worthy of the title. In dismantling the idol god, however, we want to be careful that we do not simply construct another idol. We should be mindful again of Weil's warning when she explains, "We have to be careful about the level on which we place the infinite. If we put it on the level which is only suitable for the finite it does not much matter what name we give it."[19]

The way to avoid the hubris of speaking too confidently about God is to acknowledge both that God is essentially mysterious and ineffable and that this mystery and ineffability have a profound effect on what it means to speak of God. Denys Turner explains the situation this way: "It follows from the *unknowability* of God that there is very little that can be *said* about God: or rather, since most theistic religions have a great number of things to say about God, what follows from the unknowability of God is that we can have very little idea of what all these things said about God *mean*."[20] Acknowledging God's mystery and the challenges it creates when it comes to speaking about God forces us to address two primary issues. First, how is it that we come to learn about our inability to speak accurately and literally about God? And second, what sort of mystery is the mystery of God? It is to these that I want to turn briefly.

To speak of God as mystery is to have our speech undo itself. Take the following two statements, one from Wittgenstein's *Tractatus* and the other from D.Z. Phillips:

(a) Wittgenstein: "Whereof one cannot speak, thereof one must be silent."[21]
(b) Phillips: "Instead of asking how we *can* speak of God, we must begin by noting that we *do* speak of God."[22]

The challenge, represented by these paradoxical statements, is to try to understand how both of them are in fact true. How can we be silent about God, respecting God's utter ineffability, while also admitting that we do, already, speak of God? The oddity is that in speaking about God, we claim to learn that God cannot be spoken of. But, in this case, the oddity is also the answer.

The solution to this conundrum is to see that God's mystery is a grammatical remark that we come to understand when we learn what it means to speak of God. There is, of course, something odd about using language to show that we cannot speak about God. The perplexity, however, is really what we should expect since we learn who God is by paying attention to language use. Wittgenstein once wrote that "Grammar tells us what kind of object anything is. (Theology as grammar.)"[23] It is by seeing how people speak about God that we come to see what sort of reality God possesses. The mystery of God is not an abstract metaphysical truth that we learn in the absence of speech; rather, like all truths about who God is, the meaning of divine mystery is something we learn by paying attention to the language use that is already in play in the religious form of life. Phillips explains it this way: "Similarly, Job, the Psalmist and St Paul are not telling us that God is hidden from them because of the inadequacy of their language. Rather, they are showing us that the notion of God, in their language, is that of a hidden God."[24] He later adds, "What we have seen is that language is not a screen which hides God from us. On the contrary, the idea of God in the language we have been explaining is the idea of a hidden God."[25] Wittgenstein's call for silence should come only after we recognize, with Phillips, that we *do* indeed already speak about God, but the speech that is already in play involves the need for silence as well. Jean Luc Marion affirms this grammatical remark when he writes that:

> God cannot be seen, not only because nothing finite can bear his glory without perishing, but above all because a God that could be conceptually comprehended would no longer bear the title "God" … he [God] remains God only on condition that this ignorance be established and admitted definitively. Everything in the world gains by being known—but God who is not of the world, gains by not being known conceptually. The idolatry of the concept is the same as that of the gaze, imagining oneself to have attained God and to be capable of maintaining him under our gaze, like a thing of the world.[26]

Recognizing that our language about God sets the grammatical parameters about what it makes sense to say about God, including the fact that what we say cannot be applied literally to the divine essence, helps us avoid the idolatry of thinking that we can contain God's essence in the confines of our language about God.

Even if we accept that in speaking of God, we come to realize the inadequacy of our speech, we still might wonder exactly what kind of mystery we are speaking about when we speak about the divine mystery. Mysteries are not of one sort; there are many types of mysteries that we are confronted with in the world. We may speak of the sort of mystery we encounter in detective stories, where someone is trying to assemble enough facts to solve a crime. Or, we may speak of natural mysteries, where scientists are trying to figure out what causes a certain disease or what prompted the Big Bang to occur. There are also mysteries that are part and parcel of the fact that, due to the sort of creatures we are, there are things we just cannot know. In these sorts of cases, we may not even be able to imagine what sort of creature we would need to be in order to solve the mystery. Maybe the mystery of consciousness is just this type of unsolvable mystery, unsolvable, that is, to us but solvable in principle.

In some of these types of mysteries, we are confronted with an epistemological setback such that if we had more knowledge, the mystery could be solved. The mystery is awaiting a solution if only we could get our facts straight. In other instances, the mystery may not be solvable by us, but in principle it is solvable, maybe by creatures smarter than us or by ones with a different neuro-physiological makeup. All these sorts of mysteries are similar in that they are contingent; we can, with enough imagination, conjure up what a solution to the mystery would look like (or what sort of being would be able to figure it out).

Transcending God is coming to recognize that solvable mysteries are not the only kind of mysteries there are. To speak of divine mystery is not to speak of a mystery in the way that a crime novel does. It is not the sort of mystery about the natural world that science is seeking to dispel. Nor is it a mystery that happens to escape our grasp but could, in principle, be solved by other sorts of creatures. That is, the mystery of God is not a mystery waiting to be solved at all. It cannot be solved by collecting more information or thinking harder or getting more academic degrees or even by dying. This is because the mystery of God is a conceptual rather than an empirical (or epistemological) issue. It is a necessary part of what we mean by God. It is a mystery that cannot be solved since solving it would be to dissolve God. Paul Tillich writes of this sort of mystery as the revelation of "something which is essentially a mystery, something which would lose its very nature if it lost its mysterious character."[27] A bit later he states, "Whatever is essentially mysterious cannot lose its mysteriousness even when it is revealed. Otherwise something which only seemed to be mysterious would be revealed, and not that which is essentially mysterious."[28] Coming to see who God is, is concurrently coming to see that God's mystery cannot be dispelled.

This sort of conceptual mystery brings to mind several interrelated ways that the concept of divine mystery gets incorporated into religious practice. First, it reminds us that, in some very real sense, all of our God-talk is grappling with unknowability. We may be speaking of God analogically, metaphorically, or simply by expressing human desires writ large (as in Feuerbach), but whatever our theological bent, the fact remains that our language about God is always broken and fragmented. As we will see later, the utter ineffability of God forces the focus of the religious life back to earth. Transcending the god that we think we know should lead us back to others as a reflection of divine love rather than on a linguistic goose chase hunting what cannot, of necessity, be found.

The second way that divine mystery enters the religious life, and this is related to what was just said, is by serving as a protective guard against the hubris of speaking too confidently about God. This is vitally important when it comes to avoiding idolatry and spiritual materialism since the sort of God needed in order for those practices to flourish is a God who can be known and spoken of as if it were your next-door neighbor or drinking buddy. Like physical idols, which we can see and feel, conceptual idols require a God whose ways and purposes can be known. Theology must be careful when speaking of God that it does not attempt to dispel mystery by talking too much or too confidently about God. As Denys Turner writes, in regard to the thought of pseudo-Denys (Pseudo-Dionysius), "high-sounding 'religious' language can, he [Pseudo-Dionysius] says, more easily mislead us into idolatrous anthropomorphisms."[29] Divine mystery creates an unbridgeable gap between language and God, which creates the space for epistemological humility, mystery, and faith.

Third, we may choose to see the concept of divine mystery as part of the worship of God. It is part of the liturgy, prayers, and hymns of the church, not to mention the sacred texts. Walter Charles's hymn *Immortal, Invisible, God Only Wise* begins, "Immortal, invisible, God only wise,/In light inaccessible, hid from our eyes."[30] Far from saying nothing, the mystery of God exalts the divine to a position above beings (similar to the mystical language Anselm used in his prayer when he addressed God as "That which none greater can be conceived"). D.Z. Phillips compares this to the person who says to someone, "Words can't tell you how grateful I am," and in so doing actually does express their gratitude. The limits of knowing God can be an act of reverence.[31]

Lastly, and perhaps most importantly, the ineffable mystery of God forces theology to become incarnational rather than metaphysical. It pushes the theologian to see the story of the self-emptying (*kenotic*) life of Jesus, which was lived as a model of self-sacrificial love for the other, as a goal to be imitated in his or her own life as a necessary condition for what it means to be a believer. Theology is brought down to earth, or made immanent, as a life lived, not under the ever-watchful eye of a vengeful deity, but under the soft gaze of a God in the shadows. We must learn, as Bonhoeffer said, that "The God who lets us live in the world without God is the God before whom we stand continually. Before God and with God we live without God."[32] This, however, does not lead to theological quietism since it forces the theologian to take the incarnational narrative of the life of Jesus seriously as a model for living a life of love for others.[33]

Transcending Nature

To transcend nature is to feel that somehow our common-sense view of reality, filtered as it is through the natural sciences, is incomplete. It is to feel that there is something lacking in any worldview that takes science as the sole arbiter of what is true and important in life. What I am not interested in here are arguments against scientism, even though I think those are important and have a place in philosophical discussions. My concern here is not with intellectual argumentation but with a feeling generated through the variety of subjective experiences that some have claimed to have had, which has led them to form the belief that, in some sense, reality is much richer, awe inspiring, and mysterious than usually thought. As Bishop Kallistos Ware writes, "Unless we start off with a feeling of awe and astonishment—with what is often called a sense of the numinous—we shall make little progress on the Way."[34] These experiences create a subjective change in the perspective of the one having them, and this change is often expressed as a feeling about the nature of reality in relation to the limits of human knowledge.

Of course, there are dramatic ways in which some have described these sorts of experiences. What comes to mind are the sort of experiences that William James writes of in *The Varieties of Religious Experience* or the ones that Rudolph Otto refers to as *mysterium tremendum et fascinans*. Yet, I suspect that most of us will never have these sorts of dramatic experiences, which are often, by definition, rare and transient. But there are more mundane ways of coming to see (or feel) that our common-sense view of the natural world is limited and fragmentary. While these experiences may not be described as dramatic, earth-shaking, or mystical, they do tend to create a feeling of epistemic humility that often results in a new outlook on life. It is these more mundane and natural types of experiences that interest me here. The best way to get at what I have in mind is by offering a few examples.

In a debate he had with Tony Blair, Christopher Hitchens once said:

> I'm a materialist … yet there is something beyond the material, or not entirely consistent with it, what you could call the Numinous, the Transcendent, or at its best the Ecstatic. I wouldn't trust anyone in this hall who didn't know what I was talking about. It's in certain music, landscape, certain creative work, without this we really would be primates. It's important to appreciate the finesse of that, and religion has done a very good job of enshrining it in music and architecture.[35]

On another occasion, this time in an interview, when asked about his contrast between the numinous and the supernatural, Hitchens said:

> It's innate in us to be overawed by certain moments, say, at evening on a mountaintop or sunset on the boundaries of the ocean. Or, in my case, looking through the Hubble telescope at those extraordinary pictures. We have a sense of awe and wonder at something beyond ourselves, and so we should, because our own lives are very transient and insignificant. That's the numinous, and there's enough wonder in the natural world without any resort to the supernatural being required.[36]

For Hitchens, the numinous and the transcendent are a feeling that is generated in the face of human finitude and in the midst of a vast universe. There is, in Hitchens, no mention of a change in ontology or a commitment to extraordinary beings. There is only a feeling, a new way of gazing on old things. There is "a sense of awe and wonder at something beyond ourselves."

Compare Hitchens remarks with what Wittgenstein says in his "Lecture on Ethics": "I will mention another experience straight away which I also know and which others of you might be acquainted with: it is, what one might call, the experience of feeling *absolutely safe*. I mean the state of mind in which one is inclined to say, 'I am safe, nothing can injure me whatever happens.'"[37] He later adds, "and the experience of absolute safety has been described by saying that we feel safe in the hands of God."[38] Wittgenstein's view of absolute safety is a feeling that nature is not the last word since it admits a feeling of safety that nature cannot crush. To say that we feel absolutely safe is to express a feeling that sees the meaning of life as something that is beyond, in some sense, the mere conglomeration of scientific facts.

Robert Coburn, following Rudolf Otto and much in line with Hitchens, describes transcendent feelings as a sense of the numinous, saying that people are sometimes "struck or moved, at least from time to time, by awareness of the sacred, by an apprehension of something in (or about) life or the world that is deeply mysterious, something both attractive and fearful that evokes such responses as awe and reverence, a profound solemnity, praise, contrition, and 'a bowing of the head.'"[39]

Finally, in his commencement address, published as *This Is Water*, the late novelist David Foster Wallace points out the possibility that we might be able to rethink the meaning of existence and begin to see the world, not as an isolated hellhole that we must endure, but rather as something more unified, beautiful, and peaceful. He writes that, by changing our thinking and paying attention, "It will actually be within your power to experience a crowded, hot, slow, consumer-hell-type situation as not only meaningful, but sacred, on fire with the same force that lit the stars—compassion, love, the subsurface unity of all things."[40]

These sorts of feelings are, as John Cottingham writes, experienced at "the times when the drab, mundane pattern of our ordinary routines gives way to something vivid and radiant, and we seem to glimpse something of the beauty and significance of the world we inhabit."[41] Cottingham is here describing a feeling that is often missing when we look on the world in segmented parts rather than as a whole of which we are a part.

Naturally, the feelings people describe in the face of transcendent experiences are going to be as varied as the individuals themselves, but they all point to some common themes that, when noticed, might help us see more clearly what is meant by transcending nature.

First, the experience of transcending nature has an existential—or emotional or experiential—impact on, at least some of, the individuals who claim to have had such an experience. They leave one with a feeling that might be described, *a la* Wittgenstein, as the feeling of "absolute safety," or as a feeling of awe and wonder toward existence, or as a feeling of love and compassion for all things, or as a feeling of gratitude for creation. However these feelings are described, there is general agreement that, rather than creating a feeling of "ho hum," these experiences leave one with the opposite feeling, namely the sense that reality (as it is revealed in these transcendent experiences) has a greater depth and seriousness to it than one might have previously believed.

In the *Tractatus*, Wittgenstein writes, "Not *how* the world is, is the mystical, but *that* it is."[42] In part, this mystical feeling occurs when we realize that science does not answer questions like "Why is there something rather than nothing?" or, "What is the meaning of life?" These sorts of experiences are described as involving feelings because they press the limits of language, creating a situation where speech and silence collide. To talk about what transcends language is to talk about having a sense that, even when speech fails us, there is still something important to learn, namely the possibility that reality may be much more than we assumed. The feeling of transcending nature, then, is best described as a not-knowing, but, it is a positive not-knowing, since we know that we do not know. This feeling is the feeling of mystery and of the possibility of the impossible rather than *knowledge* about the mysterious or recognition of *how* the impossible is possible. It is a feeling that is hard to describe linguistically mainly because it is not knowledge that is conveyed (or conceivable) in propositional form. Yet, despite the lack of sematic precision, the feeling of the transcendence of nature is one that carries with it a certain seriousness about how we might come to gaze upon reality given our finitude and the vastness of all that is.

Second, to transcend nature is to also feel (and maybe, at a later time, come to believe) something specific about reality; namely, it is to feel (or believe) that, for all we know, there is more to reality than science can ever discover. It is the subjective *feeling* that our view of reality is, quite possibly, limited, or it is the awareness that certain aspects of our scientific description of the world are, again, for all we know, false. While earlier I spoke of the possibility of a rational argument for the limits of science, my interest here is in the way that certain experiences give rise to a specific feeling (i.e., the feeling of a reality that outstrips science), which may get verbalized as a belief, but that essentially entails the stance that science is only one way, among other possible ways, of knowing what reality is like.

While the first theme of transcending nature pointed out the general fact that the very idea of the transcendence of nature has an experiential component (which may be described generally as a "feeling" or more specifically as the feeling of awe, wonder, or gratitude), here I argue that aside from the feeling of awe, wonder, or gratitude, the experience of transcending nature carries with it the specific feeling that our position in the world allows for the possibility that there is more (probably much more) to reality than what we can ever learn from science. What I have in mind is the sort of feelings about reality that we saw described above by Hitchens, Wittgenstein, and Wallace. These feelings are quasi-epistemological in nature, but, again, only in the negative sense that they force us to come to recognize the limits of scientific knowledge. Human limits are seen as necessitated by our finitude and situatedness within the midst of existence. This is seen most vividly when these human conditions are placed against the backdrop of infinity. The experience of transcending nature contains the feeling that there is a much vaster whole that we are not only a part of but a part that is situated, for better or worse, in the metaphorical middle of time and space—a situatedness that should, again, create in us some epistemological humility.

The third trait that should be considered when talking about what it might mean to transcend nature is the idea that these experiences often leave one with the feeling that all reality is interrelated in a way that is not captured by our common-sense scientific view of things (with the exception, possibly, of some aspects of quantum physics. But whoever thought that quantum physics was commonsensical?). This sort of view occurs when we shift our perspective of the world from within time and space to an imagined position outside of time and space. It is to see the world from the perspective of eternity (*sub specie aeternitatis*). J.R. Jones writes:

> But now, a perceiver who perceives the world from eternity is no longer a part of what he beholds. He no longer perceives objects, as it were from within their midst. He is abstracted to a point of view outside the world. And to see the world thus, without one's own involvement in it, is to see it as a single thing.[43]

Once one imagines a perspective outside of all that is, the natural perspective is to see everything as an unbounded whole. To quote Jones again:

> We seem abstracted to a point outside the world and we see it without our own involvement in it—we see it as one thing. And when this happens to you (if it ever does happen), you *know* that "how the world is" is not everything. There is something else—there is the existence of the world—"*that* the world is."[44]

Naturally this eternal perspective is imaginary, but it is an effective position to take in order to break the illusion of separateness while leaving science (the view that describes "how" the world is) untouched.

To transcend nature, then, is to have an existential feeling that creates in us a desire to take our finitude seriously in the face of ultimate reality. It is to feel that there is, for all we know, more to reality than science can ever tell us. Lastly, it is to see that, *sub specie aeternitatis*, there is an interrelatedness to all life that is missing when we try and discern ultimate reality from our bounded perch locked within time and space.

Transcending the Self

I take it that some form of self-transcendence constitutes the meaning of the Christian life. Sometimes it is called "dying to the self," "carrying our cross," or "loving our neighbors," yet, however it is spoken of, it always involves transcending our natural, selfish state. This idea of self-transcendence, which gets expressed in love for the Other, is so central to the religious life that the final chapter of Part One is reserved for a discussion of this topic. With that in mind,

I will only briefly comment on the idea of transcending the self here as a way of introducing what is to come.

To transcend the self is to overcome our natural propensity to prefer ourselves and our own desires over the needs of others. I call this sort of selfishness our natural propensity, since it seems to be an essential part of our nature as self-conscious human beings; that is, it is built into the very nature of consciousness. In *This Is Water*, David Foster Wallace writes, "Everything in my own immediate experience supports my deep belief that I am the absolute center of the universe, the realest, most vivid and important person in existence. We rarely think about this sort of natural, basic self-centeredness, because it's so socially repulsive, but it's pretty much the same for all of us, deep down."[45] This is the perspective of someone in the midst of the warp and woof of everyday existence. It is an explanation for the seemingly easy way in which some live their lives of ease while ignoring suffering all around them, suffering they could easily help alleviate. But, while this sort of natural egoism is part of what it means to possess a first-person perspective, there is also a real sense that the religious life requires, as part of what it means to be a believer, the transcendence of this very sort of natural egoism.

To transcend ourselves is to view others around us as equals. It is to help those in need when possible. It is to treat others as ends in themselves and not as a means to an end. And, lastly, it is to practice the Christian mandate to "die to self" and to "love our neighbor as our self." To transcend our self is to put love in the middle of Christian existence. The Apostle Paul writes:

> If I speak in the tongues of men and of angels, but have not love, I am a noisy gong or a clanging cymbal. And if I have prophetic powers, and understand all mysteries and all knowledge, and if I have all faith, so as to remove mountains, but have not love, I am nothing. If I give away all I have, and if I deliver my body to be burned, but have not love, I gain nothing. (I Corinthians 13:1–7 RSV)

Paul points out the radical way that love serves to imbue other activities, intellectual powers, and even virtues—such as faith—with ultimate meaning. The sort of love Paul has in mind (agape) requires a transcending of our ego since it requires we "love our neighbor as our self." Paul writes, "Let no one seek his own good, but the good of his neighbor" (I Corinthians 10:24 RSV). If the self gets in the way of love, idolatry is the result. Paul points to how all of human life is animated by agape, or the love that Jesus shows to humanity by means of giving up his life as a prototype of love. Agape is given such prominence in the Christian religion that it appears to undermine any claim that mere belief is more important than (or forms the basis of) religious practice. After quoting the verse from I Corinthians just mentioned, Mark Johnston writes, "The immanent and heroic form of first-century Christian life is nothing? Yes, nothing, zero, a waste, if it is not animated by agape."[46] No metaphysical speculation about the existence of God, no promises of eternal life, no recognition by your peers and loved ones, nothing! This sort of love is not just difficult, but impossible without learning to transcend ourselves since its only motive can be the well-being of the other. As John Caputo writes, "If love is love it does not have anything up its sleeve."[47]

Transcendence allows us to go beyond the idol god, it allows us to see more to reality than meets the eye, and it lays the foundation to begin to see other people as metaphysical equals. More importantly, transcendence can be seen as an answer (or a set of answers) to religious limiting questions. Transcendence enters the believer's life not as a set of things we need to believe but as a filter through which reality is viewed. However, this way of looking at religious belief leaves us with questions about the justification and truth of faith. If religious belief is just a useful heuristic, a way of viewing and interpreting reality, then what sense can be made of its truth? How can it be criticized? What will serve as its justification? These types of questions loosely correspond to questions surrounding what has come to be called "fideism." In the remaining part of this chapter, I want to look at how some of these questions might be answered.

Reasons, Religion, and Fideism

In *Culture and Value*, Wittgenstein writes:

> The Christian religion is only for one who needs infinite help, therefore only for one who feels an infinite need. The whole planet cannot be in greater anguish than a single soul. The Christian faith—as I view it—is the refuge in this ultimate anguish.[48]

The need for infinite help—however that tends to be manifested—is what generates the sort of religious limiting questions that, Coburn argues, are a basis of religious language. When it comes to religious belief, one question we may ask is what sort of reasons one might offer for why they believe what they do, and, naturally, we would expect these answers to be as varied as the people who give them. In the case of those who accept a logically complete religious answer to religious limiting questions, the believer's reasons for belief will probably reference the fact that in the language of religion—a language with a long, rich history—they have found a new way to live. These reasons will most likely be the sort of things that appeal to how religion helps them make sense of their existence, or how it quells the sting of finitude, or maybe how it helps them see reality as imbued with peace, love, and ultimate meaning. Religious belief (as a way of assessing and interpreting our lives) is a way of making sense of some of the puzzling aspects of existence. Since religious belief, at least much of the time, arises out of the sort of existential shock created by our finitude, why wouldn't we expect the reasons people give for their religious belief to reference the way religion satisfies these sorts of existential concerns?[49] It seems quite natural to think that this is how it should be. Someone may say that living religiously helps them make sense of life, or helps them see others with compassion, or allows them to feel at peace in the world. These are the sorts of reasons we would expect from someone whose embrace of a religious worldview has brought them peace, joy, and love. But, for some, these sorts of reasons are paltry at best and childish at worst.

The problem these sorts of reasons present, for some at least, is that they do not seem to offer a strong-enough *rational* basis for the truth of religious practice. It is not enough, some suggest, to simply say that religion satisfies our existential concerns by offering a new way of living and assessing life, since that says nothing about the actual truth of religion. Truth, they say, gives way to wishful thinking or self-deception. This concern, however, is to mistake truth found *within* religious practice for the truth *of* religious practice. It is to miss the fact that truth and falsity about this or that religious claim is made within the context of a religious form of life, but that the religious form of life itself (like any form of life) is not true or false.

The worry that some have about distinguishing between truth claims made in religion and the truth of the religious practice itself is that if we allow that it makes no sense to call the religious form of life true or false (any more than it makes sense to call the entire practice of science true or false), then we are heading down a path that leads to an unpalatable form of fideism. But this is to demand that something be true or false that is not itself a candidate for truth or falsity. It is to turn religious belief and practice into a set of propositions that are either true or false and which must be justified with objective evidence *before* they are to be believed. But the religious life is not just a set of propositions which must be believed and justified. The religious life, as I have been arguing throughout, is more like a worldview, or the background against which our whole life is assessed rather than a set of propositions about supernatural entities and miraculous events. The religious life is lived and accepted, rather than merely believed in. Religious practice itself creates the context in which we come to see what counts as true/false, orthodox/heterodox, worshipful/idolatrous. In what follows, I want to look at the charge of fideism and show why it may not be as serious an objection to religious belief as some think. In fact, there may be certain uses of fideism that are simply ways of spelling out unique aspects of the grammar of religious language, especially as this language is related to the way concepts like truth and justification get used in other contexts. To get a better grasp on the issue, I want to introduce Hilary Putnam's example of conceptual relativity.[50]

Conceptual Relativity

Hilary Putnam presents the idea of conceptual relativity in relation to an imaginary story of two people trying to decide how many objects exist in a certain room given the following three entities: $x1$, $x2$, and $x3$. (Of course, an entity is not necessarily counted as an object.) On one account, it is clear that we have just three objects, each coinciding with exactly one of the entities ($x1$, $x2$, $x3$). But, Putnam says, "Suppose, for example, that like some Polish logicians [namely, Lezniewski and his invention of the idea of mereological sums], I believe that for every two particulars there is an object which is their sum."[51] On this account, the three entities would give rise to the following seven objects: $x1$, $x2$, $x3$, $x1 + x2$, $x1 + x3$, $x2 + x3$, $x1 + x2 + x3$. The main point here is that the number of objects is dependent, obviously enough, on what one counts as an "object." More importantly, while we would easily be able to settle disputes within each "object language game" (since we would know "from the inside" what counts as an object), settling disputes between individuals who play different "object language games" would not be so simple. We would have no access to what might be called the objectively correct way of defining an object that we could then use in order to figure out who is getting it right. It isn't that we do not at the moment have access to this view from nowhere; it's rather that it doesn't make sense to talk about such a view existing at all.

What does all this have to do with religious belief, generally, and with fideism specifically? When we think of the rule for how to define an object, we might naturally ask how we learn this rule. Is the rule first formulated *a priori* and then followed in our daily practice, or does the rule actually come out of the practice of counting objects? I think, if we reflect on how we talk about the relationship between rules and practice, we can see that the latter suggestion makes the most sense. If we want to see what people mean by an "object," then we should look and see how they use this concept. Then, and only then, can we formulate the grammatical rule for what an object is, what the essence of an object is.

Suppose we observe some group that defines an object differently than we do. Now, since we notice this new way of defining objects is indeed different from our own, we already have one sense of how objects should be (or are) defined. In this case, we might want to argue for and defend our way of defining an object over their way. That seems like a reasonable-enough position. Or, maybe we just think it best to go on our way and admit that there are a variety of different ways of defining objects. In this case we might not even want to enter a dialogue about which way is the right way. This choice also seems reasonable. Now, suppose that we begin to think about the different ways of counting objects, and say we decide we want to know who is right. Within the life of each community that defines "object" in their distinct way, the practice of using and interacting with objects will have a sense in their lives (to see this, think of the way that object talk might play a role in a description of our own language game). But what sense can be given to the idea of wanting to know who counts objects correctly?

Since each group has their own definition of what an object is, it seems natural that there will be numerous ways we can see the rule being followed in the life of each community. When a parent, in either object world, says to a child, "Hand me that object please?" the parent knows whether what they receive is correct or not because they speak the language in which the practice and definition of objects has its life. But, when we ask of these two different worlds, "Who is getting it right?" or "Who is defining objects in the most objectively correct way?" or "Who is cutting the world up at its joints in the right way?" what are we asking? The question seems reasonable enough, but its unreasonableness shows itself when we try and imagine what an answer would look like. How would we even decide such a thing? What standard, outside of either practice, could we appeal to in order to decide who, if anybody, is getting it right? Most importantly, does it even make sense to ask such a question (or to try and offer an answer)? Since the rules for what counts as an object are derived from a particular practice that is already part of a life, to what authority, external to the practice, could we appeal to in order to decide who is correct in their definition of an object? I think this brief discussion may go a long way in helping us begin to see religious belief and practice in a way that avoids some uses of fideism while embracing others. Before we see how this is accomplished, however, I should say a bit more about fideism.

Types of Fideism: Meaning, Justification, and Truth

The main contemporary dispute about fideism broke out between D.Z. Phillips and Kai Nielsen shortly after Nielsen published his paper "Wittgensteinian Fideism" in 1967 in the journal *Philosophy*.[52] The dispute continued for many years—mainly with Phillips trying to explain why he was not really a fideist—until the two met to discuss the issue, one last time, at a conference in Claremont California, shortly before Phillips's death.[53] The most important outcome of this long dialogue, as I see it, is that Nielsen's complaints brought to the forefront certain aspects of the groundlessness of religious belief. To Phillips's credit, by resisting Nielsen's label of fideism in a variety of publications, he was able to keep the debate going, allowing us to see that fideism was more than one single concept and that some of its uses are not as logically egregious as one might think. The downside of the long debate is that Phillips, as far as I can tell, never did see that certain aspects of fideism arise naturally by paying attention to the unique grammar of religious belief, the same grammar, incidentally, that Phillips spent his career painstakingly describing (which makes this lacuna even more perplexing).

Fideism, in its most general form, usually gets construed as something like "faith-ism," or the idea that religious belief is simply accepted on faith and is antithetical to reason or rational inquiry. This way of talking, however, fails to say much about what is meant by reason or rationality. We have seen that religious believers are apt to give a variety of reasons for why it is they believe what they do, so to say that religious belief is antithetical to reason does not tell us very much about how reason and rationality are used in religion. If a use of reason or rationality from the natural sciences, say, is applied to religion, then all we may come to realize is that religion is not a science (but why should we have thought it was?). So, a definition of fideism that uses undefined concepts like "reason" and "rationality" will never get us very far. However, by seeing why it will not work to define fideism using undefined concepts, we can begin to see what fideism is trying to get at in the first place. The problem is that certain words that get used within the religious form of life garner their meaning from the way they are used in that context. To understand what "God" means, as we have already seen, we need to look at how that word gets used in a religious context. But does the same hold true for super-concepts like truth, reason, rationality, and justification? Does their meaning, when used in a religious context, depend on their use? To help make these amorphous questions a bit more concrete, let's return again to Putnam's example regarding the definition of objects.

Remember, in Putnam's story, I stipulated that the definitions of what counts as an object do not simply fall from the sky; rather, they are derived by looking to the "object language game" in which the inhabitants of Putnam's imaginary story participate. By describing the interactions people have with objects in each of the two different contexts, we are able to formulate the grammatical rules about what counts as an object in each context. The criteria for defining an object are internal to each practice. I take it that the individuals in one object world could, if they wanted, communicate with the individuals in the other object world and, furthermore, that each could understand how the other defines objects. However, what if one of the object counters starts to say that the other object counter is irrational in the way they define objects? What exactly are they saying? It seems like they could be saying either: (a) that the other object counter has different rules for what counts as an object than what I use, and, since I take my rules to be the correct ones, the others are simply wrong; or, they may be saying, (b) Reason (with a capital R), which applies to all definitions of objects (a sort of Platonic form of an object), shows us that the other object counters are counting objects in the objectively wrong way (their rules for object counting are irrational and false). The claim of (a) uses the context dependent rules for counting objects from one practice to argue that the other is wrong. Really the claim is that the other group is simply different and, as is often the case, different gets defined as wrong. If they want to convince the other object-defining group, then they might want to try to persuade (or convert) them to count objects the way that they count them. What they cannot do is appeal to a way of defining objects that exists outside of any practice and then try and use that definition as *the* way of defining objects.

As to what is going on in (b), there are two possibilities. First, it may be that in (b), the group is taking the rules (or reasons) they have for defining objects and absolutizing them as *the* rules for defining objects. In this case, they take their context-dependent rules, rules internal to their practice, and apply them to an area in which they have no application. The rules are stripped from their context of use and misapplied. When the definition from one context is brought into another context, one in which the concept has no application, then the other object counters can either change their definition and accept the new one, reject the new definition and go on their way, or, maybe, incorporate two senses of the word "object" into their practice. The mistake, however, is thinking that the definition of "object" from one form of life is somehow capable of serving as the standard for all uses.[54]

Now, the other possibility is that the object definers in (b) think they have a pure use of *the* rules for defining objects that dictates how objects should be counted always and everywhere. They have the definition of objects that God would give if God were asked. But from where does this rule for defining objects get its meaning? From what context was it derived? Of course, it is impossible to make sense of a rule without a context (even a private rule has a context of one person), so this idea of a context-free rule is difficult to understand at best—at worst, it is simply meaningless.

Here is the gist of this discussion. It is logically illicit to take a rule whose meaning is fixed within a certain use of language (a rule internal to a practice) and then apply it (externally) to another practice where it has no purchase. Furthermore, it makes no sense to pretend that there is a rule whose meaning is fixed free of any context, but which is (*per impossibile*) applicable to all contexts. When a rule that is internal to one practice gets applied to a different (external) practice, or when a rule is said to be free of any and all contexts, we are always going to end up in logically suspect terrain. Fideism (or more accurately Wittgensteinian Fideism) rests on ignoring this internal/external distinction of meaning. The claim that there are internal reasons that are (somewhat) unique to a particular practice means that there will often be no sense in criticizing certain aspects of a practice using rules derived from an external (or different) practice. However, rather than thinking that there is one thing called Wittgensteinian fideism, it is best to see how ignoring the internal/external distinction leads to a cluster of fideisms rather than any one thing called fideism.

Senses of Fidesim

Semantic Fideism

In *An Introduction to the Philosophy of Religion*, Kai Nielsen writes that certain Wittgensteinian philosophers "argue that religious concepts can only be understood if we have an insider's grasp of the form of life of which they are an integral part."[55] This is a fairly common claim about fideism that often gets taken for the whole story. The worry is that the meaning of religious language can never be grasped by those who do not participate in a religious form of life, and if the meaning of religious language cannot be understood by an unbeliever, then it cannot be criticized externally either. We can call this sort of fideism *semantic fideism*.

Semantic fideism, as I see it, is clearly false for the following reasons. First, religious concepts, as answers to religious limiting questions, are perfectly intelligible to those not in the grip of any religious limiting question themselves. If this were not so, conversion to a religious form of life would be impossible. How would people expressing a spiritual crisis, articulated by means of religious limiting questions, understand the religious answer as logically complete unless they first could understand what the answer meant? Furthermore, since the religious limiting questions arise out of a shared experience of human finitude and human suffering, it stands to reason that the religious response to these conditions would be understandable by those outside of the religious tradition. Even if someone does not feel the existential impact of death, suffering, and meaninglessness themselves, it does not follow that they cannot understand how someone who is in such a state feels. (This sort of thing is what we mean by empathy.) The unbeliever may be perplexed as to why anyone would need to accept a religious way of life, but that is simply a way of saying that they do not share the religious believers existential concerns; it is not to say they cannot understand the state the believer is in. This is why Wittgenstein, who may not have been a believer himself, is able to write that "The Christian religion is only for one who needs infinite help, therefore only for one who feels an infinite need. The whole planet cannot be in greater anguish than a single soul. The Christian faith—as I view it—is the refuge in this ultimate anguish."[56] Since the religious limiting questions and the religious answers are both addressed to human concerns, it seems unlikely that one could understand one and not the other. The narrow view of fideism that sees it as an inability to understand religious meaning from the outside seems unlikely, although, as we will see in a later chapter in Part Two, it may take some work for the unbeliever to accurately understand what the believer is saying. It may behoove the unbeliever to do the hard work of trying to see what the believer is actually saying so that he or she can avoid any misunderstandings; this just means that religion may appear different from the inside than it does from the outside, but this does not mean that the unbeliever cannot come to learn the meaning of what the believer is saying.

If the unbeliever can understand religious language, does it make sense to say that he or she can also criticize it? Is sematic fideism better seen as the claim that religion is insulated from outside scrutiny? I don't think this view makes much sense either. If religion could not be criticized, then it would seem to be an anything-goes affair, and there would be no such thing as a confused or mistaken use of a religious concept. However, internal to the practice of religion, there is a distinction between the standard use of a concept and a deviant (or confused) use. As we already saw in the first chapter, and as we will see in the next, there are uses of religious language that can legitimately be considered confused, mistaken, or idolatrous. Pointing out a confused use of religious language presupposes (or is parasitic upon) there already being a standard use of religious language in play. This distinction, however, is made *within* religion. It is made against the background of the lived life and tradition of faith, the historical accounts of theology, and the various sacred texts. Once we understand religious language in the context in which it is used, something I just argued is as possible for the unbeliever as much as for the believer, then spotting a confused use of a religious concept is just a matter of pointing out a use that deviates from the standard use. When we understand how the game should be played, we are able to understand when it is being played inappropriately, just as I can point out a mistaken move in chess once I understand the moves that are allowed.

Justification and Truth Fideism

Even if religious language can be understood by those who do not participate in the religious form of life (i.e., semantic fideism is false), and even if someone who is not a believer oneself could still criticize certain religious uses of language, it still stands to reason that fideism might show up at the level of justification and truth. Can the religious form of life itself be criticized and shown to be false? The question is not "can certain claims within religion be shown to be unjustified or false by appealing to internal criteria of meaningfulness?" but rather, "can the practice of religion as a whole be shown to be unjustified or false?" I call the claim that it makes no sense to criticize the practice of religion as a whole *justification fideism*, and the claim that it makes no sense to claim that the practice of religion (i.e., the religious form of life) as a whole is true or false, *truth fideism*. Here is how Nielsen describes the sort of fideism I have in mind: "It [religion] can only be understood or criticized, and then only in a piecemeal way, from within this mode by someone who has a participant's understanding of this mode of discourse."[57] We have already dealt with the question of how specific instances of religious language can be understood and criticized externally using internal criteria (rules and criteria internal to the logic of religious practice), but what about criticizing the entire practice of religion? Does that even make sense?

When Nielsen says that, on a fideistic account of religion, it is impossible to criticize religion or argue for its falsity from outside the practice of religion itself, his concern is mainly with a variety of philosophical claims that he refers to as "dark sayings," sayings which, when accepted, lead one straight to fideism.[58]

While he lists eight of these sayings, I want to focus on two of them that I take as not only representative of a certain sort of fideism but also as paradigmatic statements of the sort of Wittgensteinian account of religious belief that I have been defending here. Nielsen writes first that "Forms of life taken as a whole are not subject to criticism; each is in order as it is, for each has its own criteria and each sets its own norms of intelligibility, reality, and rationality," and then that "There is no Archimedean point in terms of which a philosopher ... can relevantly criticise a whole form of life or a way of life. He cannot even criticise a whole mode of discourse, for each mode of discourse as each form of life has its own specific criteria of rationality/irrationality, intelligibility/unintelligibility, and reality/unreality."[59]

I actually think Nielsen is correct in what he says. I think that the two points he makes about forms of life having their own internal rules and criteria, and his claim that forms of life cannot be criticized from the outside, are indicative of the best way to look at forms of life in general and religious practice more specifically. In fact, the two sayings are related. It is because forms of life have their own internal rules about meaningfulness that they cannot be criticized externally using rules drawn from another practice. Where I think Nielsen is misguided is in his belief that somehow these are negative claims that must be rejected rather than an explanation of the grammar of religious belief. Before explaining why I think Nielsen is correct in his account of fideism but wrong to fret about it, I want to make a few necessary distinctions.

The first thing to note is that religious practice takes place within a life that overlaps with other interests and areas of life. In this case we should avoid thinking that there is an isolated religious language game that has no bearing or overlap with other areas of life. This is a naïve way to think of religious language games (or forms of life) and it is one that Rush Rhees tried to amend in the writings collected and edited by D.Z. Phillips and published as *Wittgenstein and the Possibility of Discourse*.[60]

The fact that believers are competent in multiple interrelated language games allows us to see that believers will themselves have a sense of how language differs in the different areas of their life. While religious believers may interpret the meaning of reality, as a whole, differently than atheists, at the empirical level, there will be deep agreement. Believers will understand the use of reason in the empirical sciences (some will even be scientists themselves) and they will understand what it means to make a rational argument for, say, Pluto being a planet. It is just that these scientific uses of reason and rationality may not be applicable *within* the practice of religion (simply because religion is not an empirical science). In this case, it is good to remember that when we say that religious concepts get their meaning from the religious form of life, we are obviously not saying these are the only concepts the believer understands. Believers would, I assume, be able to distinguish between giving a reason in science, giving a reason in religion, and giving a reason in philosophy (say, for their belief that there are other minds or that memories are veridical). The believer, like most people, is able to discriminate quite easily between the variety of ways words get used, including the important philosophical concepts we mentioned earlier, concepts like truth, reason, rationality, and justification. So the first point to remember is that when the believer speaks as a believer, he or she is not unaware that one is using language that is related to, but also different from, other ways they use language in their lives.

Second, it may be that when Nielsen is asking about criticizing religion from the outside, he is thinking of criticizing certain religious beliefs that conflict with (or impinge on) some specific claim in science. Sometimes, under the name of religion, believers attempt to make claims that actively oppose empirical science. I have in mind things like Young Earth creationism or the belief in certain claims about divine interaction. Yet, if the religious form of life cannot be criticized from outside the practice of religion, then science would be unable to criticize religious beliefs that go against their deeply held empirical truths. There are two things to be said here. First, if religious belief begins to wander off into the domain of science, making statements that go against certain well-established empirical claims, then it may be that religious belief has strayed from religion in a purposeful attempt to look like a science. In my first book, *Kneeling at the Altar of Science*,[61] I argue that, oftentimes, theologians have indeed purposefully tried to dress religion in the garb of science in order to bolster its intellectual respectability and make it more acceptable in a culture obsessed with science's way of investigating the empirical world. This led, however, to certain philosophical confusions that affected both religion and science. The first point is that religion's encroachment on science may be due to certain individuals illicitly trying to make religious belief look more scientific.

Second, if religious beliefs are conflicting with certain scientific facts, then it would seem natural that the religious belief could be criticized from the outside. Once religion has encroached on the findings of another domain, then using the rules and norms of that discipline to criticize religion is expected. There may be no agreed-upon standards in which to sway one's opinion one way or another (a scientist may not convince the Young Earth creationists that they are wrong), but criticism of religion using arguments from science, *if religion is making scientific claims*, seems appropriate. If believers indiscriminately claim for religion meaning that is not part of its internal grammar, but is part of the grammar of another discipline, then external criticism is warranted. This sort of criticism, however, is just part of the normal process of pointing out what the grammar of religion actually is and showing when it stretches itself so far that it loses its religious sense.

Now it may be that once we agree with Nielsen about the inability to criticize the religious form of life as a whole, he would simply shrug. It may be that he has no desire to waste his time criticizing a religious belief that is simply seen as a way of assessing life or a way of interpreting the meaning of reality as a whole. Behind Nielson's criticism of fideism, however, is his claim that any religion that does not allow itself to be criticized with external criteria is rationally defective and unworthy of our participation. With his scientific bent, it is no surprise that Nielson would find a faith that uses transcendence in ways similar to those we saw above, a faith that at its center involves some form of religious practice (like worship or prayer), and a faith that is committed to a life of service and a commitment to justice, intellectually paltry at best. This sort of religious faith, however, does not deny the importance and power of science, nor does it conflict with any of the normal empirical beliefs held by science. For example, the religious life may involve the belief that any talk of God must admit God's utter mystery. It may also believe that science does not present a universe where a spiritual reality is impossible, or a universe where it is impossible that, at some deep level, everything is interrelated. The believer of the sort I have in mind here may be committed to helping those in need, he or she may see all of life as a gift, and he or she may strive to live with peace, hope, and joy whenever possible. Is there anything here which an atheist could disprove? But, for Nielson that is the point. If there is nothing he can criticize or disprove about religious practice using norms and rules from science, then it must be that religious practice has no cognitive value. But what we must remember is that Nielson is constantly insisting that religious practice conform to rules and norms that are not internal to its own rules and criteria. Nielson is asking too much and looking at religious practice far too little.

I think this last claim gets to Nielsen's concern most accurately. Sure, he might say, I can accept that believers are committed to a way of interpreting life and serving others, a way that does not interfere with the empirical claims of science. But is this way of assessing reality justified? Is it true? Both Nielson and I agree that at least part of fideism is a commitment to the idea that these sorts of meta-questions do not make sense when asked external to religious practice. The difference is that Nielson sees this as a defect for religion and I take it as a natural consequence of the grammar of religious belief. I accept justification and truth fideism because "justification" and "truth" both have a use within the practice of religion. Of course, since these concepts do get used in religion, it is important to look to that practice to figure out what they mean in that context. It does no good to simply come to the table with claims about what these words must mean and then criticize religion for not conforming to this use. The meaning of religious concepts must be understood against the backdrop of religious practice. Nielson may not like the way concepts are used in religion, but his criticisms are more like someone "booing" and less like anything intellectually persuasive. In closing, I want to make one final attempt to solidify the importance of letting religious practice speak for itself.

Letting Religion Speak

In his essay "Philosophy, Theology and the Reality of God," D.Z. Phillips makes a provocative suggestion for how we might look at the meaning of divine reality. He writes, "I suggest that more can be gained if one compares the question, 'What kind of reality is divine reality?' not with the question, 'Is this physical object real or not?' but with the different question, 'What kind of reality is the reality of physical objects?'"[62] Now how is it that we investigate the sort of reality that physical objects have? We do this by speaking about, interacting with, and living in a world of physical objects. We do things such as clean our plate, take out the trash, buy a wedding ring, mow the lawn, and watch sporting events. That is, by living in a world where we interact with the sort of things we call physical objects, we learn to reflect on, delineate, and explain the sort of grammatical sense that physical object talk has.

Now, as Phillips notes, this sort of point about the grammar of the reality of physical objects has a corollary in religion. He writes, "to ask a question about the reality of God is to ask a question about *a kind of reality* not about the reality of *this* or *that*, in much the same way as asking a question about the reality of physical objects is not about the reality of this or that physical object."[63] The question of the grammar of the reality of God comes out of, or is logically dependent upon, the practice in which people pray, worship, love agapeistically, etc. This is why Phillips, in *Death and Immortality*, writes, "In learning by contemplation, attention, renunciation, what forgiving, thanking, loving, etc., mean in these contexts, the believer is participating in the reality of God; *this is what we mean by God's reality*."[64] By participating in (or by describing) the religious form of life, we are able to explain the grammar of divine reality; that is, we are able to see what is meant by divine reality *in toto* (as opposed to the reality of this or that spiritual object).

In explaining the grammar of physical object talk and divine reality talk, we are explaining what kind of reality is being addressed when we speak of physical reality and divine reality, respectively. It is only by looking at the use of these concepts that we come to see what they mean, but this meaning is internal to their use, prompting Phillips to write that "It follows from my argument that the criteria of meaningfulness cannot be found *outside* religion, since they are given by religious discourse itself. Theology can claim justifiably to show what is meaningful in religion only when it has an internal relation to religious discourse."[65] Since the meaning of religious language (including concepts used in religion like reasonableness, justification, true, and false etc.) occurs within the religious form of life, it makes no sense to ask of the form of life itself if it is true or false. Commenting on the work of D.Z. Phillips, William Brenner writes:

> In learning to participate in these different but interrelated activities, we learned, among other things, what counts, in a given context, as good grounds for a knowledge-claim. Clearly then, in view of this, "the given" [the form of life] cannot itself be based on grounds. And so we do not earn or fail to earn the right to it, as we do with our knowledge-claims.[66]

The practice of religion is what Brenner refers to as "the given," and it is this given that brings sense to our language. So, in saying that the given cannot be criticized, falsified, or justified, I am not saying that there is an argument lacking that still needs to be discovered in order to falsify the given—I am saying that it makes no logical sense to speak this way. The given is, so to speak, groundless, and it is this groundlessness that leads to justification and truth fideism, and it is also this groundlessness that should be accepted.

In *On certainty*, Wittgenstein writes, "Giving grounds, however, justifying the evidence, comes to an end—but the end is not certain propositions striking us immediately as true … it is our acting, which lies at the bottom of our language game."[67] The religious life is a life committed to the daily practices of faith lived out with all the variety and diversity with which religiosity is displayed. A believer accepts the religious form of life as an answer to certain questions and, in practicing his or her faith and becoming a competent speaker of the language of faith, the believer, so to speak, enters into a religious worldview (or interprets existence under a religious gaze). It is this religious way of life that grounds statements of truth and falsity made within this particular form of life. Wittgenstein continues in *On Certainty*, "If the true is what is grounded, then the ground is not true, nor yet false."[68] When the practice of religion is accepted as an answer to religious limiting questions, then the believer begins to make certain discriminations within religion about what is true and what is false. It would be a mistake to ask if the practice itself is true or false. That is to mistake the grounded for the ground itself. In the object-defining example, it would be a mistake to think there is a third view from nowhere where we get the real answer for how to define objects. There is no such place. Both ways of defining objects are, strictly speaking, groundless—they are incommensurable. But groundlessness is not a defect of religion; it is simply part and parcel of all human practice. John Whittaker writes:

> They [religious beliefs] are not groundless simply because we *now* lack the evidence or the experience on which they might ideally be judged; their groundlessness belongs to their logical nature as fundamental beliefs that play a formative role in shaping our thought .... They are essentially transformative beliefs, in other words, because their adoption entails a corresponding adjustment in one's mental life and its outward manifestation.[69]

Conclusion

The mistake about religious belief that I have tried to address in this chapter is the view that sees religion as a set of metaphysical beliefs about reality, a set of beliefs that can be justified and shown to be true. In fact, religion is best seen as a way of living, of assessing reality, of accepting life's vicissitudes, and of looking on those in need with love. As Wittgenstein writes in *Culture and Value*, "a religious belief could only be something like a passionate commitment to a system of reference. Hence, although it's a belief, it's really a way of living, or a way of assessing life. It's passionately seizing hold of this interpretation."[70] Religion, as a practice, is a way of interpreting the whole of life. It is a distinctively religious way of being in the world. This was seen in the discussion of the various senses of transcendence, but, it should be remembered, these concepts are used within religion; they are part of the internal practice of religion. There is no sense that can be made of justifying the religious form of life or of asking if the religious form of life is true or false. Again, as Wittgenstein says in *On Certainty*, "You must bear in mind that the language-game is so to say something unpredictable. I mean: it is not based on grounds. It is not reasonable or unreasonable. It is there—like our life."[71] The key now is to investigate the place that certain long-held religious doctrines have within a faith that is more about living than believing. This will be the goal we will tackle in the next chapter.

3

Picturing a Religious Form of Life

In Flannery O'Connor's short story "Parker's Back," her last story published before her untimely death at the age of thirty-nine, O'Connor tells the story of the relationship between O.E. Parker and Sarah Ruth Cates. The two meet one day when Parker's truck breaks down in front of the house in which Sarah Ruth lives. Sarah Ruth, the daughter of a traveling preacher, is a woman who O'Connor describes as "plain, plain."[1] She is also a bit of a self-righteous religious prude who, "In addition to her other bad qualities, is forever sniffing up sin."[2] Parker, on the other hand, is worldlier and savvier than Sarah. As far as religion goes, Parker has little need for such things. One thing that Parker does have a need for, however, is tattoos. His body is covered in tattoos of all sorts—an eagle sitting on a cannon, a coiled-up serpent, a hand of cards, hearts with arrows shot through them, a panther, a tiger, a cobra, and even Queen Elizabeth II and Prince Phillip—tattoos that seem so randomly chosen that the only story they tell is the story of the chaos of Parker's life. O'Connor writes, "The effect was not of one intricate arabesque of colors but of something haphazard and botched."[3] The only place that Parker doesn't have a tattoo is on his back. He doesn't see the point of having one where he can't even see it. For her part, Sarah Ruth sees Parker's tattoos through the eyes of her piety, thinking Parker vain for having such a gaudy display etched into his skin.

The two characters marry but, even after their marriage, the troubled relationship, which was always present, continues. Sarah Ruth remains stuck in her pretentious self-righteousness and Parker remains discontented, thinking every night that he might choose to simply not return home. When feeling discontented, the only solace Parker gets is when he thinks of getting another tattoo, but he hates the thought of having to use mirrors to be able to look at his back, which is where the new tattoo would inevitably have to go. Sarah Ruth, conversely, tells Parker that at the judgment seat, God will want to know what else he did with his time other than getting all those ridiculous tattoos. As Parker continues in his unhappy existence, he comes around to the fact that if a tattoo is going to make him feel better, he will have to go ahead and get one on his back. He begins to think it a good idea to get a religious tattoo that might grab the attention of Sarah Ruth and maybe even make her feel good, or at least placate her nastiness a bit. O'Connor writes, "but as urgent as it might be for him to get a tattoo, it was just as urgent that he get exactly the right one to bring Sarah Ruth to heel."[4] The tattoo begins to consume Parker's thoughts until it becomes all that he can think about.

One day, while baling hay in the field, Parker is flung off his tractor by a tree branch. As he flies off the tractor seat, he finds himself yelling "in an unbelievably loud voice, 'GOD ABOVE!'"[5] The tractor crashes into the tree, causing the tree to burst into flames. Parker's shoes get knocked off his feet, leaving him shoeless in front of the burning tree (reminiscent of Moses). This event changes Parker in an inexplicable way, so much so that he gets in his truck and drives straight to the tattoo parlor knowing "that there had been a great change in his life, a leap forward into a worse unknown, and that there was nothing he could do about it."[6] In the language of faith, we might say that Parker was struck by the gratuitous grace of God. It may have been unexpected and even undesired, but it showed up in the form of a burning tree and a broken tractor.

At the tattoo parlor, Parker, requesting a tattoo of God, shuffles through the images in the tattoo artist's book. "Parker sped on, then stopped," O'Connor writes. "His heart too appeared to cut off; there was absolute silence. It said *as plainly as if silence were a language itself,* GO BACK. Parker returned to the picture—the haloed head of a flat stern Byzantine Christ with all-demanding eyes."[7] After getting the tattoo of the icon of the Byzantine Christ on his back, "Parker looked, turned white and moved away. The eyes in the reflected face continued to look at him—still, straight, all-demanding, enclosed in silence."[8] Underscoring the role the eyes of the tattooed Christ play in the story, O'Connor later writes, "The eyes that were now forever on his back were eyes to be obeyed. He was as certain of it as he had ever been of anything."[9]

After a stop at the bar, which ends in a fight, Parker finally heads home to show his new tattoo of God to his wife, hoping he has finally found a way to please her. Back home, Parker knocks on the front door, but Sarah Ruth keeps asking who it is, partly fooling with Parker and partly showing her dissatisfaction with him. Finally, after being asked again who he is, Parker whispers into the door: "'Obadiah' …, and all at once he felt the light pouring through him, turning his spider web soul into a perfect arabesque of colors, a garden of trees and birds and beasts. 'Obadiah Elihue!' he whispered."[10] For one of the few times in his life, Parker willingly self-identifies with his given biblical name. O.E. Parker has died and Obadiah Elihue is born.

After some resistance from his wife, Obadiah finally gets her to look at the new tattoo of the Byzantine Christ, but Sarah Ruth not only gives no indication that the tattoo pleases her; she also indicates that she doesn't even recognize the image on Obadiah's back. "It ain't anybody I know," she says. Parker lets her know that it is a tattoo of God, but Sarah Ruth simply insists that it can't be since he doesn't know what God looks like, reminding him that "He don't look, He's a spirit. No man shall see his face."[11] Just then she begins to scream that Parker is an idolater and, since she does not want an idolater in her house, he must get out. She grabs a broom and begins to beat Parker, chasing him out of the house and into the yard. As welts form on the face of the Christ figure tattooed on Parker's back, Parker lays outside on the ground. O'Connor ends the story saying, "There he was—who called himself Obadiah Elihue—leaning against the tree, crying like a baby."[12]

Idolatrous Religious Symbols

There is no doubt that O.E. Parker and his wife Sarah Ruth see different things when they look at the tattoo of the Byzantine Christ, and the differences in what they see are instructive for us today. When Sarah Ruth reminds Parker that his tattoo cannot be God because no one has seen God since God is a spirit, Parker reminds her that it is only a picture (as opposed to a portrait). In that one sentence, we see their differences plain as day. When Parker says the tattoo is only a picture, he is both trying to get Sarah Ruth to see that it is not like a photograph and get her to see that, as a picture, it has a different use than just trying to accurately represent God. Parker has learned something that his pious wife cannot grasp. He has learned that an image can have a use that goes beyond its pictorial representation. When Parker says the tattoo is of God, and Sarah Ruth says it isn't, they certainly aren't disputing whether or not the tattoo is a good likeness of God. It is rather that they see the picture in different ways, or better yet, they are each using the picture in a different way. When Parker sees the Byzantine Christ, he sees it as an icon, as an image that represents the divine by pointing beyond itself to something ineffable, but the image also represents an experience he had. It represents the way that the divine has entered his life and taken on a central role in his way of looking at the world. To see the tattoo as an icon that points to the divine is to realize that the tattoo is not meant as a portrait of God (good or bad); rather, it is representative of an experience that he had in relation to divine mystery. The God that Parker saw in the eyes of the Christ was the One who first saw him when he fell off the tractor and lay on the ground shoeless in front of the burning tree.

Sarah Ruth's seeing, on the other hand, stops at the image itself. She can't move her gaze beyond the mere lines, shadings, and colors of the tattoo. In her husband's tattoo, she sees only an idol because she sees it as a rendering of what can never be portrayed. Her only use for the image is to see it as not just a poor representation of God, but as an idolatrous attempt to create an image of the ineffable. Sarah Ruth's inability to see God in the image turns her into an iconoclast who needs to destroy the idol. While O'Connor presents Sarah Ruth as the more "religious" of the two at the outset, her piety blinds her to possibilities when it comes to seeing God. Her iconoclasm is leveled not only against the idol on Parker's back but also against Parker himself, who, in having an experience of God (seen, not the least, in his referring to himself as "Obadiah"), comes to present a challenge to the real idolatry, which is Sarah Ruth's life. Sarah Ruth's seeing is stuck at the level of the material—unable to see God in the image, she is content to see it as an idol. The change in the life of Sarah Ruth is all on the surface. Her religious life lacks depth; therefore, she is unable to see the image as an icon.

What O'Connor describes in "Parkers Back" is still with us today. That is, there are those who see religious doctrines as simple statements of fact that must be assented to, full stop. However, this sort of belief is often severed from their life. There is no ethical transformation, no concept of a life that must be changed, no concept of the "eyes of Christ" demanding something of them. Religious doctrines are often used as a way of escaping life or encouraging a status-quo existence of selfishness. This is the sort of thing we called idolatry earlier. Nicholas Lash, commenting on Martin Buber's concept of religion, summarizes the sort of idolatry we mentioned in chapter one. Buber writes, "We build little shelters to divinity, in which we huddle in order to escape from ourselves, from each other, from the world—and from God."[13] With contemporary religious doctrines, this can occur, as we will see, in a variety of ways, but the goal is always a form of escape from guilt, suffering, meaninglessness, and, ultimately, death. The goal of idolatrous religious belief is to manipulate the anthropomorphic God so as to proffer a divine ally in our escape from reality, an ally that will allow our ego and our needs to occupy center stage. Religious doctrines, on this account, lead to a form of life similar to what we saw in Johnston's account of "spiritual materialism" in that the idolatrous practice occurs under the guise of spirituality.

Religious belief is often discredited on the claim that it is anti-scientific, requiring individuals to accept things that any modern-day individual should find outrageous. I do not believe this is the case. I think the belief in an anthropomorphic God should be rejected not because it conflicts with our knowledge of science, but because it is simply irreligious. Supernatural theism lends itself to a theological system that preferences correct belief over religious practice, creating an intellectual system that lacks the required ethical robustness that one would expect from someone who claims to model one's life on the life of Jesus. Nietzsche writes, "The Christians have never practiced the actions Jesus prescribed them; and the impudent garrulous talk about the 'justification by faith' and its supreme and sole significance is only the consequence of the Church's lack of courage and will to profess the works Jesus demanded."[14] What a wonderful description of the state we are in today. Christian faith, as it often gets presented, is not unbelievable due to its metaphysics or epistemology; rather, it is unbelievable because those who profess to believe it lack the courage to live by the moral precepts of its founder. This, naturally, shows up in the way certain beliefs get interpreted. The doctrines become cowardice shrouded in religious garb. They become a way to maintain the privilege of the "I" in the face of the call to "die to self." They become a desire for compensation in the face of suffering and they display a need to have the world make sense *for us*. While this way of thinking may placate fear and help us feel that all is well, the cost is true faith being replaced with an idolatrous practice. In what follows, I want to look at a few specific examples of religious belief in contemporary faith that may help give us a glimpse of modern-day idolatry in action.

Atonement and Idolatry

In his article entitled "The Power of Forgiveness," the famed evangelical preacher Joel Osteen writes:

> Jesus paid the ultimate price for our sins on the cross. He lived a perfect and sinless life and gave it as a sacrifice for your sins and mine. And when all hope seemed to be gone He miraculously came to life again. What this means is: When we accept Him as our Lord and Savior we are completely forgiven … for anything … for everything … forever![15]

While Osteen himself represents the extreme right in most of his theological views, the concept of substitutionary atonement serves as the centerpiece of the faith of many people. This idea, at least on its surface, is not an odd concept. Regarding the doctrine of the atonement Daniel Migliore writes, "the cross has been the center of attention in most doctrines of atonement in Western theology."[16] First Corinthians, a letter attributed to the Apostle Paul, states, "For I delivered to you as of first importance what I also received, that Christ died for our sins in accordance with the scriptures" (I Corinthians 15:3 RSV). While there are a variety of different atonement theories, most of them see the cross as a sort of transaction, whereby a debt is paid to God (or possibly the devil, depending on whose theory we are talking about) through the death of Jesus in order to forgive human beings of their sins. On the human side, what is required, so the story goes, is the acceptance that the substitutionary death of Jesus was indeed a penalty paid for the punishment that we, as sinners, rightfully deserved.

Forgiveness and Belief: Subjective and Objective

When I was a teenager, I remember praying the "prayer of faith" with a friend who announced afterward that I was now forgiven of my sins and, henceforth, an acceptable candidate for entrance into heaven. I remember thinking how easy this process was compared with my Catholic upbringing. All I did was recite a few words from the book of Romans (the "Roman Road," it was called), assent to their truth, and boom, I was saved! But does this sort of forgiveness represent the essence of faith—the heart of the Christian message—or is it an easy way to deal with our misdeeds, a way to assuage our guilt, without the hard work of personal transformation? Or maybe, in accepting a quick and easy form of forgiveness, we are seeking, as I was, a way to help rid ourselves of our fear of death by doing whatever it takes to earn eternal life. While being forgiven by just praying a simple prayer is sold as God's ultimate act of Grace, there seems to be something trivial and easy about it, something that fails to take human striving and the natural propensity for human selfishness seriously.

What could be wrong with the claim that "Jesus died for our sins"? Of course, it depends on what one means by that phrase. If atonement arises from a desire to be reconciled with divine love (to accept that we are ourselves accepted by God, to paraphrase Tillich), then it seems that there is nothing more theologically important than claiming that Jesus died for our sins. My argument here is that there are some ways of speaking about the atonement that are more religiously acceptable than others and some ways that are simply idolatrous and irreligious. It is not the idea of atonement in and of itself that is problematic, but the way that this doctrine gets used or the way it shows up in the life of the believer. Since meaning depends on use, there will naturally be some ways that the concept of atonement gets used that lead to confusion rather than clarity. It is the problematic use of atonement that I want to look at here.

The idea of "atonement" has both a subjective side and an objective side. In the sort of atonement story mentioned above—let's call it the transactional view—the objective side is the historical execution of Jesus on the cross by the Romans, while the subjective side is an individual's accepting the objective event as being sufficient for the forgiveness of sins.[17] When forgiveness of sin is seen as the result of praying a certain prayer and believing a certain set of facts, the subjective side of the atonement gets overemphasized. The objective side of the atonement is a necessary condition for forgiveness, but without its subjective acceptance, it never actually gets applied to the individual's life. The objective side of the atonement fades into the background as the subjective side takes center stage.

In this case, if no one ever accepted that Jesus died for their sins, then, supposedly, not only would no one ever be forgiven, but the objective death of Jesus would have been for naught. If we see forgiveness this way, then the individual's acceptance of the death of Jesus becomes more important than the crucifixion itself. Furthermore, if the really important thing about the atonement is that it be accepted subjectively by individuals, then it seems that any old death of Jesus would have succeeded. What if Jesus just lived to be eighty and died in his sleep—couldn't people still believe that he died for their sins? Some might want to say that the death of Jesus had to be a bloody public death so that his death could be seen on par with the Old Testament sacrifices, thus serving as a fulfillment of prophecy. But if that were so, then it seems that it is the objective event that matters most and not our subjective acceptance of it. When we make the atonement about our believing something, it seems to trivialize the objective event itself, yet, if the objective event is supposed to somehow secure forgiveness, then the subjective aspect appears unnecessary. What we need is a way to see the atonement as something we participate in *with* Jesus—we need to see the life and death of Jesus as a model for our own lives. But more on that later.

"Cheap Grace" as Idolatry

A second problem that arises when we stress the subjective side of forgiveness is that when forgiveness is seen as the simple assent to a few propositions, it trivializes forgiveness, making it an easy path to tread with little need to change or reorient our lives. The individual may feel bad about things he or she has done in the past, and may even desire to not repeat such bad behaviors in the future, but the main requirement needed in order to be forgiven, on this account at least, is to just believe that Jesus died for their sins. Forgiveness is done to the believer; it is imputed without reference to how life is lived or how one's character is transformed. This is a form of what we might call a magical conception of forgiveness. Sin is wiped away like a stain from a carpet or spilled wine on linoleum. More specifically, there is little to no cost to the individual except the cost of believing that something, at some time, in some far-off place, happened, and happened for their benefit. If simple belief becomes the cost of following Jesus, then the story of the gospel makes no essential ethical claim on the believer's life. The claim on this account is mainly epistemological, namely, it is about amassing enough evidence to be able to believe that Jesus died for one's sins. So, while the first problem with the atonement is that if we stress the subjective act of believing, we lose the importance of the objective fact itself, here the problem is that making forgiveness of sins a matter of simply believing creates a logical problem, rendering the idea of atonement impotent when it comes to personal transformation.

The logical problem created here is that, when belief (taken as mental assent to a proposition) becomes the main requirement for forgiveness, there is a logical gap created between believing something and living a certain way. Forgiveness, imparted just for the asking, may simply seem like the definition of grace, but what sort of grace is it? What sort of grace allows for forgiveness to be obtained by simply assenting that a certain fact occurred without making a real ethical demand on the individual who has been forgiven? Forgiveness, seen as an instantaneous act, negates the need for an inner transformation. If you keep persisting in nasty behavior, or if you neglect the poor or ignore others in need, then the sort of forgiveness that simply requires believing the right thing allows you to just repent and move on. This sort of forgiveness allows for the logical possibility that the "saved" go on living a life unchanged, a life where there is a disconnect between professed beliefs and the life lived. This sort of religious nonsense is what Dietrich Bonhoeffer called "cheap grace."

Dietrich Bonhoeffer, in *The Cost of Discipleship*, had no patience for the sort of forgiveness story just outlined. Bonhoeffer defines cheap grace in the following way: "Cheap grace means grace sold on the market like cheapjack's wares. The sacraments, the forgiveness of sin, and the consolations of religion are thrown away at cut prices. Grace is represented as the Church's inexhaustible treasury, from which she showers blessings with generous hands, without asking questions or fixing limits. Grace without price; grace without cost!"[18] Cheap grace uses religion to escape the real cost of forgiveness that the believer must incur and work through as one's life is realigned as a response to grace. Cheap grace robs the individual of the need to be transformed, a transformation that is necessary in order to deal with certain innate aspects of who he or she is, aspects that serve to maintain the believer's selfishness and keep him or her from those in need. Cheap grace trivializes the need to deal with the conditions that have led the sinner to a state of perpetual sin in the first place. Bonhoeffer continues:

> Cheap grace means grace as a doctrine, a principle, a system. It means forgiveness of sins proclaimed as a general truth, the love of God taught as the Christian "conception" of God. An intellectual assent to that idea is held to be of itself sufficient to secure remission of sins. The Church, which holds the correct doctrine of grace, has, it is supposed, *ipso facto* a part in that grace. In such a Church, the world finds a cheap covering for its sins; no contrition is required, still less any real desire to be delivered from sin.[19]

When forgiveness is proclaimed as a "general truth," the transformative power of grace is reduced to a mental property or a commodity bought with a nod of approval toward the cross. With cheap grace, guilt is assuaged but robbed of its power to compel us to change. More importantly, seeing grace as a mental act of acceptance creates a situation where we no longer see the need to model and pattern our life after the life of Jesus. We are forgiven, and heavenbound—what more needs to be done? Changing our orientation to life, in general, and to others in particular, becomes a contingent fact that may or may not occur rather than the necessary condition of what it means to be forgiven. This sort of story about "amazing grace" is not only not amazing; it is idolatrous. Bonhoeffer again:

> Cheap grace means the justification of sin without the justification of the sinner. Grace alone does everything, they say, and so everything can remain as it was before ... The world goes on in the same old way, and we are still sinners "even in the best life" as Luther said. Well, then, let the Christian live like the rest of the world, let him model himself on the world's standards in every sphere of life, and not presumptuously aspire to live a different life under grace from his old life under sin.[20]

The concept of atonement whereby Jesus died for my sins and all I must do is accept that fact leads to an unredeemed life, a life led by self-will seeking to escape guilt on the cheap. It is a life without religious merit which is lived under the guise of religiosity, or, better yet, an instance of metaphysical self-help. It is, again, the epitome of an idolatrous faith that places our own comfort and ease at the center of existence.

Bonhoeffer juxtaposes cheap grace with costly grace, writing:

> Costly grace is the Gospel, which must be *sought* again and again, the gift, which must be *asked* for, the door at which a man must *knock*. Such grace is *costly* because it calls us to follow, and it is *grace* because it calls us to follow *Jesus Christ*. It is costly because it costs a man his life, and it is grace because it gives a man the only true life.[21]

To say that costly grace costs us our life is another way of saying that we must, in some sense, die while still living. That is, we must die to ourselves, to our wants and our desire for compensation, while yet living a life of love in relation to those in need. This, of course, is the demarcation line between idolatry and transformative faith. Belief in a doctrine that leads us away from ourselves and to the Other frees us from manipulating divine love and using it as a tool of self-interest. Any explanation of the meaning of the death of Jesus must pay attention to the relationship between the story of the death of Jesus and the fact that accepting this story costs us our egocentric way of living. What we need is a shift in how we view reality and a shift in how we look upon those we share the world with. Believing in the salvific effect of Jesus's death must show itself in a changed life that turns us from ourselves and toward the Other. If there are no external criteria for the internal acceptance of forgiveness, then the result is idolatry.

Temporal Immortality and Idolatry

Paul Tillich writes, "Estranged from the ultimate power of being, man is determined by his finitude. He is given over to his natural fate. He came from nothing, and he returns to nothing. He is under the domination of death and is driven by the anxiety of having to die."[22] I would expect that this sort of death-anxiety is fairly common, although it probably manifests itself in a variety of ways.[23] Some wear death-anxiety on their sleeves Woody Allen style, while others try to escape the mere thought of their own death by working obsessively, exercising to excess, or, possibly, by studying philosophy. My way of dealing with it as a teenager was, as I mentioned above, to get "saved" in order to secure my spot in heaven. My main interest here is not with how death-anxiety feeds into religious belief, but rather with how the belief in—and craving for—eternal life can easily get turned into something idolatrous.

The fear of death and an idolatrous use of the concept of eternal life are bound to be natural soul mates. This is because the fear of death is essentially a fear about what will happen to *me*? Where will *I* go? Will *I* cease to exist? Once this sort of self-obsession is turned toward death, the result is a natural propensity to try and replace our finitude with something more palatable and acceptable to our ego. Simone Weil writes, "The imagination is continually at work filling up all the fissures through which grace might pass."[24] Once the imagination goes to work to protect itself from what Tillich called the "threat of non-being,"[25] an idolatrous false eternity results. If you are not sure if the promise of eternal life plays a role in why some choose to practice religion, ask yourself what church attendance would look like if Jesus announced tomorrow that there really was a place called heaven, but, unfortunately, it has reached capacity and its borders are henceforth closed.

How is it that the concept of "eternal life" gets turned into something idolatrous? I think there are several important ways that this can happen. Before looking at these, however, I want to look at how eternal life shares the same sort of logical challenge that we just saw above with the concept of the "forgiveness of sins."

Belief without Practice Revisited

Much like the forgiveness of sins, eternal life is often gained on the cheap. Reminiscent of Bonhoeffer's concept of "cheap grace," we get a form of "cheap immortality" when eternal life is seen as something that we are guaranteed just by believing the right things. In fact, forgiveness of sins and eternal life are usually thought to be secured by believing the exact same set of facts; this is because the forgiveness of sins is generally taken as a sufficient condition for inheriting eternal life. Sometimes we tend to think that this sort of theology is only reserved for the fundamentalist and evangelical. I have, however, learned through experience that many old-fashioned Protestant liberals and practicing Catholics also believe that some sort of heavenly existence is secured by believing the right things. The point being that the key to heaven is, again, being in a certain belief-state, no strings attached: "Whosoever believeth in him should not perish but have everlasting life" (John 3:16 RSV). "He who believes in the Son has eternal life; he who does not obey the Son shall not see life, but the wrath of God rests upon him" (John 3:36 RSV).

I remember when I was a young evangelical attending a small Bible college, we would be sent out to a shopping mall to "witness" to people. The goal was simply to get people to pray with us so that they might get saved, avoid hell, and make it into heaven. I never thought about the poverty, illness, or social/emotional struggles that these people might be facing—my goal at that time was not to help them with this life but get them to the next one. We often see this same sort of attitude when the goal of religious proselytizing or missionary work is to save souls rather than feed bodies and mend broken emotions. This is all predicated on the idea that eternal life is gained if we can simply get the person to utter the correct prayer. People become commodities, and the missionary becomes the peddler of the secret words that will save souls. The proselytizer is like a gnostic salesman who works on commission.

This, of course, gets us back to the argument that we saw above when we looked at the forgiveness of sins; namely, there is the logical possibility that someone could believe the "right" things so as to secure eternal life but still live any old way they please. Of course, it would not be expected that those who "believe on the Lord Jesus Christ" would actually live any old way they please, but if eternal life is secured by simply believing the right things, a logical space is opened up that allows for this possibility. If proper belief is what it takes to inherit eternal life, then practice gets pushed aside, allowing for the possibility that someone who lives a pretty nasty life may find themselves in heaven sharing space with some wonderfully loving believer like, maybe, Jimmy Carter (when he gets there) or Saint Francis or Dorothy Day. This is a possibility since all that is supposedly required to get to heaven is that one assent to the right set of facts (of course this all requires we think of heaven and the deceased in realistic terms).

Now, someone may respond that believing on (or in) Jesus is more than just believing certain facts to be true. To believe in Jesus means to trust Jesus, and such a belief entails (necessarily) that the believer live a virtuous life, a life that displays love toward others and strives to manifest (as much as possible) the virtues of peace and joy. The argument here is that it is a mistake to think that believing in Jesus is enough *all by itself* in order for us to inherit eternal life. What is also needed is a life that displays the fruits of that commitment.

I think this is the correct response, but it hides an ambiguity. Maybe we take the relationship between belief and practice to be something like this: "If you believe X then you will do Y." Now the natural question is what does it mean to say someone "will do Y"? It may mean either (a) "if you believe X then you should do Y (although you might not)" or (b) "if you believe X then you must do Y," which would be the same as saying that "believing X means that you actually do Y," where doing Y is part of what believing X means. If it is argued that, while it is hoped (or even expected) that those who believe in Jesus live a certain way, but, in reality, they may not, then we are back to the same argument noted above; namely, that there is a logical disconnect between belief and practice.

However, if the argument is that believing in (or on) Jesus only makes sense if one also lives a certain way (or if one's life is transformed in such a way that the change is exhibited in how the person lives), then I agree. In this case, the *meaning* of eternal life would have to refer to how the concept shows up in the life of the individual believer. The meaning of eternal life would not just be about some far-off place that we are going to go to someday since its meaning would be interrelated with how it affects the earthly life we live now. Believing in eternal life would be more about how we interpret our life on earth and less about what happens after our death. This way of linking belief and practice avoids what I call the "idolatry of mere belief," an idea which allows individuals the assurance of heaven without the need for a transformed life. Patrick Horn seems to be talking about avoiding something like the "idolatry of mere belief" when he writes, "Belief in the resurrection is not a relation to a proposition concerning the future; it is a relation to God concerning whether one lives in Christ, in humility and love."[26]

Eternal Life, "I," and Compensation

All we have done so far is to try and show that, again, there is a certain oddity that occurs when beliefs are logically separated from practice. However, showing the irreligious nature of what I have called "cheap immortality," or immortality secured through mere belief, does not deal with all the ways that eternal life can become idolatrous. There are at least three other crucial ways that this can occur that should be mentioned.

First, the thought of eternal life can easily be turned into a selfish concern to see our own egos continue on after death. Simone Weil writes, "The sin in me says 'I.'"[27] For Weil, one of the most important religious acts we can accomplish is to give ourselves over to God so completely that the "I" is lost in divine love. Weil writes, "We possess nothing in the world … except the power to say 'I.' That is what we have to give to God."[28] Yet, there is a very real sense in which a desire for eternal life can easily become the most egregious sort of anti-religious selfishness that one can imagine. This occurs when the "I," and its desire to be kept safe, is given pride of place over God. In this case, there is a refusal (or inability) to deny the self, causing the self to construct a concept of eternal life that grants the "I" such importance that its demise becomes unthinkable. Here, what is most important is the survival of us (or me). This is why so many philosophical accounts of eternal life make the survival of human consciousness, or the maintaining of personal identity after death, the test of the truthfulness of the concept itself. Eternal life, on this reading, is not so much about God; it is about us and our fear that we will somehow lose our self-identity (or our very self) after death.

We cannot imagine a world (heavenly or otherwise) where we are not there to bless reality with our presence. Simone Weil seems to have something like this thought in mind when she writes that "The principal claim which we think we have on the universe is that our personality should continue … The instinct of self-preservation makes us feel this continuation to be a necessity, and we believe that a necessity is a right."[29] Maybe, as a friend of mine used to say, heaven is a place for those who are surprised to be there.

The second way that eternal life can be turned into something idolatrous is when it is seen as a form of compensation for the good things we've done while on earth. We see this when people talk about gaining jewels in their heavenly crown or when they say, "there'll be a special place in heaven for that one."[30] Heaven, on this view, is seen as a reward for living. It is like an achievement party or awards ceremony for the winners. In thinking of the relationship between life and death in this way, the good things we do are not seen as part of what it means to have inherited eternal life (while still on earth), they are done in order to *obtain* eternal life. This kind of attitude, while rarely admitted—who wants to admit they help others just to get to heaven?—undoes the purity of the work we do to help others. This is not because the good deeds do not actually help—they very well may—but rather because our self-seeking motives negate our claim to love. Doing good is our way of earning an entrance ticket to the party. This makes it look as if we worship God rather than, say, the devil simply because God happens to be the one with the most power, the one who can secure the promise of our living forever if we do good deeds. Rush Rhees criticizes this way of thinking, writing,

> Is the reason for not worshipping the devil instead of God that God is stronger than the devil? God will get you in the end, the devil will not be able to save you from his fury, and then you will be [in] *for* it. "Think of your future boy, and don't throw away your chances." What a creeping and vile sort of thing religion must be.[31]

This sort of belief is creeping and vile because the motivation to serve God is a disguised way of saving ourselves. If we are doing good works simply to secure heaven, then our supposed good deeds become another instance of a vile practice. Religious faith, like acts of love, cannot be practiced for something (except for the love of neighbor). Patrick Horn writes, "In light of the Christian call to sacrificial living, the intellectual search for a vindication of one's belief is itself an irreligious act; inconsistent with the life of self-denial to which Christ calls the individual."[32] Using eternal life to validate (or reward) your actions and practices as a believer, again, simply shows that you never had much of a grasp on the meaning of Christian belief and charity in the first place. Doing good as a way of earning eternal life negates one's belief in God and falsifies one's supposed love for his or her neighbor.

The final way that eternal life can get used in an idolatrous way is when we conceive of it as something like our earthly life that simply continues on forever. This is related to the earlier claim that we sometimes seem to prefer our own existence so much so that we think it intolerable to conceive of it not continuing forever, and, not continuing in a state that mimics, to some extent, this worldly existence. This is not so odd since it would be challenging, if not impossible, for humans to imagine a heavenly state as being anything other than this earthly life writ large (modified, of course, so as to meet heaven's standards). We simply do not have the conceptual repertoire to imagine what an eternal state might be like, so we imagine what it is we are familiar with and spice it up to look more heavenly. Wittgenstein refers to this as temporal immortality and writes that, since it is a life much like our temporal life, it is inept at helping us solve the problems that we hoped it would help us solve. He writes,

> The temporal immortality of the soul of man, that is to say, its eternal survival also after death, is not only in no way guaranteed, but this assumption in the first place will not do for us what we always tried to make it do. Is a riddle solved by the fact that I survive forever? Is this eternal life not as enigmatic as our present one? The solution of the riddle of life in space and time lies *outside* space and time.[33]

The claim here is that any account of eternal life that is patterned on this life (consciousness, spiritual bodies, mansions, streets of gold, chats with dead historical figures), is one that would carry with it the same perplexities that this life exhibits. Nothing would be solved by simply making this life (or something like it) longer in duration (eternally long, in fact). A temporal immortality would still be an enigma since it would still have to account for the riddles of existence created by time.

There is nothing, in and of itself, religiously significant about the prolongation of life, even if the venue is changed to a far-off beautiful place populated with really nice historical characters (like a spiritual Disneyland). Simone Weil summarizes the way eternal life can be robbed of meaning if we simply see it as a prolongation of our earthly life, writing, "Belief in immortality is harmful because it is not in our power to conceive of the soul as really incorporeal. So, this belief is, in fact, a belief in the prolongation of life and it robs death of its purpose."[34] Temporal immortality is just another way of fleeing from the religious significance of seeing death as an opportunity to renounce the self and embrace the eternal. By trying to conceptualize eternal life using the image of this life, we strip eternal life of its religious context thereby stripping it of its religious power to guide and transform this life. The only rectification for this sort of thinking is to place the concept of immortality within the context of the religious life as a whole. D.Z. Phillips observes that seeing death as a result of grace is to see "the contrast between the temporal (that is, the concern with the self) and the eternal (that is, the concern with self-renunciation)."[35]

In all of these examples, the problem with eternal life boils down to thinking we can actually conceive of what eternal life must be like. Thinking that eternal life is obtained by believing the correct things or thinking of it as something we earn by doing good all rely on the belief that we can accurately conceive of what it will be like to experience life after death. In a way, the idolatrous use of eternal life is a problem that centers on a lack of epistemic humility. We think we know what heaven is (or must be, or should be) like, and then we try and figure out what we must do to get there. In a sense, it becomes like looking at vacation brochures and then trying to save for airfare. Yet, in conceiving of what eternal life is like, we ignore the fact that we cannot conceive of it at all. Wittgenstein gets at this point when he says that "The solution of the riddle of life in space and time lies *outside* space and time."[36] Conceiving of life without the categories of space and time is not only hard work but also impossible (and probably senseless) given that our concepts are always filtered through the categories of space and time. Weil also points out the conceptual challenges of trying to imagine immortality when she writes that "it is not in our power to conceive of the soul as really incorporeal."[37] At the heart of eternal life is not just its logical relationship to the life we live on earth but also the fact that whatever it is, it is an utter mystery. We may appeal to it as something worth obtaining, but we have no idea what it might be like. This is why I am drawn to Marcus Borg's saying that the goal should be "To die unto God and hope for the best."[38]

The Problem of Evil and Idolatry

Evil and Supernatural Theism

Human suffering has always been a challenge for those who profess belief in God. The difficulty is trying to explain why seemingly gratuitous suffering and pain exist if God is perfectly good and also, presumably, powerful enough to create a world without the sort of suffering we see around us on a daily basis. This dilemma has led many atheists, including Richard Dawkins, to conclude that a world like the one we inhabit is simply incompatible with the God of supernatural theism. Here is how David Hume, citing Epicurus, states the problem of evil: "Is He willing to prevent evil, but not able? Then He is impotent. Is He able, but not willing? Then He is malevolent. Is He both able and willing? Whence then is evil?"[39]

The problem of evil, however, is not a problem for theism in general; it is rather both generated and propagated by a commitment to supernatural theism.

For the problem of evil to get off the ground, God must be seen as a person, a sort of pure consciousness with desires and plans. God must also be a moral agent much like us, someone who demands a reason for suffering, reasons that fall within the general scope of the sort of reasons we can think up. Most importantly, God must be omnipotent so as to guarantee that the divine plan is not thwarted, and God must act in the world to manipulate and control events so that the divine plan actually comes to fruition.

So, while it appears that theism—full stop—is being addressed when someone formulates the argument from evil, the problem itself already defines the type of God that is being challenged. Hume, in the mouth of his character Cleanthes, clearly sees the relationship between anthropomorphism and the problem of evil, writing, "If we preserve human analogy, we must forever find it impossible to reconcile any mixture of evil in the universe with infinite attributes; much less, can we ever prove the latter with the former."[40] But why would we want to "preserve human analogy" unless we think of God in person-like terms? Before any response is formulated to how evil and God can coexist, supernatural theism is already present. So, it is the supernatural theist, not theists generally, who must respond to challenges presented by the existence of evil. In this case, the first challenge for the problem of evil is to understand that it is generated by a commitment to supernatural theism and so it is already open to all of the challenges that come with that sort of belief.

I believe that one way to respond to the problem of evil is to try and logically dissolve it by showing that it depends on an illicit conception of God (i.e., anthropomorphism) and on a grammatically confused understanding of the divine attributes (since these attributes rely on conceiving of God as a person without a body). This is partly what D.Z. Phillips attempts in his book *The Problem of Evil and the Problem of God*.[41] However, short of dissolving the problem by pointing out its commitment to a variety of conceptual confusions, the next best response is to allow the philosopher to speak of God in anthropomorphic terms and then show how this talk, in relation to his or her explanations of how it is that evil and God can coexist, leads to idolatrous consequences. If we proceed in this way, we get a sort of *reductio ad absurdum* of the anthropomorphic God via the problem of evil and the stories that believers create to explain the existence of evil. This is the path I will follow here by looking at three ways that the supernatural theist's explanation of evil leads us away from God and toward our own ego.

Searching for a Story

A traditional staple for responding to the problem of evil has been to develop an explanatory story (what philosophers and theologians call a "theodicy") that defends the goodness and attributes of God in the face of suffering and pain. That is, philosophers attempt to show the purpose that evil and suffering serve in God's ultimate plan. John Hick, for example, writes that "God has set us in a world containing unpredictable contingencies and dangers—in which unexpected and undeserved calamities may occur to anyone—because only in such a world can mutual caring and love be elicited."[42] The claim is that the suffering and evil we see in the world is not gratuitous at all but rather necessary in order to bring about something really good. Maybe suffering, like Hick states, exists to teach humans to be loving and caring, or to somehow grow in virtue. Or, maybe evil is the result of human freewill, or, possibly, it is the work of the devil or the result of original sin. However the theodicy gets cashed out, the conclusion is generally the same and it goes something like this: on a purely utilitarian account of things, evil and suffering in the world are allowed by God in order to bring about some greater good, and this greater good will, in the end, be worth it all. As Richard Swinburne writes, "Theodicy is the enterprise of showing that appearances are misleading, and that (probably) all the world's evils do promote a greater good."[43]

My concern here is not whether or not any of these sorts of stories actually succeed—I am not even sure what success would amount to here. Rather, my concern is with the very idea of constructing such stories in the first place. There is a very real possibility that any formulation of theodicy has the propensity to quickly devolve into something idolatrous in the following three ways. First, rather than thinking of theodicies as a way of justifying God in the face of evil, it may be best to see these stories as a way of helping humans avoid the painful reality of a world with seemingly gratuitous suffering. The theodicies, which explain the reasons why evil must exist, help us feel that evil is not so bad since God deems it necessary for some greater good. Second, theodicies are a way of placing human beings at the center of existence. It is generally human suffering that we are concerned with, and even then, our concern is really with the suffering that befalls *us*. Again, we have placed ourselves at the center. Lastly, theodicies show an insensitivity to human suffering by seeing the pain people suffer as a mere path to a greater good. In what follows, I want to briefly look at each of these a bit closer.

Avoiding the Reality of Evil

In the *Pensées*, Pascal writes:

> Being unable to cure death, wretchedness, and ignorance, men have decided, in order to be happy, not to think about such things … The only good thing for men, therefore, is to be diverted from thinking of what they are, either by some occupation which takes their mind off it or by some novel and agreeable passion which keeps them busy, like gambling, hunting, some absorbing show, in short by what is called diversion.[44]

In her book on the theological significance of Simone Weil, Rebecca Rozelle-Stone relates that Simone Weil was probably influenced by this very idea found in Pascal, namely, the idea that the natural response of humans in the face of the vicissitudes of life is avoidance. Rozelle-Stone, summarizing Weil, writes, "Thus, we are masters of avoiding (reality) by imaginarily 'filling' the emptiness that constitutes our true being as finite creatures."[45] Suffering, death, and finitude create a feeling of uneasiness, a feeling that the world is not a safe place, and we, in order to go on, must avoid this thought (or at least not dwell on it for too long).

But this sort of avoidance cannot last long. What are we supposed to do with the collective pain of all who suffer? The prevalence of seemingly gratuitous suffering, both historically and in the present, is just too much to ignore. The suffering is even more intense, and the need to offer an explanation more pressing, when the suffering hits home. Avoidance, in this case, does not involve ignoring suffering's existence (how can we ignore our own pain?), but rather trying to avoid its seemingly gratuitous nature by believing it is part of a divine plan. What we want is someone to eradicate senseless suffering or at least explain why it *must* exist. This, theologically, is the impetus for theodicies. Yet this sort of response to suffering is just an avoidance of a reality that will not submit to our desires. It is a way of turning our face away from the world. Like daydreaming, drinking excessively, or working long hours, reality is avoided by conjuring theological reasons for explaining how evil and the anthropomorphic God of supernatural theism can coexist. Our thinking is diverted away from the unpleasantness of what Robert Coburn calls "the turning world." Theodicies are idolatrous not only because they rest on a confused concept of God, but, more importantly, because they create a story that allows us to avoid the truth about the world in exchange for a fantasy of our own making.

Deliver *Me* from Evil

Theodicies, however, are not simply a turning away from reality; they are also a turning toward ourselves. Demanding an explanation for evil and suffering is usually a search for an explanation for the evil and suffering that befalls *us*. We rarely develop a theodicy to explain how God can exist in the face of the death of ants, clams, or muskrats. The suffering that bothers us most is the suffering that we endure, both individually and as a species. If suffering happens to *us*, then we feel we must have an explanation for the necessity of the suffering. It must, we think, have instrumental value for us to maintain our dignity and our faith in God. We don't avoid the hurt of suffering by developing a theodicy, but we do create a way to endure it by giving it ultimate value. Like the pain after a bad tooth is pulled, we endure suffering as a necessary condition for ultimate good. But this craving for an explanation may be an instance of bad faith because it inflates the importance of the "I." This sort of instrumentalism is anti-religious in that it places the self at the center. D.Z. Phillips describes it this way: "this instrumentalism, and concentration on the self, appears again and again in the morally sufficient reasons, advanced by theodicists, to explain why God permits the existence of evil."[46]

Once we create a deity in our own image, evil and suffering cry out for an explanation; surely we would not let ourselves suffer if we were God. Since God does not ultimately keep pain and suffering from us, there must, we reason, be some ultimate purpose for the evil in the world. In this case, the very sort of God who gives rise to the problem of evil in the first place (i.e., the anthropomorphic God) is manipulated and shown to have the same preference for us that we have for ourselves. Any suffering that happens to us must be for a reason. (I imagine if chickens believed in a deity, then they would want a rational explanation for how the chicken God can coexist in a world with pot pies.) We manipulate who God is, what God will do, and who we are in God's plan so that the sting of death and suffering will not hurt so badly. As Mark Johnston writes, "The present thought is that the central issue of theodicy, the problem of unnecessary evil, arises only with a conception of Divine Goodness that expresses the idolatrous longing for a useful god, one who will favor us with something *other than* his own self-revelation."[47] God is our strong protector who may not save us from suffering but will make sure it all has an ultimate purpose. Theodicies bring us right back to the "useful" God of spiritual materialism that we met in Chapter 1. We imagine we know the ways of God with such clarity that we can discern the reason(s) why evil exists. In this way the God we construct helps protects us from the uncomfortable fact that we must live with mystery; however, the price is not conceptual clarity but belief in a God who may not be worthy of our concern.

Trivializing Suffering

The idea that evil must serve a utilitarian purpose is not only a way of placing human beings at the pinnacle of creation and a way of manipulating the anthropomorphic God for our favor; it also leads to a trivializing of real suffering and pain. If pain and suffering are part of the divine plan, then what sort of energy do we really need to expend trying to ameliorate its existence? Even worse, it seems brutish and nasty to accept a story where the correct response to those who suffer is to say that their pain is part of a divine plan and to assure them that they will be compensated nicely in the end. This treats human suffering as instrumental, reducing it to a mere move in a game or a role in an unfolding saga. This was the mistake made by Job's comforters when they decided that his suffering was due to some hidden sin that he had committed. Job's friends tried to explain suffering as part of a grand scheme of cause and effect, but, as Howard Wettstein says, "Unwarranted suffering is no mere surface appearance, but a ground floor phenomenon, not to be explained away."[48] Seeing suffering as instrumental is most egregious and irreligious because it turns God into one of Job's friends, who, in trying to comfort, does so in a way that mocks the sufferer. This is why, Wettstein writes, "It is crucial that we not belittle suffering by seeing it, for example, as a mere appearance of some higher form of justice. It is crucial that we call injustice and horror by their right names, as did God's faithful servant, Job."[49] It is here, at the point where the sufferers are mocked by the claim that "all will be well," that the idea of supernatural theism loses its purchase on reality. If we are asked to side with suffering or with the God of supernatural theism, our religious instincts should lead us to practice a form of ethical atheism.

Letting Sufferers Have a Voice

Whenever I hear someone telling a story of how God performed a miracle in his or her life, I generally think, well, if God could do that, can't God cure childhood cancer or save a kid from abuse or torture? The simple idea is that if God can manipulate the placement of cars in order to help you get a closer parking spot at Walmart or, even more impressively, if God can make *your* cancer disappear, what about the others (especially the children)? Thinking God selectively interacts in the world, leaving some to suffer and die while healing others, leads some to declare that "all things happen for a purpose." This is the downfall of theodicy; it leads to a world where God is using us as chess pieces to bring about something good. But is this the sort of plan that would be worth the senseless suffering of innocent people (especially the children)? Do we really want (or need) to worship a God who designs his plan willfully on the backs of the most vulnerable among us? Or, should we respond, as Rieux does to Father Paneloux in Camus's *The Plague* when the priest suggests that we should love what we do not understand? Rieux responds by saying, "No, Father. I've a very different idea of love. And until my dying day I shall refuse to love a scheme of things in which children are put up to torture."[50] This response is similar to the words Dostoevsky puts in the mouth of Ivan Karamazov when he is confronted with various reasons why children suffer:

> If everyone must suffer in order for their suffering to purchase eternal harmony, what do young children have to do with it, tell me, please? It is quite impossible to understand why they should have to suffer, and why should they have to purchase harmony with their sufferings? Why have they also ended up as raw material, to be the manure for someone else's future harmony?[51]

Ivan then decides that if this is what is necessary for eternal harmony, then he wants no part of it:

> I decline the offer of eternal harmony altogether. It is not worth one single small tear of even one tortured little child that beat its breast with its little fist and prayed in its foul-smelling dog-hole with its unredeemed tears addressed to "dear Father God!" It is not worth it because its tears have remained unredeemed. They must be redeemed, or there can be no harmony. But by what means, by what means will you redeem them? Is it even possible? Will you really do it by avenging them? But what use is vengeance to me, what use to me is hell for torturers, what can hell put right again, when those children have been tortured to death?[52]

A little bit later, Ivan states that even if he were given a ticket that would grant him entrance into heaven where suffering is somehow redeemed and harmony attained, he would not accept the offer. It is not God he is rejecting, but rather the offer of eternal harmony based on the idea that something can recompense for the suffering of children. Ivan says, "I do not want harmony, out of a love for mankind I do not want it. I want rather to be left with sufferings that are unavenged. Let me rather remain with my unavenged suffering and unassuaged indignation, *even though I am not right.*"[53]

Ivan's rejection of the God who offers recompense is a religious act. It is an instance when the individual sees clearly the need to be on the side of the sufferer. To allow innocent suffering and pain to occur on the condition that all will be well (eventually) mocks the sufferer. There is no greater good hand-waving that justifies the suffering and torment of the innocent. The anthropomorphic God must be rid of in order for us to offer respect and love to those who suffer. A God who compels us to escape the reality of suffering by trivializing it as a necessary part of a divine plan is an idol that must be given up. In this sense, the problem of evil leads to atheism, but, again, it is a purifying atheism that pushes believers to turn from an idolatrous conception of a God that trivializes evil and suffering. Rather than follow this false God, we may do better to embrace mystery and gratitude for all of creation. In this way, we become less consumed with ourselves and more compelled, by love for the Other, to seek to remedy pain and suffering without appeal to a grand explanatory master narrative that trivializes suffering and mocks the sufferer.

Doctrines, Pictures, and Propositions/Truth and Meaning

In all of these examples of how religious doctrines get used in idolatrous ways, there is a common thread which states that religious doctrines are propositions that require our intellectual assent. Whether the content of the proposition is that "Jesus died for our sins," or "if we believe in Jesus we will live forever," or "evil will be recompensed for good," the idea is that these are statements of God's will that tend to serve our needs, look out for our well-being, and seek to preserve our egos. What is missing is the way that religious doctrines should be the sort of things that lead us to love God and neighbor (or to express our love of God by loving our neighbor) while learning to die to our own obsession with ourselves and our needs. What we need is a reformation in how we view religious language. The difference may be as simple as pointing out the distinction between a picture and a proposition.

Many philosophers of religion today see the sort of religious doctrines that we just looked at as straightforward propositions that are either true or false.

What we need to do, so the story goes, is look at the evidence for and against the propositions of religious belief, weigh the evidence carefully, and then make a decision as to their truth value (of course, if we wanted, we could simply ignore the doctrines altogether and go on with our life). If the doctrines are supposed to rely on historical facts—such as the claims about the resurrection or the life and sayings of Jesus—then the evidence we amass may need to also rely on the historical-critical method or some other form of historiography. In cases where the evidence needed is more conceptual—such as in the claim that God exists or the belief that we will live eternally—philosophical arguments may be called on in order to sway us one way or another.

To see religious doctrines as straightforward propositions standing in need of rational evidence is not a radical claim; it is simply the normal way that many today see religious belief. D.Z. Phillips writes:

> If the philosophical friends of religion pride themselves on anything, it is on their conception of themselves as the guardians of the propositional element in religious belief. They are unhesitating in their criticisms of any analysis of that belief which seems to them to deny that propositional element. In contrast to any such analysis, they claim to have a robust conception of truth.[54]

Even outside of worries about religious belief, this seems to be the way many think of philosophical inquiry, full stop. If we really desire to get to the truth, then all the fluff of life must be stripped down to propositional claims about reality. As John Cottingham notes, "This is the implicit assumption [of analytic philosophy] that the truth is, as it were, 'flat,' and that we reach the best results in philosophy by eliminating all ambiguity from our discourse and striving to emulate the austere, pared-down language of modern science."[55]

Thinking of religious beliefs as "flat" true/false statements leads to the possibility, which we have already looked at, that religious beliefs could be believed in without reference to the life of the believer. This is the real problem that lurks behind much of what we have looked at in this chapter. Forgiveness of sin, eternal life, and the explanation of evil all became theories about how to explain certain facts about guilt, death, and suffering. The problem is that seeing these sorts of beliefs as theories, creates the impression that they are the kind of hypothetical beliefs that exist on par with scientific claims. But to see religious faith in this way is a mistake. As Mark Johnston writes, "Belief in God is not a matter of believing in the proposition that he exists; it is an orientation in which the Highest One comes into view, with salvific effect."[56] D.Z. Phillips shows some affinity with Johnston when he writes in *Death and Immortality* that "In learning by contemplation, attention, renunciation, what forgiving, thanking, loving, etc. mean in these contexts, the believer is participating in the reality of God; *that is what is meant by God's reality.*"[57] For Johnston and Phillips, the reality of God (or God coming into view) is seen in the believer's life and actions; it is seen in the interpretation the believer places on reality. The meaning and the practices converge into a whole that is not logically separable. Any account of religious language must accomplish the following: First, it should tie the meaning of the utterances to the stance the believer takes toward life and other people. Second, it must give an account of the truth of religious language, not in reference to what the utterances refer to, but in reference to how they influence the believer's moral (or agapeistic) stance toward life and other people. Since the idea of the truth of religious belief has been touched on in earlier chapters and will also be looked at again in the next chapter, here, I will just mention how the meaning of religious doctrines might be better served if we see them as pictures that regulate behavior rather than propositions that we should believe in based on the available "evidence."

Religious Pictures

Wittgenstein, in his *Lectures and Conversations on Aesthetics, Psychology and Religious Belief*, offers us a way to look at religious belief that connects their meaning with the life of the believer. His claim is that religious beliefs function much like pictures, but only a certain sort of picture will do when it comes to these beliefs. He writes:

> How do I know that a picture is a picture of Lewy [one of Wittgenstein's students]? Normally by its likeness to Lewy, or under certain circumstances, a picture of Lewy may not be like him, but like Smith. If I give up the business of being like [as a criterion], I get into an awful mess, because anything may be his portrait, given a certain method of projection.[58]

For many pictures—primarily those we call "representational"—the efficacy or success of the picture is judged by how accurately it represents what it is picturing. If we did not refer to how well a picture represents its subject, then we would lose our grasp on what it means to be a "good picture." But, naturally, not all pictures are representational in this way. Earlier in the same lecture, Wittgenstein writes, "The word 'God' is amongst the earliest learnt—pictures and catechisms, etc. But not the same consequences as with pictures of aunts. I wasn't shown [that which the picture pictured]."⁵⁹ Wittgenstein then immediately says, "The word [God] is used like a word representing a person."⁶⁰ It is taking this picture too literally that leads to confusion when some speak of God as if God were actually an object among objects. It is also indicative of what went wrong above when we looked at the various religious beliefs. The surface grammar of things like forgiveness of sins, eternal life, and the omnipotence of God in relation to evil was taken too literally, resulting in a confused use of these concepts, a use that was logically separated from the life of the believer. What is needed, if religious language is going to be more than idolatrous, is a means of linking religious language inextricably with the life of the believer. This, I suggest, is what Wittgenstein is getting at when he suggests we see religious language as a sort of picture (or set of interrelated pictures). Of course, we would have to understand how the religious picture pictures.

Since there are a variety of different ways that pictures picture, Wittgenstein wants to stress the importance of knowing what "method of projection" we are attributing to the picture(s) we are using. This is why, in the *Philosophical Investigations*, Wittgenstein spells out the importance of knowing what sort of picture you are dealing with before you start drawing any conclusions about meaning. He writes, "If we compare a proposition to a picture, we must think whether we are comparing it to a portrait (a historical representation) or to a genre picture. And both comparisons have a point."⁶¹ Wittgenstein's reference to genre pictures is especially enlightening. Wittgenstein continues, "When I look at a genre-picture, it tells me something, even though I don't believe (imagine) for a moment that the people I see in it really exist, or that there have really been people in that situation. But suppose I ask: *What* does it tell me, then?"⁶² At this point, all we need is a recognition that some pictures function not as representations of some state of affairs but as meaningful representations of some aspect of reality that garner their meaning when they are put to a specific use. This is why Wittgenstein said that for some pictures, "The whole *weight* may be in the picture."⁶³ As I see it, saying that the "whole weight may be in the picture" is not to say that the picture carries its meaning with it—as if meaning was a sort of magical aura that was attached to the picture—rather, it says that some pictures are such that their meaning is secured in some way other than representing some empirical state of affairs. When a believer uses a religious picture, the use does not depend on the accuracy of the picture any more than the meaning *Aesop's Fables* depend on an accurate depiction of the linguistic capabilities of animals. Pictures can picture reality in a variety of ways.

The move from genre pictures—which picture something by not picturing representationally—to religious pictures is a short and easy step. Wittgenstein makes this point clear by thinking about Michelangelo's painting of the *Creation of Adam* on the ceiling of the Sistine Chapel. He writes, "If we ever saw this, we certainly would not think this the Deity. The picture has to be used in an entirely different way if we are to call the man in the queer blanket 'God,' and so on."[64] The point is not that poor Ole Michelangelo was doing his best and probably got some of the features of God correct if only we could travel to where God lives and compare the painting with the real deal. No, that would be silly; the point is that religious pictures are not used that way at all (or at least they should not be). What is important when attempting to see how a picture is (or can be) used is to pay attention to the way the picture takes up residence in the life of the believer.

Religious pictures (or doctrines) get their meaning, not in abstraction, but rather, the meaning of the pictures are fixed in two primary ways. First, the pictures are part of a more complete story which is itself part of the sacred texts of the religious community. In this case, pictures are just "scenes" abstracted from a larger narrative. Their meaning is partly dependent on the role they play in the overall narrative. Second, pictures gain their meaning when they are used by the religious believer. These are sacred pictures embedded in sacred stories, so the use they are put to will show up in the religious life of the believer, but they will not be things that float around on the periphery of the believer's life; they will be pictures that lie at the center of their religious existence and identity. Wittgenstein stresses the important link between the role of religious pictures and their use, writing, "Here believing obviously plays much more this role: suppose we said that a certain picture might play the role of constantly admonishing me, or I always think of it. Here, an enormous difference would be between those people for whom the picture is constantly in the foreground and the others who just didn't use it at all."[65] Religious pictures guide the believer's life by serving as a reference point from which he or she views reality. In this sense, the pictures serve as an interpretation of the meaning of life and as a regulative guide for action. They are there as a constant reminder to the believer about how they should live. However, since the pictures are indeed religious in nature, they also point beyond themselves to the ineffable, transcendent God. That is, the pictures imply (presuppose) a spiritual reality whose essence is spoken about in the language of agape and shown in our inability to say anything more. In this way, the pictures are icons that reveal the inexpressible while also serving to guide the believer's actions. The pictures have a vertical and a horizontal component, even though the vertical component serves to remind us that there is nothing (or no thing) there to speak of. In revealing the ineffable, the pictures semantically refer back to the life of the believer, thereby collapsing the ineffable into concrete action. The transcendent is conflated into the immanent life of agape.

Religious pictures have a relationship to human life similar to what we saw with idols. In the first chapter, I argued that idols only become real when they are used as part of a "religious" practice where the practitioner has turned inward and away from others, choosing to focus (perhaps unconsciously) on themselves. The doctrines mentioned above are idolatrous since in all three instances (forgiveness of sin, eternal life, and omnipotence/evil) the result of belief was an inordinate concern with the self and a turning away from (or neglecting of) others. Non-idolatrous religious pictures, conversely, are pragmatically true if they are used as a guide to living a selfless agapeistic life. This means that there is a constraint put on the meaning of religious pictures. If the pictures are used so as to feed the ego and draw one away from others, then an idol is present. But the self-same picture used to bring one strength to live a transformed life of love can be religiously significant. Religious pictures must have ethical constraints, constraints that show up in the believer's life as a way of pointing to the fact that they are being used in a way that avoids the claim of idolatry. In chapter five, I will look more closely at the relationship between religious pictures (or stories) and the life of agape. In closing this chapter, however, I want to point toward some ways that the religious beliefs mentioned above can be transformed from idolatrous beliefs to beliefs that display religious import.

Believing the Right Things and Acting the Right Way

Taking up Our Cross

The death of Jesus need not (and should not) be seen as something that is done to us if (and when) we believe the right set of facts. It should, rather, be seen as a model for something that we must do ourselves with the help of divine grace; that is, we must "die to self" by carrying our own metaphorical cross. The life of Jesus is a prime example of where the life of faith leads; that is, it is a picture of the death of self that must be incurred if agape is going to be possible. Jesus led a selfless life in solidarity with the outcast, marginalized, and poor, resulting, ultimately, in his execution. His death on the cross is a radical reminder of the sort of ego death that must occur if we are going to be able to live a life focused on agape. Jesus's death was not a death that replaces our need for a continual subjective death; it is rather a model of the cost incurred if we desire to follow this first-century Palestinian rebel. The cross can be taken as a picture (or model) that points to the fact that in order to overcome the constant pull of our ego—the cause of much of the problems we incur—we must die to self. As Lisa McCullough writes in relation to the theology of Simone Weil, "We must imitate God's renunciation in creation and crucifixion."[66] Since the self is the root of all our actions that preference our own needs over the needs of others, the death of self is an effectively powerful way to view the meaning of the "forgiveness of sin" while avoiding the pitfalls of self-love. Simone Weil writes:

> We possess nothing in the world—a mere chance can strip us of everything—except the power to say "I." That is what we have to give to God, in other words, to destroy. There is absolutely no other free act which it is given us to accomplish, only the destruction of the "I."[67]

Of course, this interpretation of the atonement is not without precedent. The Apostle Paul writes, "I have been crucified with Christ; it is no longer I who live, but Christ who lives in me; and the life I now live in the flesh I live by faith in the Son of God, who loved me and gave himself for me" (Galatians 2:20 RSV). Jesus also seems to have something similar in mind when he is "quoted" as saying, "If any man would come after me, let him deny himself and take up his cross and follow me. For whoever would save his life will lose it, and whoever loses his life for my sake will find it" (Matthew 16:24–25 RSV). In the life of Jesus, dying to self was manifested not only as a preference for the outcast and marginalized but also as a struggle with both finitude and alienation, this is seen most clearly when Jesus is wrestling with the fear of death in the Garden of Gethsemane and with the feeling of abandonment while he was dying on the cross.

The self never goes quietly, of course, but this sort of living-death is something that can bring new life. This is displayed in the story of the resurrection that follows the crucifixion. As the self wiggles and writhes its way to a slow death on our own cross, we find ourselves better able to live in union with God and others. Through death, we are resurrected as individuals whose life is in God, stripped of our own selfish desires. The cross is not just a moral model of the cost of love meant to inspire (à la Abelard); rather, it is a reminder of what the criteria of forgiveness looks like in the human subject. Dying to self (which is, or can be, the meaning of the cross) is a gift to the living who, through self-denial, are freed from the bondage of ego. The cross both reveals the cause of sin and offers the solution. The cross offers a metaphor for the fact that we must make the death of self a daily reality if agape is going to be possible. This is one way to look at the meaning of the Gospels' portrayal of the forgiveness of sins. The forgiveness of sins is not something that happens to us but something that we express in our lives as we die to self and live, sacrificially, for the Other.

Dying to Self and Living in God

When we think of eternal life as temporal immortality, what happens to the religiously important concepts of dying to self, of loving others more than (or as) ourselves, and of seeing our life as a sacrifice offered to God? Part of the problem is that the idea of the soul is intimately related to our concept of the survival of the self, a self whose desires we must die to. We often want to think of the soul as the eternal part of our consciousness that will never die, but this is a religiously questionable idea. D.Z. Phillips writes, "The immortality of the soul, by contrast, refers to a person's relation to the self-effacement and love of others involved in dying to the self."[68] The sort of temporal immortality that we noted above, which appears to have little to do with religious faith, forces us to look to this self-sacrificial sort of explanation of eternal life in order to avoid idolatry. Phillips was constantly trying to admonish the philosopher to see the religious importance of the believers' use of eternal life and immortality. He wanted to get away from the simplistic idea that what was important was solely the claim that we (whoever "we" are) would continue on forever and ever. Phillips writes, "I am suggesting that eternal life for the believer is participation in the life of God and that this life has to do with dying to the self, seeing that all things are a gift from God, that nothing is ours by right or necessity."[69]

On this way of looking at things, eternal life is not an assurance of the continued existence of our consciousness, or of an immaterial soul living forever, or even of a resurrected body floating off to a new home; rather, it is the religiously significant claim, as Phillips writes, "that where God is, there will we be also. God is a spiritual reality. We become more than ourselves at death when we become part of that spiritual reality."[70] If that seems mysterious, then that is the point. Mystery replaces idolatry. The mystery, however, should not negate the fact that eternal life has a meaning for us while we are still alive, one that goes beyond simply waiting to "see" what happens at death. The eternal imbues the temporal with seriousness and meaning even in the face of utter mystery. Phillips again:

> In the religious belief in immortality I am concerned to elucidate, the mortal does not determine the immortal. Rather, it is the eternal which gives sense to the temporal ... For a religious person, it can show that life is given and taken

away; that we are not the centre of the universe. The religious expression of this fact is to say that we are in God's hands."[71]

Even more religiously poignant, Phillips, earlier in the same essay, writes that "To believe in the immortality of the soul is to want to give one's soul to God."[72] This is one possibility for how the believer can use the picture of eternal life—it is a chance to die to our desire to see our ego go on forever. It is our chance to fully die to self and give our (eternal) life to God. As Phillips explains in a beautiful passage, "To die in God is to be able to see one's death as part of the majesty of God's will. Saying farewell is not a negative act. It is part of what is meant by giving glory to God."[73]

Gratitude and the Displaced "I"

What happens when we stop trying to offer divine reasons for why suffering and pain exist? D.Z. Phillips notes that once we accept that we are not at the center of the universe, we risk accepting a certain fatalism since we realize that anything may happen to us, and there is little we can do about it. He responds that this reaction

> omits the essential fact that in recognizing that life itself is a gift and that the ways things go in it are a grace, *the believer dies to the "I"* that sees itself at the centre of the universe. In fatalism, there is acceptance of the inevitable, but no love of it. In the religious response I am talking of, there is a requirement to love the fact that God has given life with its contingencies to human beings. This love is gratitude for existence.[74]

But loving all of creation may lead to simply accepting all that occurs without striving to alleviate suffering. If everything that occurs in life is an instance of grace, then why try to change things? This response, however, is what Phillips resists when he writes in the above quote that we can accept the inevitable but not love it. We can accept that the world, as a whole, is a gift of God while still fighting against injustice. This is partly because injustice is often the result of individuals, groups, or nations desiring to exert their will or power over others. Since this sort of exertion of the self (individually or collectively) is what religion says we must die to, any injustice that is the result of this sort of sin must be resisted. There is also the fact that any genuine expression of religiosity requires that we be on the side of those suffering, not as a means of garnering divine favor, but for their own sake. In this case, injustice should be resisted for the sake of the sufferer as well as being a means of fighting against the consequences of ego and selfishness. This is why Phillips writes that "we should now be able to see why belief in creation, seeing oneself as the recipient of grace, cannot lead to quietism, since it involves fighting against everything in the world, and in oneself, that regards other people, and that world, as creatures to be exploited, possessed and used for one's own selfish purposes."[75]

The important point here is that we cease to place ourselves at the center of creation. To think that our suffering must be for something is to think that we are at the center of all that is important, but this is simply another manifestation of our ego. What I am suggesting is that we come to displace the importance of the self in such a way that we are then able to take our place as one among many within the created order. Our values and way of judging existence, including suffering, tend to prefer our own needs and desires, but, as Howard Wettstein writes, regarding what Job learned from his encounter with God:

> The world seen by Job through God's eyes is exquisite, awe-inspiring. But by stark contrast with, for example, Genesis chapter 1, it is a strikingly non-anthropocentric world. It is a wild and violent world, and we are not its tamers. Most important, it is not teleologically organized with respect to human needs, ends, or values.[76]

The non-idolatrous picture of God in the face of suffering is one that allows us to offer gratitude for all of existence—it is a refusal to place oneself, and one's epistemological desire to know, over God's grace. D.Z. Phillips explains that "To see oneself as nothing, and grace as everything, is pure love of God. That is what loving God amounts to."[77] No theory is needed to explain evil away since the religious response is not to seek to explain why evil exists but rather to love others in the midst of pain and suffering as we learn daily to die to self. This is one possibility for how the believer can use the picture of God in relation to the existence of evil and suffering.

Conclusion

Religious beliefs are regulative guides for behavior whose meaning is intricately and logically tied to a life that involves dying to self and putting others' needs above (or on par with) our own. They are pictures that help us see and pay attention to what is important in life as we seek to follow the model of Jesus. This means, however, that a confused concept of God can get between us and our love of others, causing us to retreat from religion in the name of religion. On the reading of the religious life that I have been presenting, a reading that sees religion as a way of interpreting existence and living for others, some may worry that we have exchanged religious truth for religious practice. In the next chapter, I will attempt to respond to this concern by looking specifically at the role that truth and criteria play in religious discourse.

4

Truth Pluralism: On Criteria and Religious Belief

In his long philosophical career, D.Z. Phillips attempted to provide a clear explanation of the meaning of religious belief by looking at the role that these beliefs played in people's lives. Of course, his distinctly Wittgensteinian approach to philosophy was not a philosophical method that was applicable only to religious discourse. All of the various ways that human beings speak on a variety of different topics and in a variety of different settings are susceptible to rules of correct usage, rules that delineate sense from nonsense. Phillips came to refer to his way of doing philosophy as "contemplative" in nature.[1] He wanted not only to give an account of the various uses of language by contemplating the relationship between grammatical rules and sense but also to see how all of the various ways that humans speak (all of the various language games that are played) are interrelated and overlapping. He wasn't interested in positing a common measure by which all reality can be judged; rather, he was content to let reality be seen from a plurality of perspectives; reality for him was diverse and multifarious. He writes, "My question is, how can philosophy give an account of reality which shows that it is necessary to go beyond simply noting differences between various modes of discourse, without invoking a common measure of 'the real' or assuming that all modes of discourse have a common subject, namely, reality?"[2]

Phillips's contemplative account of philosophy is pluralistic but not disjointed. While he allows that there will be differences in the accounts that different aspects of language give as an answer to the question, "What is real?," there is still more philosophical work to be done, since, as Phillips writes, "They can only be the differences they are because their reality depends on the place they occupy in human life."[3] So contemplative philosophy will be interested in how all of these various forms of life make up what we might call the "human language game" (a term Phillips would probably not have approved of). The very fact that human beings communicate with each other shows that we share much in common when it comes to language use. The variety of language games come together in the fact that human discourse is possible and by the fact that we inhabit the same world.

One way to understand contemplative philosophy is to simply see it as an attempt to offer a clear explanation of the meaning of concepts as they are used in a variety of different contexts. In short, it is a philosophical commitment to Wittgenstein's dictum that "meaning is use." But the idea that meaning is dependent on how words are used is something that I find trivial and commonsensical. It seems to me a truism to say that in order to see what a word means, we must look and see how competent speakers of a language use the word (or concept) in question. How else could meaning be fixed? But that does not mean that meaning-as-use is unimportant, and part of its importance has to do with the fact that this sort of thinking has repercussions for what we mean when we speak of truth in a given context. We must allow that, as we observe language use from context to context, the use of the concept of "truth" (or saying that something "is true") may end up having both similarities and differences across a variety of contexts. Furthermore, since truth is parasitic on meaning, it is paramount to fix meaning before inquiring about truth. Here is how the story goes.

Most words that have a variety of meanings are fairly mundane and we are able to pick up their meaning as children. To say that "the bank is closed" or "the bank is overflowing" forces us to pay attention to context in order to fix meaning. The same is true for "please butter the toast" and "that treadmill is toast today." While the same word is used, the meanings in the two different contexts are different. If we are unable to infer meaning from context in these sorts of everyday cases, we are quickly corrected by our linguistic community. The real trouble comes when philosophers fail to see the contextual dependence of the meaning of concepts that are taken as the philosophical heavyweights, words like: "exist," "real," "fact," and "refer." In these cases, there is a tendency to take these words as meta-concepts that have a meaning that floats above the contextual fray. It is thought that these words are important enough that they mean the same thing without any reference to their context of use. The philosopher often operates with the following sort of abstract definitions: "X exists iff Y," or "X is real iff Y," or "X is a fact iff Y." In these cases, the explanation of Y would give the necessary and sufficient conditions for what it means for something to "exist" or for something to be "real," or for something to be considered a "fact." Many philosophers have gone on this way, applying a univocal definition of concepts across the board, without taking the time to consider how these concepts are used or how their meaning might change across contexts. In this case, they end up being conceptually confused when they try to apply a concept, which obtains its meaning from one context, into other contexts without doing the work to see if such an application is justified.

Allowing that concepts can take on different meanings in different contexts isn't too surprising in and of itself, but what is more interesting is the fact that within the one human reality, we have a plurality of realities with a plurality of (sometimes conflicting) truth claims. It isn't simply the differences in meaning that show up upon investigation that matter, but rather what these differences reveal about the nature of what we call "reality." That is, what is interesting is that reality is not one big thing but a variety of "realities," a plurality of realities that show up in the various ways that language gets used in the human form of life. Phillips writes, "What we need to recognize is that in human activities there are many conceptions of 'the real' and 'the unreal'. Philosophy must settle for pointing this out, clarifying the differences between them, and locating the confusion of attempting to transcend them in a more comprehensive account of reality."[4]

It is this "reality of realities" that poses interesting possibilities for those interested in the plurality of truth, since a "plurality of realities" would also entail (at least possibly) a plurality of truth claims and maybe even a plurality of truths. This is because the concept of truth is going to appear in a variety of different contexts just like the other philosophical heavyweights mentioned above ("fact," "reality," "exist," "refer," etc.). This sort of pluralism would mean that the very idea of a world that exists out there, independent of the way we speak about it, is nonsense. Reality is seen in our descriptions about what is real, and this is multifarious and diverse. This does not mean there is no independent reality, but rather that what an independent reality means will, possibly, be different in different contexts. In this chapter I want to attempt to outline a way of looking at truth that allows for several things to coexist at one time. First, I want to see how it is possible to give a singular account of truth that still allows for a diversity of applications as it gets used in various contexts. Second, I want to investigate how this singular account of truth can be used in a plurality of ways as we begin to see the relationship between truth, meaning, and criteria. After looking at some perplexities that occur when we look at the idea of truth and criteria, I want to conclude by offering a possible way to make sense of truth in religious practice.

A Singular Account of Truth?

Oftentimes, truth is taken to be a substantive predicate (or property) that is assigned to propositions (or thoughts, judgments, beliefs, sentences, etc.). In a certain sense, calling truth a predicate presents no serious problem on the surface since we would still need to do the work of figuring out what the truth predicate actually means. The bigger problem is that we often take predicates to be a substantial property—a property that we can identify upon investigation and a property that has the same meaning across all uses. Take the following examples[5]:

a) The ball is purple.
b) The iron filings are magnetic.
c) The chemical is pungent.

In all of these cases, a property (*purpleness, magnetism, pungency*) is assigned to an object such that each could, in principle, be identified upon investigation. We see the ball has the property of being purple, we observe the iron filings moving in a specific pattern displaying magnetism, and, having uncorked the flask, we smell that the chemical is pungent. This is all quite natural as it goes. Predicates attach to things, and we can generally tell when something has a certain property. If we know what the property of being purple is, then we know that all purple things share exactly that property (the same goes for the other properties as well). We could even investigate purpleness scientifically and give a precise empirical account of exactly what we mean when we say, "X is purple."

We can, however, be led astray when we enter the domain of truth, for it seems perfectly normal to say:

a) "The ball is purple" is true. (It is true that the ball is purple.)
b) "Iron filings are magnetic" is true. (It is true that iron filings are magnetic.)
c) "The chemical is pungent" is true. (It is true that the chemical is pungent.)

Now in these cases, what we have is a *truth predicate* attached to each proposition. On the face of it, as I just noted, there is nothing inherently wrong with talking about a truth predicate. In these sentences, we know what it means to say that each proposition is true because we are familiar with the sort of things each proposition is referring to; that is, we know the meaning of the things the propositions speak of. If we know what purple (as a color) is, what iron filings and magnetism are, and what a pungent smell is, then we can add "is true" to the above propositions and know that these things obtain in reality.

Challenges occur, however, when we are tempted into looking for a single predicate (or property) that all "true" things have in common. It seems that since we know (or can figure out) what all magnetic things, all purple things, and all pungent things have in common, we should also expect that all true things would also have something in common (since "is true" is just a predicate attached to the propositions.) Paul Horwich writes:

> Just as the predicate "is magnetic" designates a feature of the world, *magnetism*, whose nature is revealed by quantum physics, and "is diabetic" describes a group of phenomena, *diabetes*, characterizable in biology, so it seems that "is true" attributes a complex property, *truth*—an ingredient of reality whose underlying structure will, it is hoped, one day be revealed by philosophical or scientific analysis.[6]

However, as Pascal Engel writes, "the truth predicate does not seem to be on a par with such properties as 'is square' or 'weighs 3 kilos.'"[7] Again, if something is square or weighs 3 kilos, then we know what property is being predicated of a thing. But this does not seem to be the case when we add "is true" to sentences (or propositions). It is not at all clear that a substantive property is being predicated of a proposition when we say of it that it is true.

Philosophers have tried mightily to identify *the* truth predicate that all instances of truth possess (i.e., truth is "correspondence," "coherence," "assertion under ideal epistemic conditions," "what your peers will let you get away with saying," etc.), but finding such a univocal application has proven difficult—truth, as a univocal predicate, has proven to be too diverse and slippery to fit into a simple mold that can be transported to all its varied uses. While some theories of truth work fine in certain contexts, trying to apply one theory across the board has not been very successful. In light of such difficulty in locating *the* truth predicate, we may think that there is little we can do. Maybe we should continue our search for a univocal view of truth or, possibly, simply proclaim truth to be far too amorphous to be captured by finite mortals such as ourselves. The problem is that we already use truth perfectly well in a variety of contexts, contexts where the speaker gets along just fine without confusion or misunderstanding. So, since truth is already in use in a variety of contexts, it would be beneficial to come up with an explanation of truth that can explain these pluralistic uses.

Letting the Air out of Truth

The way forward is to admit that while there is a truth predicate ("is true" is added to much of what we say), it does not function in a single univocal way like the more substantive predicates we looked at above. As a corrective of looking for a single use of the truth predicate, the best thing to do is to follow the long tradition of philosophers who have deflated the concept of truth down to something reasonable, effective, and consistent—a way of looking at truth that can make sense of the diversity of ways in which the concept is actually used. In doing so, it might seem that we will have stripped truth of its plurality since we are offering a single way of looking at truth, but, as I shall argue in the bulk of what follows, what we get is a sort of *E Pluribus Unum* view of truth, that is, a single deflated concept (i.e., a single deflated truth predicate) with a plurality of uses.

Gottlob Frege once wrote somewhere that "It is also worthy of notice that the sentence 'I smell the scent of violets' has the same content as the sentence 'it is true that I smell the scent of violets.' So, it seems, then, that nothing is added to the thought by my ascribing to it the property of truth."[8] Frank Ramsey, in a similar vein as Frege, writes:

> Truth and falsity are ascribed primarily to propositions. The propositions to which they are ascribed may be either explicitly given or described. Suppose first that it is explicitly given; then it is evident that "It is true that Caesar was murdered" means no more than that Caesar was murdered, and "it is false that Caesar was murdered" means that Caesar is not murdered. They are phrases that we sometimes use for emphasis or for stylistic reasons, or to indicate the position occupied by the statement in our argument. So we can also say "it is a fact that he was murdered" or "that he was murdered is contrary to fact."[9]

Finally, Alfred Tarski adds:

> Consider the sentence "snow is white." We ask the question under what conditions this sentence is true or false. It seems clear that if we base ourselves on the classical conception of truth, we shall say that the sentence is true if snow is white, and that it is false if snow is not white. Thus, if the definition of truth is to conform to our conception, it must imply the following equivalence: The sentence "snow is white" is true if, and only if, snow is white.[10]

Now compare all of these with what Wittgenstein writes in the *Philosophical Investigations*:

> At bottom, giving "This is how things are" as the general form of propositions is the same as giving the definition: a proposition is whatever can be true or false. For instead of "This is how things are" I could have said "This is true." (Or again "This is false.") But we have
>
> "p" is true = p
>
> "p" is false = not-p.
>
> And to say that a proposition is whatever can be true or false amounts to saying: we call something a proposition when in our language we apply the calculus of truth functions to it.[11]

What all these quotes have in common is the claim that to say of a proposition that it is true is the same thing as simply asserting the proposition. This way of talking about truth is often called the deflationary theory of truth. The deflationary theory of truth has been aptly defended by a number of philosophers, most notably by Wittgenstein's friend Frank Ramsey and, more recently, by Paul Horwich. In his book *Truth*, Horwich gives an account of what his deflationary theory amounts to in the following way:

> in order for the truth predicate to fulfil its function we must acknowledge that (MT) [The minimal theory] The proposition *that quarks really exist* is true if and only if quarks really exist, the proposition *that lying is bad* is true if and only if lying is bad, ... and so on,
> but nothing more about truth need be assumed.[12]

Horwich then generalizes (MT) to a simple equivalence schema (E), which he describes as follows: "(E) It is true *that* p if and only if p."[13] This is equivalent to Wittgenstein's formulation that "'p' is true = p," or to the simple claim that to assert that "p" is true is to simply restate P. For instance: "God exists" is true iff God exists. It is true that "unicorns do not exist" iff unicorns do not exist. It is true that "Jack cheated on his Spanish test" iff Jack cheated on his Spanish test. You get the idea.

Horwich's minimalist conception of truth, of which much more can be (and has been) written, is elegant in that it is easily translatable to a variety of different contexts where truth is used. So, while there are many different uses of the concept "true," each use will have a similar property, namely, the non-substantive logical property of being equivalent to simply asserting the proposition. When we look at the meaning of "is true," we see that the predicate adds nothing to the simple assertion that *p* is the case (whatever *p* stands for). In introducing what he calls the "transparency property" of truth, Simon Blackburn makes a similar point, writing that "This [the transparency thesis] is the fact that it makes no difference whether you say that it is raining, or it is true that it is raining, or true that it is true that it is raining, and so on forever."[14] In his little book *Truth*, Pascal Engle makes a similar point when he writes:

> "The volcano has erupted" and "It is true that the volcano has erupted" do not exactly mean the same thing, for the latter contains the mark of approval, but in so far as what is said is concerned, they have the same cognitive content. In this sense the words "is true" do not designate a *further* characteristic from the fact that the sentence has this content.[15]

The importance of the deflationary theory of truth is that it allows the truth predicate to come alive only within the context in which it is used. Since truth is the simple assertion of a proposition, we can only know what is being stated as true when we know the meaning of what is being asserted. In this case truth becomes subservient to meaning. It is to this idea that I turn next.

Semantic Priority

In an earlier chapter, I quoted D.Z. Phillips saying, "It follows from my argument that the criteria of meaningfulness cannot be found outside religion, since they are given by religious discourse itself."[16] What Phillips refers to as the criteria of meaningfulness includes the various ways that words get used in a religious context and the importance that paying attention to their use has for understanding what such words mean. Of course, while Phillips is referring here to only the religious use of words, the same sort of thing applies in other contexts as well. Consider what Phillips's long-time friend and former teacher, Peter Winch, writes:

> criteria of logic are not a direct gift of God, but arise out of, and are only intelligible in the context of, ways of living or modes of social life. It follows that one cannot apply criteria of logic to modes of social life as such. For instance, science is one such mode and religion is another; and each has criteria of intelligibility peculiar to itself.[17]

What Phillips and Winch point to is the important way that paying attention to the context in which language is used gives us access to what Philips calls the "criteria of meaningfulness" and what Winch calls the "criteria of logic." Now, since one of the concepts that gets used in a variety of contexts is the concept of "truth," there is no way to understand the meaning of truth in a given practice short of understanding its use. Of course, based on the discussion above, we know that truth is best seen as being equivalent to simply asserting a proposition. Without knowing the meaning of the proposition that is being asserted, we would have no idea under what conditions it makes sense to state that "*P* is true." That is, we would have no idea what the criteria are for asserting *P*. We can now see that since the truth predicate is equivalent to the assertion of a proposition and since a proposition secures its meaning in the context in which it is used, it only makes sense that truth be taken as utterly reliant on the meaning of the proposition that is being asserted as true. This is a long-winded way of saying that the sense of truth is dependent on propositional meaning, an idea I call "semantic priority."

To get a grasp on the meaning of semantic priority, it is helpful to turn again to Hilary Putnam's example of conceptual relativism. To summarize Putnam's story in a slightly truncated fashion, we remember that the imaginary Rudolf Carnap and the Polish logician are presented with three entities—$x1$, $x2$, and $x3$—and then asked to identify the number of objects that exist. Carnap, employing our ordinary concept of object, reports that there are exactly three objects: $x1$, $x2$, and $x3$. By contrast, the Polish logician, who accepts a particular mereology of objects according to which for every two particulars there is a new object, counts the objects and reports that there are exactly seven: $x1$, $x2$, $x3$, $x1 + x2$, $x1 + x3$, $x2 + x3$, $x1 + x2 + x3$. The two define the meaning of object differently and, hence, come up with different answers as to how many objects exist.

Again, in this little story Putnam packs in a few really important points, especially when it comes to the relationship between meaning and truth. The most important one for our purposes here, and I take it the most obvious as well, is that truth cannot be spoken of intelligibly until meaning is fixed. In Putnam's story, there is simply no way to decide on the truth of how many objects there are until the meaning of "object" is determined. Of course, once the meaning of "object" is fixed, an answer to the question "How many objects are there?" can be determined. Possibly the most interesting aspect of Putnam's story is that the Polish logician and Carnap are both correct in their given answers. This doesn't mean that there are two different correct answers to the question about how many objects there are, but rather that given the divergent meaning of "object" (neither of which is more correct than the other), they both offer the correct answer. It is true that in one context there are three objects, and it is true that in another context there are seven objects. Understanding truth, in each case, is part and parcel of understanding meaning.

From Putnam's example, we can see the obviousness of the fact that we cannot judge whether "it is true that *x*" is justified without knowing the meaning of "*x*." This obvious platitude is what is meant by semantic priority. Take the deflationary theory mentioned above in which, again, Horwich writes "that the meaning of the truth predicate is fixed by the schema; 'the proposition that *p* is true if and only if *p*.'"[18] Now, of course we need to know what it means to assert *p* if the meaning of "*p* is true" is going to be the same as simply asserting that "*p* is the case." But what does it mean to assert *p*? That, of course, depends on the meaning of *p*, which, naturally, depends on how *p* is used. Meaning must precede truth.

Now, semantic priority has some interesting entailments that should be mentioned. The first is that semantic priority gives us, quite naturally, any and all truth conditions that we might need in order to know what would need to be the case for something to be true. Michael Dummett, writing about those who adhere to a certain sort of truth minimalism, writes, "On such an account, you can know the condition for a sentence to be true only when you know what the sentence means; the explanation of what it means, and of what it is for it to have that meaning, must therefore be given in some manner that does not appeal to the notion of the sentence's being true."[19] It would be odd to know the meaning of a proposition and not know what, in principle, would have to be the case for it to be true. (This is a semantic claim not an epistemological claim, though the two are related.) In this way, truth attaches to the meaning of propositions in the way that the deflationary theory of truth states it does. Horwich writes:

> the advantage of relying on *use* in giving a naturalistic characterization of understanding is that it is obvious how knowledge of the use of a word is manifested (namely, by accepting certain sentences containing it in certain conditions), whereas it is not at all clear how knowledge of truth conditions is manifested; that is unless such knowledge is construed ... as the product of a knowledge of meaning (which is in turn explained in terms of use) and a grasp of the concept of truth.[20]

This does not mean that the conditions that make a sentence (or proposition) true are dependent on meaning, but only that when we learn what a sentence (or proposition) means, then we also learn what would need to be the case for that self-same sentence (or proposition) to be true. So, meaning allows us not only to see that truth amounts to the same thing as asserting a proposition (deflationary theory of truth) but also to know what conditions must obtain for us to justifiably say of a proposition that it is true. The important link between meaning and truth is the idea that there are certain criteria that we appeal to when we are asked, "How do we know that *x* is true?" It is to the central topic of criteria that we now turn.

Truth and Criteria

In her book *Wittgenstein's Account of Truth*, Sara Ellenbogen writes, "Wittgenstein holds that truth conditions are determined by criteria, that is, by rules which determine, by linguistic convention, the circumstances under which we may predicate 'is true' of the sentences in language which we treat as being true or false."[21] When we are asked if such and such is the case, we might say, "Yes, that's true." If we are then asked, "Well how do you know that?" then we might respond by saying, "Because … " It is what replaces the ellipsis that serves as the criteria for why (or how) we claim to know that something is true. So, criteria, in the narrow sense (criteria regarding truth), are the sort of things we appeal to when we want to explain to someone how it is that we know certain things are true. In a broader sense, as we have seen, criteria are also answers offered, within a language game or practice, to various why questions: "Why do you believe that?" "Why do you say that is true?" "Why do you claim to know that?" and "Why do you believe that word has that meaning?" Before defining criteria more perspicuously, a few things should be mentioned about some of their general characteristics.

Criteria as Part of Language

First, criteria are explanations (or elucidations) of what is already implicitly present when language is being used. Ellenbogen writes that:

> we acquire the concept of truth by learning how to apply the predicate "is true" to statements in our language, that is, by learning what counts as establishing our statements as true. And we learn what counts as establishing statements as true by participating in the linguistic practices of a community. For just as within a linguistic community we agree on correct uses of words, we also agree upon methods of testing the statements which we treat as being true or false.[22]

When linguistic communication occurs, criteria are already present—hiding in plain sight—guiding sensical dialogue. Without agreed-upon criteria, language would degenerate into pure nonsense. We may even want to go so far as to say that linguistic communication is parasitic on criteria, but criteria rarely show themselves until it is necessary to settle some form of dispute or to clear up some confusion that has occurred. Since language is rule-governed, learning the criteria of sensible speech happens naturally as we learn a language; this includes learning the criteria for truth and falsity as well as the criteria for meaningful discourse.

Take, for example, the claim that "Joe has a toothache." If asked by someone how I know that Joe has a toothache, I would appeal to certain outward criteria of pain behavior that I learned to associate with individuals who have a toothache. When we learn the meaning of "toothache," we also learn the criteria that we would normally appeal to in order to show why we think that someone is experiencing a toothache. Wittgenstein writes, "to explain my criteria for another person's having [a] toothache is to give a grammatical explanation about the word 'toothache' and, in this sense, an explanation of the meaning of the word toothache."[23] The criterial link between pain behavior and a toothache is learned as we learn what it is for someone to have a toothache.

In all of the various situations in which we need to explain the meaning of a word or explain why we hold something to be true, we will need to appeal to the criteria that we learned as we learned to speak competently. Here is how Rogers Albritton, again using the standard toothache example, explains the way that criteria are reliant on language: "If a kind of behavior is a criterion, in Wittgenstein's sense, of having a toothache, then it is part of the 'use,' the 'grammar,' of the word 'toothache,' among others, that in at least some circumstances another person who so behaves may be said to have a toothache."[24]

The discussion of the logical relationship between criteria and language raises a possible confusion that should be addressed before moving on. Some may think that if criteria are already present when one is using language, then it must be that all language use whatsoever is in perfect logical order, and if one desires to learn the grammar or rules of a language, all one needs to do is listen to people speak and note what it is that they say. To put this differently, some may take it that any speaker who is saying something is a competent speaker. This, however, misses an important point about what it means to be a competent speaker. A competent speaker is not simply someone who speaks but rather someone who speaks competently. This implies that there are some ways in which language use can be confused or illicit. To think that delineating the grammatical rules of a language is simply a matter of listening to someone speak misses the point of what is meant by offering a grammatical description of a practice; in fact, it runs together two different senses of what is meant by a practice. Here is how D.Z. Philips makes this important point:

> It is essential to distinguish between a grammatical and a sociological use of "practice." In its grammatical use, the appeal to practice is an appeal to the conceptual character of what is said or done. ... On the sociological use of "practice," however, we are simply referring to what happens, to what, in fact, goes on. Such activities may be riddled with confusions. It is only by conflating

the grammatical and sociological use of "practice" that we arrive at the conclusion that, according to Wittgenstein, there are no confused practices.[25]

A competent speaker is not someone who is simply dubbed to be such (no matter who the person is); rather, a competent speaker is someone whose use of language shows a certain grammatical sense when it comes to the way his or her use of words is tied to his or her form of life. Not all uses of language are in logical order just because they happen to be spoken. When we look at how words are used in any specific context, we will see that sometimes words get used in such a way that sense breaks down and the words lose their meaning. Think of people who construe the existence of God on par with the existence of other substantives or think of someone speaking as if going to heaven is like going to Pittsburgh (only farther away and requiring a different mode of transportation). In both cases the grammar of religious language is ignored and traded for a language use that has a similar surface grammar but none of the religious connotations demanded by this use of language. In such cases, religious language loses its sense and God and heaven become just another existent thing and another far-off place respectively. Again, what is missing is the religious context from which "God" and "heaven" get their meaning. It is when we see a certain logical sense between the use of words and the practice in which they occur, that we come to see what it means to be a competent speaker. The idea of a competent speaker who is baptized to be so is a myth, since a competent speaker is only determined after a grammatical investigation into the sense of language is conducted.[26]

Criteria as Social Conventions

Second, criteria are best seen as social conventions of language. As Ellenbogan noted above, criteria are "rules which determine, *by linguistic convention*, the circumstances under which we may predicate 'is true' of the sentences in language which we treat as being true or false."[27] It is best here to think of the use of "convention" as indicating some form of agreement between speakers of a language. Since communication is always a social activity (we communicate with others), it is essential that we remember that criteria are a part of the social interactions arising out of our sharing a language (and a life) with others. However, without agreement between speakers about the rules of sensible discourse, no communication would be possible (this is similar to what we saw above regarding criteria). Stanley Cavell writes, "criteria are specifications a given person or group sets up on the basis of which ... to judge ... whether something has a particular status or value."²⁸ It is the social nature of criteria that compels Cavell to say of them "that they are only human, nothing more than natural to us."²⁹

Seeing criteria as social conventions should not, however, make us think that they are either the sort of things that we overtly agree on or the sort of things that we can decide to *fully* give up on.³⁰ Even though criteria are social conventions, they are deeply tied to what it means to be human. In fact, it may be profitable to see criteria as grounded in human nature. This is because criteria are deeply embedded in, and tied to, human social interaction. Wittgenstein writes, "'So you are saying that human agreement decides what is true and what is false?' It is what human beings *say* that is true and false; and they agree in the *language* they use. That is not agreement in opinions but in form of life."³¹ Cavell, mentioning the depth in human life from which criteria (as conventions) spring to life, writes:

> The conventions we appeal to may be said to be "fixed," "adopted," "accepted," etc. by us; but this does not now mean that what we have fixed or adopted are (merely) the (conventional) *names* of things. The conventions which control the application of grammatical criteria are fixed not by customs or some particular concord or agreement which might, without disrupting the texture of our lives, be changed where convenience suggests a change .... They are, rather, fixed by the nature of human life itself, the human fix itself, by those "very general facts of nature" ... and, I take it, in particular, very general facts of *human nature*.³²

Criterial agreement, while shown in language, is fixed (contingently) by the human form of life (or by human biology). In this sense, as we will see, we may opt out of certain linguistic practices, but opting out of all practices would be tantamount to simply ceasing to communicate with others. Espen Hammer writes, "Since my language with all its grammatical nodes and everyday logic was there before me ..., I cannot help voicing my words as a representative speaker, as one among many to whom I belong in a community of speakers."³³

The Groundlessness of Criteria

Finally, it is important to realize that criteria are the final appeal when it comes to disputes about meaning and/or truth. The appeal to criteria is a kind of "groundless foundation"; it is, to use Wittgenstein's words, the place where "we have reached bedrock" and "our spade is turned."³⁴ Noting this fact is to notice that, for the most part, our lives get along quite well without our knowledge claims ever being called into question. However, when certain things are questioned—usually when things go awry in some way—we offer an explanation that is generally an appeal to agreed-upon criteria. At this point there is nothing more to be said. Criteria are such that if someone were to ask for a further explanation for something after the criteria have been offered as an explanation, the only proper answer is "This is how we act" or "This is how we go on." Our general agreement in forms of life shows that criteria lie at the bedrock of sensible communication. In a way, criteria function a bit like what Wittgenstein called "hinge propositions," in that asking for a further justification for criteria is as nonsensical as it would be if we asked for some justification for the fixed hinges that thought swings on.[35] Michal Williams writes:

> According to Wittgenstein, there are—indeed, must be—basic certainties: propositions or judgements that we *do not* doubt because we *cannot* doubt them. These basic certainties can be thought of as "framework judgements" in the following sense: by lying "apart from the route travelled by inquiry", they constitute the framework within which practices of inquiring, justifying beliefs, arguing, asking for and giving reasons, making knowledge-claims, etc. take place. This has nothing to do with practicality and everything to do with the conditions for making any judgements at all.[36]

Criterial agreement represents the end of the discussion. This, of course, does not mean that we must always agree with the criteria offered to us on any given occasion. We may fight to change the way we see certain things, or we may simply refuse to participate in certain aspects of language. Whatever our revolt, what we cannot do is look beyond criteria for another rule to justify the ones we already have in place.

Recognizing that (a) criteria are appealed to as an elucidation for a language game that is already in place and being played, (b) that criteria are social conventions that we learn as we become competent speakers of a language, and (c) that agreed-upon criteria represent the bedrock of appeal in disputes regarding meaning and truth are all important points to keep in mind as we look at a more nuanced definition of criteria.

Defining Criteria

In the *Blue and Brown Books*, Wittgenstein explains his idea of criteria in a longish passage that I think is worth quoting in full. He writes:

> Let us introduce two antithetical terms in order to avoid certain elementary confusions: To the question "How do you know that so-and-so is the case?", we

sometimes answer by giving "criteria" and sometimes by giving "symptoms". If medical science calls angina an inflammation caused by a particular bacillus, and we ask in a particular case "why do you say this man has got angina?" then the answer "I have found the bacillus so-and-so in his blood" gives us the criterion, or what we may call the *defining criterion* of angina. If on the other hand the answer was, "His throat is inflamed", this might give us a symptom of angina. I call "symptom" a phenomenon of which experience has taught us that it coincided, in some way or other, with the phenomenon which is our defining criterion. Then to say "A man has angina if this bacillus is found in him" is a tautology or it is a loose way of stating the definition of "angina". But to say, "A man has angina whenever he has an inflamed throat" is to make a hypothesis.[37]

The distinction Wittgenstein makes between a defining criterion and a symptom is important. If a defining criterion is present, then the presence of what it is a criterion for is, of necessity, also present (even if it is not visible). A defining criterion is part of what we mean by the thing itself; it is learned as we learn how to use language. A symptom, on the other hand, is simply something that coincides (or is empirically correlated) with certain things. A symptom gives us an *indication* of the presence of something else, but not its necessary existence, so what we do in such cases is make a hypothesis that the other thing is present as well. The real difference between a defining criterion and a symptom is the surety with which each one points to something else. One way to look at a defining criterion is to see it as representing a necessary connection between the presence of the criterion and the truth of what it is a criterion for, such that if c is present, then p is true (where c is a criterion, or a set of criteria, and p is a proposition logically connected to c).

John Canfield writes that there are two features that defining criterion have: "The first is that the tie between criterion and the state of affairs governed by the criterion is a conventional one."[38] This is simply part and parcel of the view of criteria that we mentioned above, namely that criteria appear as a social convention. Canfield continues, "The second feature of the view of criteria is … the criterion's being met is decisive for establishing that the corresponding state of affairs exists, that is, the state of affairs for which the criterion is a criterion."[39] This is simply to claim that the presence of criteria (as opposed to a symptom) guarantees the presence of what the criteria represent (or stand for).

When we appeal to criteria to explain why we take something to be true, it isn't always clear if we are appealing to a defining criterion or to a symptom. What is clear is the unsettling fact (at least for the defining criterion view) that we can be wrong about something we claim is true even when it appears that the criterion has been met. This goes against the strong reading of how the defining criterion is supposed to function. If the presence of a defining criterion guarantees the truth of what the criterion is a criterion for, and if it is possible to be in possession of a criterion and yet be wrong about the truth of what the criterion is a criterion for, then we are in the midst of a paradox that must be addressed.

Criteria, Justification, and Shams

As was mentioned already, when we speak of criteria (as opposed to a symptom), it is supposed to be the case that if the criteria for some truth are met, then that truth is supposed to obtain of necessity. Yet, clearly, we sometimes *appear* to have all the criteria we need but, as it turns out, we are mistaken about what we thought was true. Take the example of someone being in pain due to a toothache. Here is Wittgenstein again: "To explain my criterion for another person's having a toothache is to give a grammatical explanation of the word 'toothache' and, in this sense, an explanation concerning the meaning of the word 'toothache.'"[40] It isn't hard to imagine, however a story showing someone who appears to see another person exhibiting all the classic signs of pain behavior that someone with a toothache exhibits, only to find out that he or she was watching the world's greatest toothache actor in action. In this case, all the criteria *seem* to have been met, but there was no toothache present, so the idea of a defining criterion must be wrong. Or, since we are making up stories, imagine a case of seeing a deer blocking your path in the road ahead of you; it is daylight and all conditions (including your own) are optimal for seeing a deer in the road. In this case, you would say (if asked) that "it is true that there is a deer in the road." Your belief in the truth of that proposition may even have behavioral consequences as you slam on your breaks to avoid the "deer." The criteria of seeing a deer in good lighting will have been met and the normal justifications given. (Seeing a deer is what serves as the criterion for claiming that "there is a deer in front of me.") But now imagine that we come to find out that Microsoft is trying out a new holographic animal machine, and the deer, though appearing very real, was in fact a sham.

Now, what is going on here with regard to the relationship between truth claims and criteria? The first thing we should note is that real criteria can be mimicked and that the sham only makes sense because of the genuine logical relationship between criteria and what they represent. We are fooled into thinking someone is in pain because they mimicked *real* pain behavior. The fact that we are normally justified in inferring pain when we observe certain behaviors is why the possibility of shams even exists. D.Z. Phillips writes, "The person's pretense is parasitic on our normal understanding. The pretense does not violate our criteria for understanding; it reinforces them."[41] The possibility of a sham is actually part of the grammar of our language; it is built into our understanding of criteria. By learning the relationship between pain and pain behavior, we realize that we generally get it right when we ascribe real pain to someone in the presence of what we observe as pain behavior even though we sometimes may be fooled. The pretense itself seems to be included in the genuine article. This is what D.Z. Phillips is getting at when he writes, "In short, the concept of pain includes the different ways in which 'pain' enters our lives, including the way people lie about their pains, exaggerate about them, playact, and so on."[42] Stanley Cavell makes a similar point when he writes, "In all such circumstance [pretense, hoax, play-acting, rehearsing] he [the one pretending to be in pain] has satisfied the criteria we use for applying the concept of pain to others. It is because of *that* satisfaction that we know that he is feigning pain."[43] So, the first way of dealing with the possibility that we can be misled by criteria is to remember that, in many circumstances, the idea of a criteria being met allows for the possibility of shams, but this possibility is included in the grammar and meaning of the concept in question. Furthermore, there would be no shams without the regular success of criterial rules.

A second way of dealing with the fact that we might be wrong when we observe certain criteria is to simply admit that if we appeal to criteria and, at some later time, come to realize it was in fact a sham, then we will come to also realize that the criteria we thought were present were not actually present at all. On this view, criteria are a necessary and sufficient condition for the existence of certain things, such that if criteria are really present, then so is that which the criteria represent. If we feel we are in possession of a certain criterion and find later that we were duped, then we must admit that we were mistaken about the presence of the criterion. This possibility might be ameliorated, of course, if we begin to think of criteria as functioning temporally. That is, we might need to realize that in observing criteria, we often need to wait on the context to let us know if it is actual criteria or a sham. This temporal view of criteria admits that the situation will often resolve itself if criteria are waited on and viewed in the larger context of what is going on. It still may be the case that at times we are mistaken, but a temporal view of criteria may eliminate errors in some instances.

The two ways of taking account of the relationship between "criteria" and shams that we just looked at goes some way in helping us explain how we may sometimes go wrong when we think we are in possession of some criterion or another; however, what these possibilities also leave open is the fact that any purported dependence on criteria may simply mean that we must accept some form of local (or contextual) skepticism. If the criteria in the case of a person writhing in pain or in the case of the deer in the road actually led us to make false claims, then does this not throw doubt on all of the cases in which we must appeal to criteria? Should we not, at least for a time, be skeptical about all our claims that rely on an appeal to criteria? Is skepticism just a fact given that we all, of necessity, rely on criteria to make claims about what is true and false?

Elaborating on some of the things that Stanley Cavell has to say about criteria, Espen Hammer writes, "Since criteria are only human, natural to us in virtue of the way we agree in language but not metaphysically aligned with anything *in the nature of things*, skepticism, the repudiation of criteria, is a standing possibility of humans."[44] Cavell makes a similar point writing, "If the fact that we share, or have established, criteria is the condition under which we can think and communicate in language, then skepticism is a *natural* possibility of that condition; it reveals most perfectly the standing threat to thought and communication, that they are only human, nothing more than natural to us."[45] Given what we have just discussed about criteria, I think Cavell is correct here when he says that language use, in and of itself, opens us up to a certain sort of skepticism. But what sort of skepticism are we talking about here?

The form of skepticism that the possibility of hoaxes and pretense points to when it comes to criteria use is not the sort of classical global skepticism that we see in those who think that everything can be doubted or that no knowledge is possible. Skepticism only functions within language and it gains its sense within the confines of things we are certain about. To doubt everything would mean that we have no way to juxtapose doubt from certainty, in which case doubt (and skepticism) would be senseless. Therefore, to believe that the fact that criteria can be mimicked leads to any sort of global skepticism is simply a mistake. But what about a more restricted form of skepticism? We might call this "local" skepticism. Think of cases where we think we see something on the road on a foggy Seattle day or when we think we see mountains coming up ahead of us on a day when clouds are hanging low. In these sorts of cases, we may not be sure that what we think we are seeing is really genuine. But, in these sorts of examples there are also certain factors that help make sense of why we are perplexed. Maybe it is the fog or maybe it is dusk with poor visibility or maybe we just had our eyes dilated at the doctor's office. In this sort of skeptical situation, we simply need to wait and evaluate our criteria over time. We wait until we get closer, or the lighting is better, or until our eyes are clear, etc. There may also be times when we are skeptical about an entire practice and when we feel it is best to decide that the whole thing is a sham. In this case, we might simply refuse to participate in that aspect of language. Say someone is skeptical about whether or not the things appealed to in religion have any bearing on reality. Here, a person may opt out of the language game and simply refuse to participate. We generally refer to these people (in religious contexts, but not only in religion) as atheists (a milder form of this might be someone who exhibits doubts within the practice of religion).

So, while the possibility of being wrong about criteria does allow for some form of skepticism, it is far narrower in scope than any sort of global skepticism that seeks to throw doubt on all our practices. As D.Z. Phillips points out, when we appeal to criteria, "we are trying to elucidate forms of life that we share with the sceptics. What we have to show is how the sceptics' words fail to do justice to these forms of life; how they distance both themselves and us from them."[46] The criteria serve as an explanation of a form of life (or language game) that is already in play, already being practiced. D.Z. Phillips writes, "*The appeal to criteria is not meant to settle anything, but to elucidate what is already settled.*"[47] This point is why Cavell seems a bit ambitious when he writes, "We begin to feel, or ought to, that maybe *language* (and understanding, and knowledge) rests upon very shaky foundations—a thin net over an abyss ….Whether our words will go on meaning what they do depends upon whether other people find it worth their while to continue to understand us."[48] Cavell's claim that language as a whole is defective is only sensible within language. Choosing to question the worth of all of language is a claim that either has a context in language or is meant to float above the contextual fray. If the latter, then Cavell is not telling us anything that has any sense at all.

Truth-Pluralism and Religious Criteria

Thus far we have seen that one way of trying to make sense of a plurality of truths, without, along the way, attempting to say that truth was one univocal thing, was to hitch our wagons to the deflationary theory of truth. On this construal, we saw that what really matters when it comes to truth is the meaning of what it is we are asserting as true. This is because on the deflationary account of truth, to say that a certain proposition is true is equivalent to asserting the same proposition. In this way we are committed to semantic priority since truth is secondary to meaning. We could never understand what is being asserted unless and until we know the meaning of the proposition in question. Semantic priority, however, led us to look at the importance of criteria for two reasons. First, criterial rules guide the meaning of words as these words take up residency in the life of the speaker. To understand meaning, we must also understand the rules that delineate sense from nonsense, and this is seen in the way words get used. Second, criteria are also used when we want to justify our claims to truth. So, while asserting that something is true is one thing, offering criteria for how we know something is true is quite another. But in order to know which criteria are agreed upon within language as justification for our truth claims, we must, again, look to see how language is used in various contexts. Now we can see that not only has truth been deflated by the equivalence schema but justification is also deflated in that criteria are agreed-upon rules of language (they are social conventions) which themselves are justified by nothing.

So how does all of this relate to religious truth? First, religious truths, like all other truth claims, are best seen from a deflationary point of view (i.e., "It is true that 'God exists' iff God exists," "'Jesus died for my sins' is true iff Jesus died for my sins," or "It is true that 'God created the heavens and the earth' iff God created the heavens and the earth"). Of course, the important work is to see how these propositions are used in a religious context so that we are then able to determine what it is that is being asserted. D.Z. Phillips writes, "The criteria of what can sensibly be said of God are to be found within the religious tradition."[49] In this sense, religion is just like any other language game and religious truth is as mundane as the use of truth in any other context. The challenge is to pay enough attention to religious practice to see the relationship between the truth claims believers make and the *life* that they live.

But what then is the criterial justification for religious belief? Are there some criteria in the religious life that we can point to as evidence that a certain person has genuine (as opposed to an idolatrous) religious faith? If the meaning of religious propositions is tied essentially to the life the believer lives, then what is it about the believer's life that allows us to be justified in claiming that we are in the presence of genuine religiosity and not a sham? What are the criteria (or the criterion) for genuine faith? Before attempting to point in the direction of an answer to this question, I want to point out a few examples of why it is that whatever the criteria for religious faith turn out to be, it will have little to do with a metaphysical being called God existing "out there" somewhere. When religious meaning and truth are located in life (rather than in the metaphysical heavens), a supernatural God becomes a hindrance to faith, a distraction that leads us away from the place where criteria find their home.[50]

An Excursus on Atheism as a Prerequisite to Faith

Paul Tillich: Ontological Atheism

At the beginning of Part II of Volume I of his *Systematic Theology*, Paul Tillich writes, "The basic theological question is the question of God. God is the answer to the question implied in being."[51] In what follows, I want to present a Tillich-like (but not a strictly Tillichian) view of the nonexistence of God which, while representative of much of what Tillich has to say on the subject, will also lack the minutia and complexities that Tillich seemed to enjoy.[52] While this view might be too incomplete to be called Tillich's view, it does allow us to see clearly why Tillich favored a form of atheism. Since Tillich saw an important relationship between theological language and human existence, it might help if we can get a birds-eye view of what sort of questions Tillich believes are implied in human existence. If we can get a general sense of this idea, then we will be in a better place to understand what sort of God Tillich thinks will best serve as an answer to the sort of existential questions that bubble up as a result of the kind of life we live.

Tillich refers to his theological method as "the method of correlation," writing, "The method of correlation explains the contents of the Christian faith through existential questions and theological answers in mutual interdependence."[53] In this case, the meaning of theological language is not given in advance; that is, it is not a set of eternal propositions that are dragged through history and assented to in each successive generation. Rather, the theological answers "are 'spoken' to human existence from beyond it. Otherwise they would not be answers, for the question is human existence itself."[54] The questions that theology seeks to correlate answers to are questions that are derived from the unique existential situation that arise in each successive generation. The questions can be as vast and as diverse as the cultures and historical time periods in which they show themselves. The answers, which are correlated with such questions, are derived from the eternal truths which are contained in what Tillich calls "revelatory experience." The theologian's task is to correlate the eternal message of the gospel with the questions that surface in human existence. This "method of correlation" has some affinity with the way that Robert Coburn spoke of correlating religious limiting questions with the logically complete answers to these questions that were provided in the language of religion.

Tillich has much to say regarding the nuances of what he means by correlation and the way that theological answers get paired with existential concerns. Those nuances, while worth looking into, are not my main concern here since they would take us too far afield. One thing that should not be overlooked, however, is that Tillich (again, much like Coburn) believes that questions that arise about human existence bubble up (partly) because of a sort of shock that humans undergo when we grasp the reality of our finitude and the fact that we are constantly threatened by the possibility of nonbeing. Tillich writes that:

> Only those who have experienced the shock of transitoriness, the anxiety in which they are aware of their finitude, the threat of nonbeing, can understand what the notion of God means. Only those who have experienced the tragic ambiguities of our historical existence and have totally questioned the meaning of existence can understand what the symbol of the Kingdom of God means.[55]

In *The Courage to Be*, Tillich writes, "Courage is the self-affirmation of being in spite of the fact of nonbeing."[56] The threat of nonbeing is best taken as the *possibility* that we might cease to exist at any time and the *actuality* that we will certainly die someday (facing the actualization of the possibility of our own nonexistence). The threat of the loss of being is not like the threat of losing an eyelash, or a tooth, or even a limb; it is rather to lose all that we are. That is why the threat of nonbeing causes a sort of "ontological shock"[57] to our thinking. In this sense, to feel the threat of nonbeing is to feel the utter contingency of human existence. My interest here is in looking at the possible role that God plays, for Tillich, in helping us face (but not necessarily overcome) our finitude with courage and faith. Of Course, the problem is not just being finite but realizing we are finite; it is the very realization of the threat of nonbeing that is so existentially shocking and anxiety producing (I take it that cows are not flummoxed by their finitude). Tillich writes, "Man (*sic*) as man (*sic*) in every civilization is anxiously aware of the threat of nonbeing and needs the courage to affirm himself (*sic*) in spite of it."[58]

Tillich states that courage requires "the power of being" if the threat of nonbeing is going to be overcome. He writes, "Courage needs the power of being, a power transcending the nonbeing which is experienced in the anxiety of fate and death."[59] Of course, it would do no good if our courage was grounded in some other being that also exists under the constant threat of nonbeing, since that being would also need help in overcoming such a threat. Many of us seek an escape from life by means of finite things (money, sex, exercise, sports, alcohol, etc.). But these things are just that, things (or, more specifically, finite things), so in this sense they are part of the same category of existing things which caused the problem in the first place. An important part of Tillich's theological method is based on the fact that all humans are ultimately concerned about something, but the object of that concern is of vital importance. Now, since the human situation reveals the need to overcome finitude (or the threat of nonbeing), Tillich writes that "ultimate concern must transcend every preliminary finite and concrete concern. It must transcend the whole realm of finitude in order to be the answer to the question implied in finitude."[60] If God is to be the answer to our existential concern, then God cannot be subject to the category of existence. "The being of God," Tillich continues, "cannot be understood as the existence of a being alongside others or above others. If God is a being, he is subject to the categories of finitude, especially to space and substance."[61] Thus, Tillich writes, "it is the finitude of being which drives us to the question of God."[62] Yet, a finite God can never serve as an answer to our questions, and this is what we get if God is subject to the category of existence.

Tillich writes, "if the notion of God appears in systematic theology in correlation with the threat of nonbeing which is implied in existence, God must be called the infinite power of being which resists the threat of nonbeing. In classical theology this is being-itself."[63] It is the relationship between God and ontology (or being) where Tillich stakes his theological claim. This is why his preferred way of speaking about God is as "being-itself," which means that God is not a being at all. There is a sense in which this is the only way that we can (or should) speak of God (unless we admit to speaking symbolically). This is oddly paradoxical since in speaking of God as being-itself, Tillich is avoiding speaking of God as a being at all. Regarding Tillich's use of this way of speaking of God, George Pattison writes, "he [Tillich] insisted that this is a 'non-symbolic' statement and, in fact, the only non-symbolic statement we can make about God. Everything else we might say about God—such as that God is 'Father' or 'Lord' or 'Creator' or 'Trinity'—is symbolic, only not this."[64] Tillich himself writes that "The statement that God is being-itself is a non-symbolic statement. It does not point beyond itself. It means what it says directly and properly; if we speak of the actuality of God, we first assert that he is not God if he is not being-itself."[65]

The very idea of being itself allows God to escape the confines of existence. In this case, it makes no sense to say that God exists. For something to have being (at least for Tillich) is for that thing to have it as a contingent property (a property it might lose). That is, we, as human beings, *have* being but we can (and will) lose it someday. But the possibility of losing our being is only possible if we participate in being. Something that is being-itself (or the ground of being) as opposed to *a* being would not participate in being, but would, rather, be defined as being. Tillich writes:

The being of God is being-itself. The being of God cannot be understood as the existence of a being alongside others or above others. If God is a being, he is subject to the categories of finitude, especially to space and substance. Even if he is called the "highest being" in the sense of the "most perfect" and the "most powerful" being, this situation is not changed. When applied to God, superlatives become diminutives.[66]

On this reading, God does not exist at all since there is no threat of nonbeing in being-itself. We may want to say that God is a necessary being, but that makes it seem again as if God is participating in being rather than being defined as being itself. If God were to exist, then God would be a being who could lose existence. This is the basis of Tillich's *ontological atheism*. He writes:

> We have spoken of the transition of being into existence, which involves the possibility that being will contradict and lose itself. This transition is excluded from being-itself … for being-itself does not participate in nonbeing. In this it stands in contrast to every being. As classical theology has emphasized, God is beyond essence and existence. Logically, being-itself is "before," "prior to," the split which characterizes finite being.[67]

To ascribe existence to God is to say too much; it is to think of God on par with other beings. It would mean offering our fealty to something other than God. This is why Tillich writes, "God does not exist. He is being-itself beyond essence and existence. Therefore, to argue that God exists is to deny him."[68]

Simone Weil: Ethical Atheism

Not all atheism is centered on the idea that any God that is seen as an object or an entity or a thing must be rejected. Some forms of atheism see a certain kind of God as an impediment to living the ethical life that religious belief demands. I believe that Simone Weil had this form of atheism (or something akin to it) in mind in some of her writings. Weil once wrote that "Religion in so far as it is a source of consolation is a hindrance to true faith: in this sense atheism is a purification."[69] One of Simone Weil's main concerns is to avoid the kind of religious idolatry that was outlined in earlier chapters: a use of God that sees divinity as a way of escaping from life. As we saw, the temptation is to worship a God that we can manipulate as a way of appeasing our sense of religious obligation while also escaping the vicissitudes of life and the challenges and rigors of a religious existence, which calls us to give up our self-centered life and serve other people. In *Gravity and Grace*, Weil writes,

"We must be careful about the level on which we place the infinite. If we place it on the level which is only suitable for the finite it will matter very little what name we give it."[70] There is a tendency to place God on the level that mimics the transcendent but in actuality is simply an exalted aspect of finitude. The religious challenge is to remove this sort of being from our lives and learn to live a selfless life for others without seeking reward. The pull of a pet God ("our own personal Jesus") who will serve us, however, is not something that is easy to rid ourselves of.

In her book *Simone Weil and Theology*, Rebecca Rozelle-Stone writes, "Rather than being authentically oriented away from the self/ego toward God, theological narratives, dogmas, doctrines, and their corresponding rites more often than not are purely self-serving."[71] We come to feel that we deserve compensation for all that we do. In this sense we fill up our feeling of meaninglessness with a God who will guarantee us such compensation, and we seek this God's approval, since it is this being that holds all the cards. Rather than live with a God who is wholly other, we fill the void in our life with a deity who is always on our side. Simone Weil writes, "It is the same with religion at a certain level. Instead of receiving the [imaginary] smile of Louis XIV, we invent a God who smiles on us."[72] The religious goal, however, is not to rush too quickly to fill the void in our life with a compensatory deity but rather to linger with ourselves while we wait on God to arrive. We must allow the emptiness to remain empty, so we do not fill it with something unworthy of our affection or worse, something that will help us avoid the void altogether. Weil writes, "We must leave on one side the beliefs which fill up voids and sweeten what is bitter. The belief in immortality. The belief in the utility of sin: *etiam peccata*. The belief in the providential ordering of events—in short the 'consolations' which are ordinarily sought in religion."[73]

Existing in the void (without God) is a means of creating space for grace to show up. Alexander Nava writes that "The void is the recognition that God is present in the world only under the form of absence, as the *deus absconditus*."[74] But God's coming as absence can only occur if we reject the temptation to fill the void in our life and instead become comfortable waiting on grace. Weil writes:

> Grace fills empty spaces but it can only enter where there is a void to receive it, and it is grace itself which makes this void.
>
> The necessity for a reward, the need to receive the equivalent of what we give. But if, doing violence to this necessity, we leave a vacuum, as it were a suction of air is produced and a supernatural reward results. It does not come if we receive other wages: it is this vacuum which makes it come.[75]

It is only by God's absence that we are made ready for God's appearance in the void, but this requires living a life free of idolatry. It requires allowing for the feeling of emptiness to invade our being as we rid ourselves of the need to always be the center of cosmic attention. In words reminiscent of Tillich, Weil writes, "Nothing which exists is absolutely worthy of love. We must therefore love that which does not exist."[76]

Naturally, the risk in bidding *adieu* to the idolatrous God is the uncomfortable feeling that comes with realizing there are no guarantees either in this life or in some life to come. Our desire for security must die in order for us to see God anew. Weil writes, "The implicit love of God can only have three immediate objects, the only three things here below in which God is really though secretly present. These are religious ceremonies, the beauty of the world and our neighbor."[77] In this sense the meaning of the love of God (or the love of God itself) is shown in the here and now. However, in order to see God in the world, we must die to our ego. The focus on the "I" keeps us from seeing God in the stuff that surrounds us. Weil writes, "The sin in me says 'I'. I am all."[78] Weil's idea of what she calls "decreation" is the necessary next step in keeping the void free of ego so that grace is possible. In creation, something is brought about by sheer power, but in decreation, our egos are eliminated through humility.

Simone Weil explains decreation by comparing it with destruction, writing, "Decreation: to make something created pass into the uncreated. Destruction: to make something created pass into nothingness. A blameworthy substitute for decreation."[79] It isn't that we are trying to rid ourselves of existence, to literally become nothing; rather, we are trying to remove ourselves, ethically, from the place that gets in the way of grace. To pass into the uncreated *via* decreation is to exist where God is but in such a way that God can exist through us. Stephen Plant writes that "Decreating the self ... meant transforming it from something that belonged to the natural world, into something that belonged to God."[80] By dying to self (decreating the ego), we are able to allow God to love through us without us expecting (or worse, demanding) recompense. Weil writes:

> He emptied himself of his divinity. We should empty ourselves of the false divinity with which we were born.
>
> Once we have understood we are nothing, the object of all our efforts is to become nothing. It is for this that we suffer with resignation, *it is for this that we act*, it is for this that we pray.
>
> May God grant me to become nothing.
>
> In so far as I become nothing, God loves himself through me.[81]

The atheism that Simone Weil presents can be seen as a form of *ethical atheism* since it removes any God that is a hindrance to living the self-sacrificial ethical life required by religious faith. Her atheism is an offer of not only good riddance to an idolatrous God but also good riddance to an ego that hampers our ability to see God in the world or in the face of our neighbor. This is an atheism that makes room for faith, an atheism that allows God to show up in the absence of the void, a void devoid of compensation and ego. In this way, the religious life can truly be religiously significant as the believer embraces—rather than flees from—the world.

Wittgenstein: Semantic Atheism

What would it mean to say that language pictures reality? In one way the meaning is clear enough. If we think again of how a picture represents what it is a picture of (if it is a representational picture), then we can imagine that language links up with reality by having words accurately represent objects in the way brushstrokes on a canvas accurately represents the Eifel Tower. The words that represent things could then be combined in various ways to picture (or describe) the world. It is said that Wittgenstein got the idea for thinking of language as a picture of reality when he saw little models of cars used in a Parisian court to picture how accidents occurred. In this case, each little model represented an object in reality; similarly, if the accidents were being described linguistically, words would act as stand-ins (models or pictures) for objects in the world. In the *Tractatus*, Wittgenstein writes:

2.1 We make to ourselves pictures of facts.
2.11 The picture presents the facts in logical space.
2.12 The picture is a model of reality.
2.13 To the objects correspond in the picture the elements of the picture.
2.131 The elements of the picture stand, in the picture, for the objects.[82]

A bit later, in proposition 2.15, he adds, "That the elements of the picture are combined with one another in a definite way, represents that the things are so combined with one another [in the world]."[83]

If we think of these statements as a rudimentary example of what it means for words to picture reality, then it appears to make perfect sense. Language represents reality by sharing with it a similar logical structure. The picture that language gives us of the world corresponds with the arrangement of the facts that make up the world. Now this is an incredibly simplistic representation of Wittgenstein's complex picture theory that is presented in the *Tractatus*, but it is a good-enough representation for our purposes here.[84] The main claim is that language represents reality in the way that a picture or model represents what it stands for (when it is a representational model). Elements in language correspond to facts in the world. If language accurately represents what is real, then it is said to be true; if it does not, then it is false. However, true or false, the model (or picture, or linguistic token) has a sense in that it could obtain even if it happens not to and it could fail to obtain even if it happens to be true at the moment (assuming it is not a necessary truth that is being expressed). For language to have a sense means that it is a candidate for truth or falsity. To say that something cannot be either true or false is to say that it lacks sense—it is meaningless.

The real question is what sort of language is it that is best suited to pictorially represent reality? Avrum Stroll writes:

> This theory of the picturing relationship between language and reality provides a further reason why it is necessary to use a formal language for philosophical purposes. It is only in a symbolic language, such as the *Principia Mathematica*, that one can formulate elementary propositions and therefore it is only by means of such a language that one can attain an accurate picture of the world.[85]

For the Wittgenstein of the *Tractatus*, ordinary language was just a bit too messy and loose to accurately represent reality. One way to clear up the messiness of ordinary language is to limit sensible language to the language of the natural sciences. Wittgenstein writes, "The totality of true propositions is the total natural sciences (or the totality of the natural sciences)."[86] A bit later he writes, "The right method of philosophy would be this. To say nothing except what can be said, i.e., the propositions of natural science"[87] This sort of thinking limits what can be said about reality, or rather it limits what we can speak sensibly about (we can still speak as much nonsense as we please). Wittgenstein writes in section 5.6 of the *Tractatus* that "*The limits of my language* means the limits of my world."[88] He then ends the *Tractatus* with the wonderful statement that "Whereof one cannot speak, thereof one must be silent."[89]

This is as good a statement of scientism as you're going to find, in that it restricts all meaningful discourse to the language of the natural sciences. This, in a limited way, is the sort of position taken by Richard Dawkins and his new atheist friends (as well as many others) who think that all truth is explicable only in the language of science.[90] In some ways, Dawkins and his friends are correct;

that is, if we *define* facts (or truth) as those things that are described in the language of science, then, of course, there will be no facts (or truths) which are not describable in the language of science. J.R. Jones writes, "In one sense, '*how* the world is' covers everything. And this means that, in that sense, all you have is science. The world is the totality of facts. And, looking as it were from the midst of this, how the world is, how it goes, the *facts* of it, will cover everything."[91] Since language cannot picture what transcends the world (including a transcendent God), then there is no sense to be made in speaking about such things. It is in language that we see that talk of transcendence is, strictly speaking, senseless. We might profitably refer to this view as *semantic atheism*.

The interesting thing for the early Wittgenstein is that he saw that facts, while objectively important, did not exhaust all that is important. Take the following passages from the *Tractatus* as an example:

6.41 The sense of the world must lie outside the world.
6.4312 The solution of the riddle of life in space and time lies *outside* space and time.
6.432 How the world is, is completely indifferent for what is higher. God does not reveal himself (*sic*) *in* the world.
6.44 Not *how* the world is, is the mystical, but *that* it is.
6.522 There is indeed the inexpressible. This *shows* itself; it is the mystical.[92]

In all of these statements, Wittgenstein reveals that while language does restrict what we can speak meaningfully about, what is really important (what imbues the whole with meaning) is inexpressible (or mystical[93]). While we cannot speak sensibly (or meaningfully) about the transcendent, it is exactly in the silence where the important stuff of existence resides. So, while language restricts what can be said, it does not restrict what can be revealed (or, following Wittgenstein, "shown"). Here is how J.R. Jones puts it:

> as we face our lives and in those moments when the question arises for us whether our life has any meaning at all—when we suddenly have what might be described as an awareness of existence and the whole question whether existence *has sense* arises for us, then we know perfectly well that the world is not unmysterious ... And when this happens to you (if it ever does happen), you *know* that "how the world is" is not everything.[94]

For the early Wittgenstein, language may restrict our ability to meaningfully speak about the transcendent, but this fact does not restrict the importance of transcendence in our lives.

All of these various forms of atheism (ontological, ethical, and semantic) offer reasons to dispense with God either as an object among objects, an idol that we use for self-gain, or as something that cannot meaningfully be spoken about. In all of these examples, the point of religious belief is not to assent to the existence of something that exists out there somewhere. John Whittaker writes:

> To believe in God, in other words, is not to satisfy oneself that there is a God in the ordinary sense of justifying an existential claim about the presence of an external object. To believe in God entails reordering one's basic longing for inward peace, and the concept of God is understood *in the light of this changed perspective*. God cannot be descriptively known, then, yet he can be understood as the descriptively unknowable source of an all-sustaining love. He is not an object in any ordinary sense, despite the fact that we refer to him with nominative expressions and personal pronouns.[95]

The various forms of atheism that we just looked at indicate that the criteria for the truth of religious faith have little to do with assenting to belief in a dispensable metaphysical God—a God which may very well lead us away from faith. To locate the actual criteria for religious truth, we must look to the life of the believer rather than to the empty skies.

Belief, Criteria, and Agape

To believe in God is to commit oneself to living a certain way. John Whittaker describes religious belief this way:

> to believe is to change the way in which we take life in under the guidance of religious ideas. We adjust our thinking to a new form of conceptual understanding that believers say brings them a peace that is unknown apart from a religious outlook. We do something more than saying "yes" to a thought, therefore. We transform ourselves. This self-transformation belongs to the very nature of what religious believing—Faith—is, which involve changes not only in the way one thinks—the species of one's judgments—but also in the manner of life that is involved in living out a new vision of the world.[96]

Faith, on this reading, is seen as a way of seeing and interpreting existence. The meaning of the concept "God" is seen in the sort of person the believer aspires to be as well as the daily strivings and instances of self-denial that accompanies such a life. So, belief in God is *not* superfluous. God is *not* a dispensable part of religious belief, but everything hinges on what belief in

God means; that is, everything hinges on what the criteria is for the truth of religious faith (which includes the existence of God). In concluding this chapter, I want to put forward the idea that the primary criteria of the truth of religious faith, and hence the meaning of belief in God, hinge on the internal relationship that exists between confessing belief and living a life committed to agapeistic love for others. While the next chapter will be a fuller explanation of this idea, here I hope to simply hint at just what it is I have in mind.

In his well-known essay "An Empiricist's View of the Nature of Religious Belief," R.B. Braithwaite gives one of the best accounts of how the meaning of theological language is logically tied to the use it is put to in the life of the believer. While often derided as a reductionistic account of religious belief, for reasons that will be made clear below, Braithwaite's seminal work is actually a fairly sophisticated look at how religious language secures meaning. Braithwaite, who was influenced by the work of Wittgenstein, summarizes the main idea of his essay by stating that, "The view which I put forward for your consideration is that the intention of a Christian to follow a Christian way of life is not only the criterion for the sincerity of his belief in the assertions of Christianity; it is the criterion for the meaningfulness of his assertions."[97] To believe in the assertions of the Christian faith is to intend to live a Christian life, but more importantly, the very meaning of the assertions are seen in the intention to live a certain way. Belief and practice are logically simultaneous. Braithwaite recognizes the faulty reasoning that exists in trying to say that one believes first and then, based on that belief, acts in a certain way. For Braithwaite, assenting to Christian belief *is* the expression of an intention to behave (or live) in a certain way. He writes, "To say that it is the dogmas of religion which is the cause of the believer's intending to behave as he does is to put the cart before the horse: it is the intention to behave which constitutes what is known as religious conviction."[98] But behave how? What sort of life does Braithwaite have in mind?

Braithwaite does not tie religious language to just any moral way of living life; he rather links religious beliefs with a specifically religious way of acting (which happen to also be a subset of the broader category of morality). Braithwaite writes:

> Unless a Christian's assertion that God is love (agape)—which I take to epitomize the assertions of the Christian religion—be taken to declare his intention to follow an agapeistic way of life, he could be asked what is the connection between the assertion and the intention, between Christian belief and Christin practice … Unless religious principles are moral principles, it makes no sense to speak of putting them into practice.[99]

The agapeistic way of life is characterized not only by outward actions toward others but also by a change of heart manifested by the believer's internal intentions. Braithwaite writes, "Christianity requires not only that you should behave towards your neighbor as if you loved him as yourself: it requires that you should love him as yourself ... being filled with *agape* includes more than behaving agapeistically externally: it also indicates an agapeistic frame of mind."[100] The conversion of the believer is a turn toward the neighbor in love. It is here, in stressing the relationship between religious language and *agape*, that Braithwaite is most impressive.

What makes Braithwaite so important is that he shows that the criterion for the truth of religious language is not that what we say refers to some divine object, but rather that the confessional language of faith is intertwined with the believer's commitment to live a life imbued with agape. Religious language is meaningful only in relation to love; the apparent supernatural objects that religious faith appears to be based on are meaningful in that they serve as the background against which agapeistic love is practiced. The truth of religious belief is internal to religious practice, and it is manifested in the sort of life the believer lives. The challenge with this way of seeing religious language, and the essence of the main criticism Braithwaite faced, is that it appears to turn religion into ethics, and it seems to reduce religious concepts to a way of living, making religious concepts unnecessary accoutrements, or ornaments of the ethical.

In an interesting passage, Braithwaite writes, "My contention then is that the primary use of religious assertions is to announce allegiance to a set of moral principles: without such allegiance there is no 'true religion.'"[101] However, it should also be remembered that without the religious life—including religious language—that surrounds the assertions and the intention to live agapeistically, there would be no "true religion" either; the life and the language are logically intertwined. It is a mistake to think that the language and stories of religion are only contingently related to the life of believers such that the believer may actually choose to give up their religious practice but still maintain living the same form of life. That is to misunderstand Braithwaite and the logical relationship that exists between language, faith, and practice. D.Z. Phillips, who may have actually accused Braithwaite of the sort reductionistic thinking I am denying he held, writes:

> This [religious] language is not contingently related to the believer's conduct as a psychological aid to it. On the contrary, it is internally related to it in that it is in terms of this language that the believer's conduct is to be understood. It is a language which in itself gives the believer certain possibilities in which to live and judge his life. Hence the kind of necessity connected with religious beliefs.[102]

In this case, separating religious belief and language from the agapeistic life is to misunderstand the internal criteria of meaningfulness between the religious use of language and the life that surrounds such language. If you strip away the context that surrounds the believer's life, meaning is lost and something else other than religion (maybe the aesthetic or ethical life) comes into view.

How does this all relate to this chapter's discussion of truth? It seems like we are well justified in accepting that a deflationary account of truth can be applied to religious concepts. I think there is sense in saying things like "'God exists' is true iff God exists," or that "'Jesus rose from the dead' is true iff Jesus rose from the dead." In all these instances, however, nothing is being said until the meaning of the concepts are fixed by their use. This means that the criteria for when it makes sense to say the beliefs are true will also be internal to the language game in which the concepts are used. For much of religious language, the criterion for truth is tied to the way the believer lives and the attitudes he or she takes toward life and others. So, what does it mean to say that religious belief is true? Or to say that God exists? What it primarily means (among other things) is that the believer is committed to living a certain way, to performing certain acts, to viewing life in a certain way. It means that some individuals choose to practice a religious form of life, and within that practice, the use of "is true" has a sense. It is within the practice of religion that believers talk about religious truth (including talk about the existence of God), but this truth is what gives sense to the religious life of love and service to others. As John Whittaker writes:

> The point of believing in God—and here we could just as well say the meaning of believing in God—is to displace impersonal judgments that depend objectively on evidence with self-involving judgments that incorporate personal repercussions. Thus, judgment that there is a God entails the surrender of the ordinary prudential conception of happiness and the substitution of another conception, in which our true well-being depends not on ourselves but on a trustworthy but indescribable source of unfailing love.[103]

The outward criterion for the truth of religious belief is a commitment to an agapeistic way of life.

5

It's All about the Neighbor: Agape and the Religious Life

In *War and Peace*, Tolstoy, through the thoughts of Prince Andrey, writes, "Yes, love … but not the love that loves for something, to gain something, or because of something, but that love that I felt for the first time, when dying, I saw my enemy and yet loved him. I knew that feeling of love which is the very essence of the soul, for which no object is needed."[1] In *The Death of Ivan Ilyich*, Tolstoy has Ivan come to a similar realization at the end of his life:

> And all at once it became clear to him [Ivan] that what had been oppressing him and would not go away was suddenly dropping away on one side, on two sides, on ten sides, on all sides. He felt full of pity for them [his wife and son], he must do something to make it less painful for them: Release them and release him from this suffering. "How right and how simple," he thought. "And the pain," he asked himself. "What has become of it? Where are you pain?" … "And death where is it?" He searched for his former habitual fear of death and did not find it. "Where is it? What death?" There was no fear because there was no death either. In place of death, there was light.[2]

In both passages, Tolstoy has his characters, through the lens of the finality of their own death, come to understand the vital importance of looking upon the world through the lens of love. Prince Andrey and Ivan Ilyich both have a revelation that leads them to see selfless love as the supreme virtue. Prince Andrey realizes that love can be its own reason, and we need not place any expectations or demands on the beloved. He also begins to see love as an internal virtue, a state that one is in, a state that needs no object but, when one is present, manifests itself through selfless acts of mercy, kindness, and care. Ivan Ilyich, on the other hand, comes to see that the gift he has to offer to his family is the gift of his own death. When he realizes this, his self-obsession and self-worry drop away. When his family becomes the object of his love, the sting of his physical pain lessens, and his ego retreats into the background of his consciousness. Astonishingly, his fear of death evaporates since there was no self left to die, even though his life had not yet ended.

What Tolstoy writes about is not just any old love. The fact that its realization is placed within the context of death is a hint that this is a love whose appearance is hard won. In Christianity there is a similar concept of selfless love; it is the love displayed in the story of the incarnated savior, who gives up his rights as God to live humbly in the presence of the "least of these." In the New Testament, this sort of selfless love of others is referred to as agape or neighborly love. The challenging aspect of Christianity is that while this love is extraordinary—and extraordinarily rare—it is also the centerpiece of what it means to live a Christian life. It is this sort of love that actively lives at the center of faith, it is not, as in the examples we just read, a simple last-lesson learned before the lights go out. Agape is not a life lived only by a saint, but is rather a template for the life that all believers are called to. This, however, does not mean that this sort of life comes easy. Nothing, as we shall see, comes easy when it has to do battle with the human ego.

Simone Weil once wrote:

> The Gospel contains a conception of life, not a theology. If I light an electric torch at night out of doors I don't judge its power by looking at the bulb, but by seeing how many objects it lights up. The brightness of a source of light is appreciated by the illumination it projects upon non-luminous objects. The value of a religious or, more generally, a spiritual way of life is appreciated by the amount of illumination thrown upon the things of this world. Earthly things are the criterion of spiritual things.[3]

In what sense can earthly things serve as the criterion of the spiritual? Criteria serve as evidence for the existence of something else; generally, they are the visible means by which we infer the reality of something not readily visible. When Tolstoy has his characters realize the importance of agape, there is a change that occurs in their outlook on life. As I see it, and as I want to argue in this chapter, this expression of a new outlook on life and a selfless way of looking on others is not just criteria for the existence of agape but also the simultaneous realization of, and criteria for, the existence of a spiritual reality. The way Tolstoy's characters come to see life and other people is evidence of a changed outlook. It is the visible manifestation of a light that is shone on their world. In the Christian faith, this idea is quite common. By coming to live what Weil calls a "spiritual way of life," the world is illuminated by love and the believer is called to live a life of service to others. Love is the visible criterion for belief in the ineffable. The agapeistic life is evidence, for the believer, that he or she has crossed from death to life—it is evidence of what it means to believe in and worship God. There may even be some sense in saying that this changed outlook on life, whereby all is illuminated by love, is God. But this is getting too far ahead of things. It would be helpful if we could first get a better grasp of what is meant by agape.

Agape and Care for the Other (Neighbor)

In *Surviving Death*, Mark Johnston defines agape in the following way:

> Consider the command of *agape*, the command to love the arbitrary other as oneself. It is best understood as Janus-faced. It is not just the command to be moved by the legitimate interests of any other just as, and to the degree that, you are moved by your own legitimate interests. It is the command to treat oneself as if one were an arbitrary other, albeit one whose life one is called to live.[4]

When making moral decisions about what we should do, agape demands that we count ourselves and our interests as one among many, all vying for our attention. We are, as Johnston says, to be an "arbitrary other" to ourselves in our own moral decision-making processes. But, while Johnston's definition is a good start, we can still fill in the details by looking at a variety of examples of the sort of love that I have in mind. Rather than attempting to offer a thoroughgoing account of agape, which has, of course, already been done with great skill and precision by others,[5] I want to try and grasp the meaning of agape in a fairly general way, but, also in a way that is religiously significant, a way that will allow us to grasp what claim agape makes on the believer in the face of the those in need. In fact, more than this, I want to argue that it is in the agapeistic relationship between the believer and those in need that God resides, and it is love that enlivens and awakens the meaning of religious language. As Levinas writes, "The dimension of the divine opens forth from the human face … It is our relations with men [humans] … that give theological concepts their only signification."[6] I want to begin by trying to grasp the multifarious nature of agapeistic love by looking at a few stories which try to explain something of the nature of a love that is always directed toward the needs of others.

Three Stories of Love

Tolstoy and the Hermit

In his short story "Three Questions," Leo Tolstoy tells the parable of a king who hopes to learn what it takes to never fail at anything in life. In order to succeed at this, he offers a reward to whoever can answer the following three questions: "what was the right time for every action, and who were the most necessary people, and how he might know what was the most important thing to do."[7] A lot of supposedly wise people come to the king to try and answer his questions, but the answers he gets are all different, and the king does not deem any of them worthy of his reward. However, still wanting an answer to his questions, the king sets out to seek the advice of an old hermit who is known to be wise.

The king finds the hermit at his home digging plant beds in the ground. After greeting the hermit, the king informs him of his desire to get some answers to his three questions. The hermit listens, says nothing in reply, and keeps on with his digging. After a while, the king, realizing the hermit must be getting quite tired, offers to take over the digging for a bit. After digging for a while himself, the king tries again to ask his questions of the wise old hermit. Again, however, there is no response; rather, the hermit simply suggests that the king take a little break from the digging. The king ignores the request and keeps working for a couple more hours until, finally, once again, he says to the hermit, "I came to you, wise man, for an answer to my questions. If you can give me none, tell me so, and I will return home."[8]

At just this moment, a badly injured bearded fellow runs out of the nearby woods, heading straight toward the king and the hermit. Seeing that the man is bleeding profusely from his belly, the king tends to the man's wound. After finally getting the bleeding to stop, the king gives the man some water and helps him to one of the hermit's huts so he can get some rest. The king, exhausted from the digging and all the excitement of the day, falls asleep only to wake with the bearded man staring at him. When the king asks what it is he needs, the man tells the king that he needs to plead for the kings forgiveness. The king replies to the bearded man that, since he does not even know him, he is sure there is nothing he has done that requires his forgiveness. The man then explains that he was the king's sworn enemy and that he had desired to kill him because the king had ordered his brother killed and had taken his property from him. He tells him how he had followed him to the hermit's home in order to assassinate him on his way back to his palace. When the king did not immediately return, the man came out from his hiding spot and was attacked and wounded by the king's bodyguard. It was at this time that the king saw him bleeding and wounded, tended to his needs, and saved his life. "I wished to kill you," the man says, "and you have saved my life."[9] The king, happy to be reconciled with a man who wanted to kill him, forgives him and promises to both have his doctor look after his wounds and restore to the man all the property that had been taken.

After the old bearded man departs, the king, one more time, asks the hermit if he will please finally answer his questions. The hermit finally responds by saying, "You have already been answered."[10] The king, not understanding what the hermit means, asks him how it is that his questions have been answered. The hermit reminds the king how, because he took pity on an old hermit, delayed his departure and helped him dig his plant bed, his life was spared. "So the most important time," the hermit says, "was when you were digging the beds; and I was the most important man; and to do me good was your most important business."[11] The hermit then reminds the king that it was only because of his saving the bearded man's life that reconciliation was possible and that peace was made with a man whom the king had mistreated: "So he was the most important man, and what you did for him was your most important business."[12] From these two examples, the hermit derives the following principle:

> there is only one time that is important—now! It is the most important time because it is the only time when we have any power. The most necessary man is he with whom you are, for no man knows whether he will ever have dealings with anyone else: and the most important affair is to do him good, because for that purpose alone was man sent into this life.[13]

Tolstoy's parable is a lesson in what I call "active attention." Real love for the needs of another requires that we first notice those who are near. We must pay attention to those who are present with us in a way that allows us to actually be aware of their needs. Sometimes the need is right before our eyes and easy to see, but at other times, it is hidden and internal but no less real. A definition of agape begins with attention, and that is what Tolstoy's parable points out. Simone Weil writes that "attention is the rarest and purest form of generosity,"[14] but attention alone is never enough—noticing another is simply the first step. As Mary Oliver once wrote, "Attention without feeling, I began to learn, is only a report. An openness—an empathy—was necessary if the attention was to matter."[15] Paying attention to others involves empathy for their situation. Nel Noddings describes empathy as "feeling with."[16] She states that in "feeling with":

> I set aside my temptation to analyze and to plan. I do not project; I receive the other into myself, and I see and feel with the other. I become a duality. I am not thus caused to see or to feel—that is, to exhibit certain behavioral signs interpreted as seeing and feeling—for I am committed to the receptivity that permits me to see and to feel in this way. The seeing and feeling are mine, but only partly and temporarily mine, as on loan to me.[17]

This sort of empathetic "feeling with" allows the attention that we pay to others to move from a mere report to active love and care. What I am calling active attention is attention plus "feeling with" (or empathy). Active attention is clear in the king's helping the bearded man who was wounded, but it need not involve healing a physical wound since we are rarely met with such a challenge in our daily lives. Active attention could be actively listening to another person or helping someone through a difficult time by our mere presence or by saying something kind or offering a friendly gesture. However it is manifested, empathy is the difference between attention as a mere report and attention as an act of generosity.

Tolstoy's charming little parable helps us get a grasp on the beginnings of a definition of agape, but it is clearly just a start. Agape entails, at minimum, active attention to the other; it is by paying enough attention to their circumstances that we generate empathy so as to act on their behalf. Tolstoy's parable does have the downfall of presenting agape as if it is done *for* something. The king benefits from his active attention in a way that could, if it became part of his motivation for helping others, undo his act. So, while Tolstoy's parable is a good start in that it shows us the importance of active attention, more needs to be said.

Jesus and the Good Samaritan

The Parable of the Good Samaritan is told by Jesus as a proposed answer to a lawyer who wanted to know what he had to do in order to obtain eternal life. (The lawyer obviously thought of eternal life as a commodity with a cost.) Jesus asks the man what the law requires of him, to which the lawyer responds, "You shall love the Lord your God with all your heart, and with all your soul, and with all your strength, and with all your mind; and your neighbor as yourself" (Luke 10:27 RSV). Jesus, seemingly satisfied with this answer, tells the man to do those things and all will be well. But the man, acting as a good lawyer, needs some clarification before he begins to love his neighbor. Naturally, he wants to know who exactly his neighbor is since he seemingly doesn't want to love the wrong person and miss out on eternal life. It is at this point that Jesus relates the well-known parable of the Good Samaritan in order to help clarify for the lawyer the meaning of neighbor. Here is a quick summary of Jesus's response.

In the Parable of the Good Samaritan, a man is beaten by some robbers and left on the side of the road for dead. A priest and then a Levite walk by the man but quickly pass to the other side so as not to inconvenience their plans for the day. A Samaritan then passes by the beaten man and, seeing the state he is in, he, much like Tolstoy's king, tends to the injured man's wounds and brings him to a place where he can rest. The story ends with Jesus asking the lawyer, "Which of these three, do you think, proved neighbor to the man who fell among the robbers?" (Luke 10:36 RSV). To which the man responds, "The one who showed mercy on him" (Luke 10:37 RSV). The story ends with Jesus admonishing the man to "Go and do likewise" (Luke 10:37 RSV).

This parable begins with the lawyer making a similar assumption to the one we saw in Tolstoy's story. In Tolstoy's tale, the hermit implies that all the good that happened to the king happened *because* of the good the king had done. Granted, the king does not know that his life was being spared because he was helping the hermit dig plant beds, but once the hermit relates this fact to him, there is a risk that the king might believe that such a result is what doing good is for. Similarly, the lawyer speaking to Jesus thinks that if one is going to inherit eternal life, then there must be a cost. His initial question is "What must I do to inherit eternal life?" Jesus's story turns this assumption on its head by not even mentioning eternal life in the answer, but rather by simply pointing out what neighborly love looks like. Jesus ends by telling the lawyer to go practice neighborly love himself—not to go do it *in order to* inherit eternal life, but just to "go and do likewise."

As with Tolstoy's story, the Parable of the Good Samaritan stresses the importance of attention. All three parties walking by noticed the injured man, but only the Samaritan paid active attention to him—he was the only one who displayed empathy, which produced active attention. Commenting on the work of Simone Weil, Miklos Vetö writes:

> The Parable of the Good Samaritan shows how "supernatural" attention is a process creating reality. Those passing by the inert and bloody body of the assaulted man hardly notice him, whereas the Samaritan stops and turns his gaze toward him. The resulting actions are the automatic consequences of that moment of attention; this faculty is creative … and constitutes love of neighbor itself.[18]

To call the Samaritan's actions "the automatic consequences of that moment of attention" points to the fact that the neighborly act is part of the character of the Samaritan, an automatic response to another human's need for help. It is automatic because it is generated by something already in the Samaritan that compels him to offer his help. Agape, which is displayed toward the injured man by the Samaritan, is described not simply as an outward act but as an inner virtue, it is something the Samaritan possesses. In Jesus's parable, the act of love is not seen as a simple relation between someone in need and someone meeting the need; rather, in this parable, we begin to get a picture of agape as an internal virtue rather than just an outward act. This can be seen more clearly if we look at the specific way that Jesus changes the lawyer's question when he offers his answer.

In his book on *Christian Ethics*, the late theologian Paul Ramsey writes that the lawyer's "question asked for a definition of 'my neighbor'; Jesus told a story defining instead 'neighborly love.'"[19] To be given a definition of neighbor would, of necessity, have allowed the lawyer to identify those people who should be loved and those who do not need to be loved. If there was a property in people that made them our neighbor, then we could ignore those who did not have that property and love only those who possess it. But active attention does not allow that possibility since it is something practiced toward those who are with us at each moment of time. Jesus, in his answer to the lawyer, creates a situation whereby it makes no sense to discriminate between neighbor and non-neighbor—there are only neighbors, with some being in greater immediate need than others. Ramsey continues a bit later: "What the parable does is to demand that the questioner revise entirely his point of view, reformulating the question first asked so as to require neighborliness of himself rather than anything of his neighbor."[20] Tolstoy's story is instructive in that it directs us to the importance of being actively attentive to the needs of those who are present with us at each moment; it gives us a Zen-like lesson regarding attention to the now. On Jesus's account, however, agape has the added property of being an internal disposition to act in a loving way. It is a disposition that can be seen as flowing from the virtuous nature of the Samaritan; his love is as much an act of character as it is an act of love. While the act of love is important, it cannot be isolated from the individual from whom it flows. Neighbors are those who are the object of neighborly love, but neighborly love is not just an act but a disposition to act that flows from an inner virtue.

In this sense, the virtue of agape (or neighborly love) is part of who the Samaritan is; it is available and readily manifested when needed (thus the distinction between virtue and the virtuous act). It is much like what is described by Prince Andrey when he says of love: "I knew that feeling of love which is the essence of the soul, for which no object is needed."[21] In the case of the Good Samaritan story, the Samaritan is simply traveling from one place to another when he comes across the injured man; therefore, since the virtue of agape is part and parcel of who he is (i.e., part of his character), he is ready to act in a selfless, loving way.

This distinction between virtue and an act of love may appear as just an ad hoc way of distinguishing Jesus's story from Tolstoy's, but I think the difference is important. I believe the distinction between the virtuous *act* of agape performed by the king and the *virtue* of agapeistic love displayed by the Samaritan is important because it allows us to see agape as a virtue that flows out of the character of the individual, with no strings attached. Of course, maybe there were hidden motives that the Samaritan had, but the story is told so as to point to the virtue of neighborly love as a selfless act based on love of, and empathetic concern for, the well-being of the Other. As a virtue, the motivation for agape is love itself, and since the motivation to act is internal to the individual, no extrinsic, nullifying motivations will be present. The story told by Jesus adds to Tolstoy's story by showing the possibility of agape as an inner virtue and by removing the temptation to see agape as being done for something other than the well-being of the Other. To make this point a bit more forcefully, I will appeal to one more story.

Peter Singer and the Drowning Child

In his book *The Life You Can Save*, Peter Singer reintroduces a story he has been using for many years in order to make an important ethical point.[22] He writes:

> On your way to work, you pass a small pond … As you get closer, you see that it is a very young child, just a toddler, who is flailing about, unable to stay upright or walk out of the pond. You look for the parents or babysitter, but there is no one else around. The child is unable to keep his head above the water for more than a few seconds at a time. If you don't wade in and pull him out, he seems likely to drown. Wading in is easy and safe, but you will ruin the new shoes you bought only a few days ago, and get your suit wet and muddy. By the time you hand the child over to someone responsible for him, and change your clothes, you'll be late for work. What should you do?[23]

Singer thinks that what we decide to do here rests on whether or not we accept the following principle: "if it is in our power to prevent something very bad from happening, without thereby sacrificing anything of comparable moral significance, we ought to do it."[24] This principle seems obvious given that we normally do not equate the value of suits and shoes with human life. I take it that it is obvious to most of us that the right and moral thing to do in this case is to save the child despite the fact that our shoes will get ruined, our suit dirty, and we will certainly be late for work. Singer's example has some commonalities with the stories of both Tolstoy and Jesus. His example involves someone paying attention to someone in need, and, even though it is not clear if the individual in the story turns "mere reporting" into active attention, it is obvious that Singer is trying to get us to see that active attention toward the drowning child is the right and ethical response. The main difference between the Singer parable and the other two is that Singer makes explicit the fact that there will often be conflicts standing in the way of our choosing to do the right thing. By showing that the individual approaching the pond would have to sacrifice some new clothing and maybe ruin his or her on-time record at work if the person were to save the child, Singer is trying to get us to see the silliness of comparing the need for material trivialities with the life of a human being.

In the parable of the Good Samaritan, the Samaritan ends up paying for the suffering man's room at the inn so he could rest and recuperate. What we do not see, however, is an internal struggle within the Samaritan as to what he should do. In Singer's example, the cost to the passerby becomes a possible barrier to acting. Singer intentionally leaves us in the lurch as to what will happen. What will the imaginary person do, standing there in his or her new suit and shoes? The fact is that when the person stops to consider if he or she *should* act given one's suit, shoes, and work schedule, the person has already shown a moral deficiency. The immediate move to help that we saw in the Samaritan, and even in Tolstoy's king, is missing in Singer's example. But this is an intentional plot twist in Singer's case since this story is just the beginning of a larger, more important point, as we shall see shortly. Singer's argument is morally compelling because it is so obvious what should be done—even if there are costs to us personally, saving the child is clearly the moral thing to do. But once we admit this, Singer has us. Before looking at his extended argument, we need to see that agape is not reserved simply for those present at hand.

A Widening Responsibility: The Neighbor as Those in Extreme Need

In all of the stories we have looked at so far, the individual in need is directly present to the person called on to help. But, especially in this technological day and age, we are capable of giving our attention and aid to those who are not directly in front of us, but who are still in dire need of aid. The most important fact to consider when seeking to alleviate suffering is the amount of suffering an individual is going through rather than the sufferer's physical proximity to us. Shouldn't there be a sort of *agapeistic* triage we perform when we are considering what is the most loving thing to do? Shouldn't we try and figure out who it is that is most in need of our help at any given time? If someone right in front of me breaks their toe and is hollering for my help as I am running past him or her in order to get to the post office before it closes so I can send a next day air package to a child in another country in order to save the child's life, then, it would seem that I am justified in ignoring the person with the broken toe. This is what is meant by *agapeistic* triage. Singer's example of the drowning child is just a sort of intuition pump that Singer uses to get us to see how radical his real argument becomes when he draws the ethical circle wider.

Earlier, we saw that Singer's principle, which he derived from the example of the drowning child, stated that "if it is in our power to prevent something very bad happening, without thereby sacrificing anything of comparable moral significance, we ought to do it." Singer then uses the intuitive plausibility of this principle and adds to it the fact that "If it were taken seriously and acted on, our lives and our world would be fundamentally changed. For the principle applies, not just to rare situations in which one can save a child from a pond, but to the everyday situation in which we can assist those living in absolute poverty."[25] Singer, using a definition offered by the World Bank, defines absolute poverty as "not having enough income to meet the most basic human needs for adequate food, water, shelter, clothing, sanitation, health care or education."[26] Singer takes it as a noncontroversial fact that there are many, many people in the world who die daily from preventable illnesses and depravations that are the direct cause of just this sort of poverty. He also takes it as a truism that some people are affluent enough that by making some small (or even big) sacrifices in their lives, they could help save some of these individuals who are dying as the direct result of poverty. He then presents the following argument:

> First premise: Suffering and death from lack of food, shelter and medical care are bad.
> Second premise: If it is in your power to prevent something bad from happening, without sacrificing anything nearly as important, it is wrong not to do so.
> Third premise: By donating to aid agencies, you can prevent suffering and death from lack of food, shelter and medical care, without sacrificing anything nearly as important.
> Conclusion: Therefore, if you do not donate to aid agencies, you are doing something wrong.[27]

This argument is a logical extension of the story of the child and the pond with the scope of the example being wider and the conclusion made a bit more explicit. All Singer does is to turn the child that we actually *see* in distress and are compelled to help into someone we can also save but whom we may not be directly acquainted with. Since many people are actually able to save the ones who are suffering and dying, even though they cannot see them directly in front of them, the conclusion is that they should do just that. The real challenge is to take Singer's argument as something more than just a philosophical exercise, something discussed for a day or two in an introduction to ethics class at your local college, and to begin to see it as a part of what is meant by our ethical obligation to others. The real challenge is the move from this philosopical argument to actually taking action in our everyday existence, an existence that sees some of us using our extra cash to buy Seahawk's tickets, concert tickets, or expensive coffee, not to mention taking vacations to foreign countries, buying new (but unneeded) clothes, or buying new books rather than using the library. If we place these sorts of things over the life of those we could save by donating that money, does it follow that we are actually responsible for the deaths of those we ignore?

It is this last suggestion—that we are responsible for someone's death if we refuse to help when we can—that is most challenging. Someone literally died because we refused to help when it was/is in our means to do so. Here is how Singer puts it: "If, then, allowing someone to die is not intrinsically different from killing someone, it would seem that we are all murderers."[28] This example applies to all the cases we looked at above: the king and the bearded man, the Samaritan and the injured person, the drowning child, and now those dying in distant places. What Singer adds to our definition of agape is the need for the sort of triage I mentioned earlier. Agapeic love requires a form of triage so we can decide who is the person(s) in our purview whose life we can save, and even more important, coming to realize what is at stake if we refuse to help.

Anecdotal Agape

From these examples, we can extrapolate a tentative but useful anecdotal definition of agape (neighborly love). First, agape requires that we treat others' needs on par with our own. In our ethical decisions, as Johnston notes, we are one among many. This requires that we overcome our ego and the desire to place our needs above others. Second, as we have seen, agape requires active attention to the one in need. Active attention is not just noticing that someone is suffering but turning toward that person in empathy and then acting to help. Third, agape requires that we act solely out of love for the well-being of the other.

The other's well-being is an end in itself and our help is solely motivated by love. We should not act because we are trying to create good karma, or have some sort of good come to us, or to earn the praise of others, or even to get into heaven. All of these external reasons for loving our neighbor make it certain that we are not loving them but rather using them as commodities to gain something else. Fourth, agape is a dispositional act that flows from an inner virtue of the one who acts with neighborly love. It is not just something we do but someone we are. It is an inner way of seeing (or perceiving) the world that generates the sort of loving action that we are defining here. It is a desire to manifest agape where and when possible. Lastly, agape may (and probably will) require some cost or sacrifice on the part of the one helping. It may cost time and/or money, but as long as contributing these do not cause more harm than the harm we are trying to alleviate, these costs are not considered valid reasons for not acting. To pay a price for agape is not necessarily to say that all agape requires suffering, but it is to say that it will (at least often) require sacrifice, even if the sacrifice is simply the pain caused by overcoming our ego and our selfish attachments to the things we desire but do not need.

It should be mentioned that knowing what agape means is not the same as knowing when or how it should be applied. To ask about the application of agape is to begin to see the diverse way in which agape is used. In Tolstoy's story, the neighbor is whoever is in front of us at any given time. In Jesus's parable, agape is directed toward the ones we come across who are in immediate physical need of active attention (although immediate need may not always be physical). Singer initially presents a case for why we all should do what the Samaritan does (although Singer does not mention the Samaritan), but then he extends his example to include all who are in, what we might call, extreme need (i.e., those who might very well die if we do not help them).

So, who is our neighbor? I think all of these situations represent different contexts where agapeistic acts or neighborly love, are in play. Since neighborly love is an internal virtue held by individuals, acts of love will be a natural property of individuals in that virtuous state. We may love all as our neighbor, being actively attentive to those we are with, but agape also requires we act toward those in extreme need who would not live (or would not be able to thrive) without our help—help, by the way, that we can easily offer. So, those who posses neighborly love are responsible to the individuals they are present with at any given time (Tolstoy), those they come across who have some sort of serious acute need that we can fill (Jesus), and those who, without our intervention, will suffer greatly and/or die (Singer). It is this broad definition of the application of agape that makes the agapeistic life so challenging, difficult, and seemingly impossible, especially in a culture that measures success by material possessions and accumulated wealth. But agape is not an abstract exercise, especially for the religious believer. Rather, it is a way of life that must grip each person as an individual. The agapeistic character (or virtue) is a property of individuals, so the agapeistic life should always be an individual decision. Agape is a first-person challenge. If it becomes simply a philosophical argument, then its point is lost and we can easily slip back into an idolatrous religion or some form of spiritual materialism. If Jesus's admonition to "Go and do the same" is not addressed to us as individuals, then it is addressed to no one at all. But what makes agape so challenging? This obviously is not a call to live what we think of as the ordinary ethical life—no, this is an extraordinary call to love. Unfortunately, it is so difficult because it is met at every turn by a sort of innate selfishness that runs deep in all of us.

The Self at the Center

Obviously, there is a difference between what we actually do and what we ought to do. Sometimes we shirk our responsibility by arguing that we surely cannot be expected to love in such a radical way, or, within the context of religion, we might argue that agape is just a religious heuristic to motivate us to strive to do better. Surely, we may say, the Gospel does not really require we "love our neighbor as our self" in the wildly radical sense outlined above. Or, even more likely, we might just define loving our neighbor in a broad enough way so that "love your neighbor" becomes tantamount to saying, "Be good to each other." Indeed, agape is a goal of the Christian life, but, as it defines what we mean by the Christian life, we should also expect that it is not utterly impossible to practice. These tendencies to try to wiggle out of our moral/religious obligation or define it so it becomes an easy path to traverse are just a symptom of a bigger problem, and that is, our natural propensity to serve ourselves and our own needs at the expense of the Other. The key here is to try and come to terms with why it is that we really tend to love ourselves more than others and to see if there are ways to begin to alleviate ourselves of this propensity.

Self-awareness and Selfishness

Mark Johnston introduces Immanuel Kant's concept of radical evil in the following way: "Kant's doctrine that we are radically evil is not the doctrine that we are bad to the bone, bad through and through; it is the manifestly true claim that there is something at the root of human nature that disposes each one of us to favor himself or herself over others."[29] In his Kenyon College commencement address, published as *This Is Water*, David Foster Wallace presents his view of what he takes to be the root cause of human suffering. At the heart of Wallace's discussion is a claim that we are all gripped by a sort of epistemological hubris, or an inability to realize that we may be wrong about certain things that seem so obviously self-evident to us. Wallace believes that part of what it means to be taught how to think—which is the self-proclaimed goal of a good liberal arts education—is to help us be a little more humble and open to the idea that the sort of things of which we think we are certain of just might, in the end, not be true "because a huge percentage of the stuff that I tend to be automatically certain of is, it turns out, totally wrong and deluded."[30] This self-assurance is, for Wallace, something that is part and parcel of who we are. It is, like Kant's radical evil, described as part of our natural propensity to prefer ourselves and our desires over others. The fact that this propensity is so ingrained in us is why overcoming this way of thinking takes so much work on our part.

Wallace notes that one of the "facts" that we tend to be certain of, which stakes its claim on us as a self-evident truth, is the idea that "Everything in my own immediate experience supports my deep belief that I am the absolute center of the universe, the realest, most vivid and important person in existence."[31] This is a sort of innate truth we carry around with us. It is, as Wallace says, "hardwired into our boards at birth."[32] This idea, for better or worse, arises out of the fact that we are the sort of beings who possess self-awareness. In having a first-person perspective, the world appears to us to be revolving around our heads as we peek out from our eyeballs, and this creates the possibility for us to develop an internal feeling that we are special, since we are aware of our own existence in a way that we are not aware of the existence of other people. This feeling of a self that is immediately present from the inside is what we generally refer to as "I."

In a very real sense, part of Wallace's claim is simply a natural fact of human existence. We are physically constituted as self-conscious beings to see ourselves as the center of our world. As Mark Johnston writes:

> One's own consciousness, the arena of presence and action in which and out of which each one of us lives our lives, presents itself as a fundamental context for the worldly happenings that make up the details of one's life. So long as we are alive, we ourselves are always around; every time we wake up in a chair or in bed, there we are, coeval with the appearance and reappearance of the world. And so we operate as if the world just wouldn't be the world unless we were here, as it were, at the center of it.[33]

There are obviously two separate but related claims here. One is that, due to our neurophysiological makeup, we sit at the center of our world. The second claim is that this special position leads naturally to the situation where we prefer ourselves over others. The first claim is simply a biological truism; the second is ethical. It is not just that we see the world from a first-person perspective; it is that this perspective *can* lead to us taking a privileged view of our own importance. Richard Taylor writes, "If I think of myself as a separate being, I at once become, to myself, a center of existence. 'Here' becomes simply where I am, and, without thinking about it, I seem to myself to be the only person, virtually the heart of creation."[34] This puts us in a bit of a predicament since we have a natural propensity to prefer ourselves over others and a moral/religious obligation to love other people as ourselves.

Two Senses of "I"

In his book *Surviving Death*, Mark Johnston makes a distinction between two different uses of the first-person pronoun "I"; that is, he distinguishes between two different ways that we have of thinking about ourselves. One use he mentions, referred to as the *de re* use, is a statement that is made by us that also just *happens* to be about us, even though we do not recognize that this is the case. Johnston gives the example of Muhamad Ali taking a fancy to the career of Cassius Clay not realizing that he and Clay are one and the same. In this case, any time Ali mentions Clay, he is also speaking about himself even if he does not know that he and Clay are the same person. The other use, referred to as the *de se* use, "involves the recognition of who one, in fact, is, thought about oneself as oneself, thought characteristically captured by identifications involving the first-person pronoun and its cognates."[35] The *de se* use is our normal use of "I," since most of us know we are referring to ourselves when we use the pronoun "I." Johnston writes, "What Ali has forgotten is the *de se* truth that he would express by saying, 'I am Cassius Clay.'"[36]

Johnston uses this distinction to then talk about the difference between derivative *de se* reasons and nonderivative ones. He uses an example borrowed from John Perry about a man who comes to notice, as he pushes his buggy through the supermarket, that someone has a bag of sugar that is leaking and it is leaving a sugar-trail all through the grocery aisles. The man thinks to himself, "Whoever is making this mess should clean it up!" Following the trail around, he notices, to his own chagrin, that the sugar is coming from his own cart. He then realizes that "I need to clean up the mess that I have made." The man has taken a general principle, namely, whoever makes a mess should clean it up, and applied it to himself when he realizes he is the one making the mess. Johnston calls the application of a general principle to ourselves (or our own situation) a "derivative *de se* reason for action."[37] He writes:

> in Perry's case [the case of the sugar], there is an impersonal reason we might capture by saying, "Everyone has reason to see to it that the mess he makes in public places is cleaned up." When Perry discovers that the mess is his mess, he also discovers that this reason applies to him, and he cleans up the mess or sees to it that it is cleaned up.[38]

Now, what Johnston calls a nonderivative (or basic) *de se* reason is one that does not derive a principle of action from a general principle like we see in the case of the spilling sugar. Johnston applies the idea of a nonderivative *de se* reason to what he calls our "everyday egocentrism," or the idea that we expect (or grant) premium treatment for ourselves (or those in our inner circle) over the needs and desires of others. Johnston describes it this way: "It [the nonderivative *de se* reason] is not experienced as having its source in the application of general impersonal principles of preference and action to one's own case; it is the felt expression of the apparent specialness of one's own case."[39] The claim is that there is no general principle that states that we *should* prefer ourselves over others, a principle which we could apply to our own case to explain our natural egocentrism. Our natural egoism is a basic feeling "of the apparent specialness" of ourselves over others—again, there is no basic principle to explain why we *should* think this way.

Johnston uses three examples to explain the difference between our subjective interest in something happening to us and the objective feeling of something happening to someone else. First, when I find out that I have won the lottery, I also find out that someone, in general, has won it, but my feeling toward the fact that I won is vastly different from thinking about someone, in general, winning. Thinking of the lottery winner, in general, I may think of how that person should responsibly invest his or her money, but in my own case, as Johnston says, "I am elated that I have won the lottery, and an ever-growing shopping list fills my mind."[40]

The second example involves sitting in a booth at my favorite brewery and overhearing two local bad guys talking about beating up someone. I begin to feel bad for that poor soul. Then, when I hear them mention my name, my vague concern becomes something more like terror. "Not me, I thought, as if that would somehow be worse than having someone or other beaten up."[41]

The final example of this sort of subjective self-concern is the reaction we have to our own death over the death of others. There is something existentially different about the way we see our own death as opposed to the deaths of others (even if those others are our own loved ones). Johnston writes, "My subjective death seems to me more ominous than the death of an arbitrary other, and here I seem to be responding to something about the situation I anticipate, something that is real, and reason-giving."[42] This is reminiscent of a passage in the death of Ivan Ilyich where Ivan feels the subjective impact of the fact that *he* is dying:

> The syllogism he had learnt from Kiesewetter's Logic: "Caius is a man, men are mortal, therefore Caius is mortal," had always seemed to him correct as applied to Caius, but certainly not as applied to himself. That Caius—man in the abstract—was mortal, was perfectly correct, but he was not Caius, not an abstract man, but a creature quite, quite separate from all others … "It cannot be that I ought to die. That would be too terrible."[43]

A subjective concern for myself is *de se* since I realize it is me I am concerned with. Yet, this concern differs from Perry's example of the spilling sugar in that there appears to be no general moral principle that we can formulate (a principle like "everyone should prefer oneself and one's situation over others"), which is then applied subjectively to our own individual case ("therefore I should give preference to myself and my situation over others"). Rather than being in possession of a derivative *de se* reason, it appears that we are operating with a nonderivative or basic *de se* reason when we, quite naturally and easily, fall into an egocentric concern for our subjective self. In the case of the sugar, we derived our reason for why we must clean up our mess from the general principle that "whoever makes a mess should clean it up." However, in the "egocentric concern" cases, there is no general moral principle to apply. Johnston writes, "the realization that it is my friend who drowned, or that it is my child who is in danger, seems to register something more than the impersonal reasons which govern friendship and family devotion. It is not at all like the case where I discover that I have made a mess."[44] Since there is no general principle for why we should be egocentric, we cannot derive our behavior from a general principle (the principle that we *ought* to act selfishly). Therefore, our principle must be nonderivative or basic.

Johnston uses the difference between derivative and nonderivative *de se* reasons to develop a sophisticated and complex argument purporting to show that "there is no persisting self worth caring about, and that this undermines the thought that our ordinary egocentrism is in fact a response to basic de se reasons."[45] However, rather than trying to get rid of the persisting self in order to escape our natural selfishness, I want to accept that there is no derivative *de se* reason to support why we *should* act selfishly but also show that there do exist normative reasons to show why we *do* act egocentrically.

Selfishness as a Basic Principle

As I noted above, there are two claims that get mixed together when we recognize that physiologically, as self-conscious beings, we are constructed so as to see the world as emanating from our center. The first claim, that Wallace and Johnston both note, is almost trivial; we are made such that the world literally appears in such a way that we are at the center. As Wallace says, this is just a hardwired fact about us. In a rather commonsensical way, this is a derivative physical principle that gets applied to a person simply because of the type of creature he or she is. The principle is something like, "Human beings are so constituted that the world appears to revolve around them," or, "Human self-consciousness makes it so we appear at the center of the place from which all the action of the world takes place." This is a general principle about human psychology that we generally apply to our own individual case.

The more challenging claim is the ethical one rather than the psychological (or neurophysiological) one. This was seen when Wallace says that this person (the "I") at the center of our world appears to us as the "most vivid and important person in existence,"[46] or when Johnston says that "we operate as if the world just wouldn't be the world unless we were here, as it were, at the center of it."[47] Both of these comments show how easily the natural fact about the type of creatures we are can slip into a form of ethical egoism. This is why, I believe, Kant took the problem of selfishness so seriously, referring to it as "radical evil." There is a natural and easy slide from self-awareness to granting the "I" a privileged place in our moral universe. For example, in our daily life, we constantly bump up against other individuals, people who are similarly constituted as ourselves and who also are aware of themselves in a privileged way. When we, peeping out from our privileged vantage point, see the variety of other people bumping up against us as we move through the world, our natural propensity is to see this as part of a production that is being directed by us such that, if others go off script (as they inevitably do), they become irritants to our show. We are each, so we think, the individual who is directing the show, and others (the bit players) need to remember that and play their part without impinging on our space.[48]

The funny thing is that this preference for ourselves over others is insidious because it is so natural. Most of us do not think of ourselves as utterly selfish. We tip at Starbucks, we let others cut in when traffic is bad, and we make sure we make eye contact when we wave to the person at the freeway exit holding a sign. The sneaky nature of egoism is that it is so embedded in who we are that we fail to notice its presence in almost everything we do. In his book *Ego Is the Enemy*, Ryan Holiday writes:

> Most of us aren't "egomaniacs," but ego is there at the root of almost every conceivable problem and obstacle, from why we can't win to why we need to win all the time and at the expense of others. From why we don't have what we want to why having what we want doesn't seem to make us feel any better.[49]

So where does this leave us? It appears there actually is a derivative *de se*-like principle that we apply to ourselves, not to explain why we *should* act selfishly, but rather to explain why we so easily *do*. It is a principle derived from the sort of creatures we are, an extension of our self-consciousness and the natural evolutionary propensity to prefer ourselves and our kin over others. We are selfish because we are placed at the center of our world. This condition makes others appear as visitors in our world, a situation that creates a space where our decisions are made in order to protect our autonomy and the autonomy of those we love against these intruders who pop in and out of our world. This 'selfishness principle' is important for an understanding of why agape is such a challenge because it shows that, while there is a principle that explains why we *do* act selfishly, there is also the moral/religious principle that we *should* not act this way. In this case, we do have a negative derivative principle that we can apply to ourselves which states that the preference for our own needs over the needs of others is wrong. Since we are self-aware and have a natural propensity to prefer ourselves, we apply this principle to ourselves and then conclude (for religious reasons) that we should not act this way.

The reason it is so difficult to love our neighbor as ourselves is because it calls upon us to go against our nature. It commands us to see others as equals, to share our stuff with those in need, and to look on others in need in the same way we look on those close to us. Agape is challenging because there is a clash between a psychological state of affairs and a moral/religious ought. We need to learn to reorient our world, to see things anew. In order to overcome ourselves, we must see things (and others) *sub specie aeternitatis*, which is a challenge given our conscious situatedness at the center. Before looking at how religion helps to offer a solution to this problem, I want to see how religion also offers a theological explanation for its existence.

Sin, Separation, and Acceptance

In his essay "You Are Accepted," Paul Tillich gives a theological account of sin in terms of the concept of separation. Tillich sees separation as an interpretation of the meaning of sin or, possibly, as an expression of sin.[50] Tillich begins by stating that it is best if sin is not equated with a simple laundry list of immoral acts (i.e., our sins): "Do they, and do we, still realize that sin does not mean an immoral act, that 'sin' should never be used in the plural, and that not our sins, but rather our sin is the great all-pervading problem of our life?"[51] Tillich wants to get behind the sort of acts that we generally call "sin" or "sinful" and penetrate to the root cause of such things. He does this by interpreting sin as a threefold form of separation (or estrangement): we are separated from others, from ourselves, and from God (or from what Tillich calls "the Ground of Being"). Tillich sees this separation as something universal, something that is the fate of all of us. It is a separation we are aware of and in which we participate. Being aware of our separation, and aware of our own participation in separation, causes a certain amount of guilt. This threefold separation is part and parcel of existing, which explains the universality of sin. Tillich writes, "Existence is separation! Before sin is an act, it is a state."[52] It would be helpful to look more closely at each of these three forms of separation.

Separation from Others

To be separated from others is partly constitutive of being creatures with inner lives that are cut off from others. Tillich explains, "Each one of us draws back into himself. We cannot penetrate the hidden centre of another individual; nor can that individual pass beyond the shroud that covers our own being."[53] To feel that we are ontologically separated from others makes loving them, at best, a challenge, since it makes the Other appear as a threat to our own freedom and autonomy. Richard Taylor writes, "In this presence of this other, which carries with it the possibility of threat to what I think of as mine, my natural response is to withdraw into my shell, into an acknowledged separateness and abandonment."[54] This feeling of separation from others causes us to lash out at them in order to prop up our fragile feeling that others might be better than us. We secretly take pleasure in the failures of others (including those we call friends), all "for the pleasure of self-elevation."[55] In comments similar to those we saw in Singer, Tillich shows the effects of our radical separation from others when he writes, "let us just consider ourselves and what we feel, when we read

... that in some sections of Europe all children under the age of three are sick and dying, or that in some sections of Asia millions without homes are freezing and starving to death."[56] It isn't just the tragedy that these things are happening, but that "the strangeness of life to life is evident in the strange fact that we can know all this, and yet can live today, this morning, tonight, as though we were completely ignorant."[57] We are separated from others.

Separation from Ourselves

To be separated from ourselves is to exhibit a certain amount of self-disdain that keeps us from living with (or in) the acceptance of the fact that we are accepted by God. Tillich sees in the human condition a certain inward self-hatred that keeps us from others, including the divine. This separation is sometimes thought to be caused by an inordinate love for oneself, but Tillich rejects this claim, writing, "We are wont to condemn self-love; but what we really mean to condemn is contrary to self-love. It is that mixture of selfishness and self-hate that permanently pursues us, that prevents us from loving others, and that prohibits us from losing ourselves in the love with which we are loved eternally."[58] In fact, for Tillich, a certain amount of self-love is necessary in order to love others. Our ability to overcome our selfishness and self-hatred is proportional to our ability to turn to, and help, others. The fact that we do not love ourselves gets manifested in an inability to love the Other. The troubling aspect of all of this is the depth in which our failure to love ourselves goes and the fact that this failure is often kept alive by unconscious drives. This is manifest in our sincere desire to do the right thing and our concomitant failure to persistently do what we know we ought. Tillich expresses this concern by quoting the Apostle Paul's well-known passage: "For I do not do the good I desire, but rather the evil that I do not desire."[59] Our separation from ourselves runs so deep that it appears that there are two actors within us, one chronically acting illicitly and doing the wrong thing and the other observing these happenings but powerless to stop them from occurring. Terry Eagleton, in his new book *Radical Sacrifice*, says something similar to Tillich when he writes, "The sinful subject is a split subject. To sin is to be decentered or self-divided, an enigma to oneself, as one's most reputable intentions are derailed by forces that cannot be controlled and of which one is a mere helpless function."[60] Tillich continues the quote of the Apostle Paul, stressing this duality that exists within: "Now if I should do what I do not wish to do, it is not I that do it, but rather sin which dwells in me."[61] "Sin" is the word the apostle uses for what Tillich describes as the separation we experience within ourselves when we act against our better judgment.

Separation from the Ground of Being

Lastly, Tillich believes that our separation from others and our separation from ourselves are all related to our separation from God ("The ground of our being"). Tillich writes, "the state of our whole life is estrangement from others and ourselves, because we are estranged from the ground of our being, because we are estranged from the origin and aim of our life."[62] Tillich sees human life lacking a sense of meaning and direction because of our separation from the divine. Without being grounded in the center of all existence, we tend to experience a separation from others and ourselves. Yet since God is defined as the ground of being, we can never be totally separated from the divine. Faith represents a desire to be reunited, having our state of separation overcome. In *The Dynamics of Faith*, Tillich writes, "The concern of faith is identical with the desire of love: reunion with that to which one belongs and from which one is estranged."[63] Given that God is the ground of being, there is a constant realization that something is missing, that we are separated from something important. As Tillich writes, "we feel that something radical, total, and unconditioned is demanded of us; but we rebel against it."[64] The feeling that we are both within the divine (as the ground of being) yet in rebellion against God, unable to escape the divine grasp, is what Tillich refers to as despair. Despair gets manifested as meaninglessness, emptiness, cynicism, and doubt, all things which Tillich sees as evidence of our separation from the ground of being.

Accepting Our Acceptance

Tillich's key to overcoming estrangement is to accept that we are already accepted by God. Our accepting that we are accepted by God is, for Tillich, what is meant by grace. However, grace is an act of accepting rather than believing. It is not to believe in the existence of God or in Jesus as our savior or in the importance of the Bible. Grace does not mean we have become moral heroes or saints. Grace rather comes to us when we are in despair or in the depths of meaninglessness, feeling the effects of separation. Grace comes to us in these moments as a spark, only asking that we accept our acceptance. In my favorite passage in all of Tillich, he writes:

It is as if a voice were saying: "You are accepted. *You are accepted*, accepted by that which is greater than you, and the name of which you do not know. Do not ask for the name now; perhaps you will find it later. Do not try to do anything now; perhaps later you will do much. Do not seek for anything; do not perform anything; do not intend anything. *Simply accept the fact that you are accepted!*"[65]

The acceptance of radical divine acceptance is pure grace; it requires nothing of us, but it transforms everything. In accepting our acceptance, we are reconciled not merely to our ground of being but more importantly to others and to ourselves.

Now naturally, as he is wont to do, Tillich is simply trying to define "sin" in contemporary language, language that makes sense in the current situation in which he (and we) lived (live). His account is not true or false but adequate or inadequate to our situation as this situation gets correlated with the eternal truths of God as these get interpreted in the language of contemporary culture. Accepting that we are accepted—being in a state of grace—is the foundation for a life of faith. It creates a freedom where we can turn to ourselves and our neighbor and begin to live and love agapeistically. But the inner acceptance that we are accepted (the acceptance of grace as a gratuitous gift) is not without an outer criterion. It is in turning toward others and living a life where loving our neighbor is a reality that we see the outward manifestation of grace. All of faith is meaningful only in relation to a lived life of love. In closing, I want to make a case for what might be called agapeistic atheism, which, in some way, is really just theism without idolatry.

God as the Story of Love

Agapeistic Atheism

In his masterful book *God as the Mystery of the World*, Eberhard Jüngel writes, "Christian theology has given many answers to the question of the being of God. But among all those answers, it has always assigned unconditional primacy to this one: God is love."[66] To say that God is love is, of course, not a very radical idea in and of itself. Probably one of the best-known Bible verses is I John 4:8, which states that "God is love." Too often, however, I am afraid we take this statement to mean that God is loving (or the most loving of all who love). In this case, we get a subject (God) who has a certain predicate (love). But, of course, saying that God "has love" or "is loving" is not the same thing as saying God *is* identical with love. Is it wise to identify God with love such that God is love is equivalent to saying that love is God? Many, I take it, would want to resist equating God and love since it seems to push God out of the picture, leading to a form of atheism. Here, the theologian may want to say, rather, that God is essentially (or necessarily) loving such that where God is, love is there as well. But wouldn't this then allow us to also say that where love is God is also? Or, as Jean Valjean says at the end of the musical *Les Miserable*, "To love another person is to see the face of God"?[67] There are good religious reasons to be an atheist about a subject God who has love (or is loving).

In *The Essence of Christianity*, Ludwig Feuerbach writes:

> Is God something besides love? A being distinct from love? Is it as if I said of an affectionate human being, he is love itself? Certainly; otherwise I must give up the name God, which expresses a special personal being, a subject in distinction from the predicate. Thus love is made something apart. God out of love sent his only-begotten Son. Here love recedes and sinks into insignificance in the dark background—God.[68]

When Feuerbach mentions the way we sometimes tend to mix up how we speak of humans with the way we speak of God ("Is it as if I said of an affectionate human being, he is love itself?"), he is making an important grammatical point. When we think of God as a loving being (or as a being who loves), the being (or the subject) is always there, since that being is God. But then the being we call God, whatever that might be, becomes primary, and love becomes secondary. A situation is created where love is always called on to play the supporting, rather than the lead, role. Even if this being is essentially love, it is always there watching over our shoulders, making sure we are doing the right thing or serving as the reason why we must love our neighbor. This being's existence undermines the freedom and autonomy necessary for love to exist. The loving being becomes the condition that makes love at best difficult and at worst impossible. Who can escape the gaze of an eternal, necessarily existing being? In this sense, atheism is the proper attitude for the believer to have when faced with this sort of metaphysical subject. This, naturally, does not mean that there is no God, but rather that all we can say about God is that love is God, and this love is best seen in the absence of a metaphysical being who is always looking over our shoulder. In fact, this sort of atheism turns us toward the story of Christianity, toward an incarnation where God escapes God to become human. Feuerbach writes, "the essential idea of the incarnation, though enveloped in the night of the religious consciousness, is love. Love determined God to the renunciation of his divinity ... thus love is a higher power and truth than deity, Love conquers God."[69] The biblical basis for this sort of agapeistic atheism is seen in "The Parable of the Sheep and the Goats" and the incarnation of Jesus. I will deal with both of these in turn.

Love without Reason

In "The Parable of the Sheep and the Goats," the Son of Man returns and gathers everyone around him, separating them into two groups like a shepherd separates the sheep from the goats. The sheep are moved to the Son of Man's right side and the goats to the left (this was before political labeling I assume). The Son of Man then turns to those on his right—the sheep—and welcomes them into his Kingdom, saying to them, "I was hungry and you gave me food, I was thirsty and you gave me drink, I was a stranger and you welcomed me, I was naked and you clothed me, I was sick and you visited me, I was in prison and you came to me" (Matthew 25:35–36 RSV). These folks on the right seem to recognize the Son of Man (since they call him Lord), but they are pretty sure he was not one of those that they helped feed or clothe or one of the ones that they visited. So, they ask him when it was that they ever helped him? The Son of Man replies, "Truly, I say to you, as you did it to one of the least of these my brethren, you did it to me" (Matthew 25:40 RSV). Now, those on the left probably didn't know the full extent of what was coming, but they probably did know that they didn't spend a lot of their free time feeding the poor or clothing the naked, so they probably had some idea that they were not going to get the same reward as the sheep. I doubt, however, that they ever expected what was about to occur. The Son of Man turns to the goats—the ones on the left—curses them and sentences them to—get this—eternal fire with the devil and all the devil's angels! Somewhat shocked, I would imagine, they ask the Son of Man when exactly it was that they ever refused to help him? To which he replies, "Truly, I say to you, as you did it not to one of the least of these, you did it not to me" (Matthew 25: 45). The story ends with those on the Son of Man's right marching off to eternal life, while those on the left sullenly shuffle off to eternal fire.

The most amazing fact about this story is that it turns much of what we think about religious life on its head. The entire reason that the sheep inherit eternal life is that they had acted lovingly toward those in need. Eternal life had little to nothing to do with propositional belief in the Lord or accepting any supernatural facts. The story just mentions that the sheep acted in love—there is no mention of them doing what they did for any external reason at all. They simply loved their neighbor, and by loving their neighbor, they (inadvertently?) loved their

God. Love was their reason, full stop. Here is what John Caputo says about this wonderful story:

> What interests me about this text is that all these works are carried out in the weak mode, or in the mode of folly—by which I mean in the absence of any deeper cause or purpose to be attained, of any Categorical Imperative or Divine Command, of any promises or threats. If there are rewards at stake here, they are an absolute secret. These works are undertaken unconditionally.[70]

What Caputo calls the "weak mode" is love for love's sake. It is by living this way that we are able to display God's love. We can compare what Caputo writes to what Lissa McCullough writes in the context of her commentary on Simone Weil:

> We prove that we belong to God by refracting God's love into the world, sacrificially and sacramentally, through our action and our work. Love of the world is finally the whole point of talking about God, since loving God is simply a means of radically transcending ourselves and our attachment to lesser goods in order to return to the world, detached, purified, and transfigured by supernatural love—which is God's love for the world active in us.[71]

If the heart of the Christian life, and the criteria for the meaningfulness of religious language, is that one loves one's neighbor selflessly, this gives us the means to see the radical importance of the Christian story of the incarnation. Christianity is not reduced to ethics; rather, the Christian faith is a means to see the life that faith requires, and it offers the model for how to live such a life. The point of religious stories is not only to present the content of faith but also to continually encourage us to live a radical life of self-sacrificial love. Living agapeistically is often seen as foolish (see I Corinthians 1:8 and I Corinthians 3:19) not because it is trite or silly but because it is a life that is against our selfish nature; it is countercultural and at times counterintuitive. With all this working against the life of agape, is it any wonder that, for some, the stories, language, and beliefs of faith are what propel them to keep going? In the story of the incarnation, we see the paradigm of self-giving. It is the prime example of the overcoming of self in the service of others. However, it isn't just a story for entertainment's sake, but rather a guide and model for both the cost of love and the price of living against the ways of the world.

The entire New Testament story of faith is a story of dying to self or of self-emptying (*kenosis*). Kenotic theology is not just a form of theology—it stands at the center of faith. It is the prerequisite for entering, the agapeistic life. In an earlier chapter, we saw transcendence as entailing a form of divine self-emptying as the god of supernatural theism died in order to give rise to the ineffable God of mystery, a God who only shows up in acts of love. The paradigm example of *kenosis*, however, is seen in the incarnation of Jesus. In the New Testament book of Philippians, the author writes:

> Have this mind among yourselves, which is yours in Christ Jesus, who, though he was in the form of God, did not count equality with God a thing to be grasped, but emptied himself, taking the form of a servant, being born in the likeness of men. And being found in human form he humbled himself and became obedient unto death, even death on a cross. (Philippians 2:5–8 RSV)

This self-emptying, or *kenosis*, of Jesus was a way for God to shift the paradigm of what it means to live a good life. No longer would salvation come from above as something imposed on believers from the outside; it would rather be found in the muck and mire of earthly existence. In his book *Beyond Words*, Frederick Buechner writes of the incarnation:

> "The word became flesh," wrote John, "and dwelt among us, full of grace and truth" (John 1:14). That is what incarnation means. It is untheological. It is unsophisticated. It is undignified. But according to Christianity, it is the way things are. All religions and philosophies that deny the reality or the significance of the material, the fleshly, the earthbound, are themselves denied. Moses at the burning bush was told to take off his shoes because the ground on which he stood was holy ground (Exodus 3:5), and incarnation means that all ground is holy ground because God not only made it but walked on it, ate and slept and worked and died on it. If we are saved anywhere, we are saved here.[72]

The incarnation is the model for a self-emptying that began when Jesus was born, but one that continually happens to us as we empty ourselves of our ego. The incarnation was the first step taken toward the drawing of our eyes back down to earth, that is, to the place where we live with others, the place where agape is possible, and the place where daily striving for *kenosis* is a religious norm. The incarnation is a model for what is required of us.

The incarnation, as the self-emptying of Jesus that occurred at his birth, was just the beginning of what we might call a kenotic model of life. Jesus's ministry was spent with the downtrodden and the needy, the poor and the lame. His life was lived as a model of what it means to serve others. From feet-washing to parables about how the first would be last and the greatest the least, Jesus's life presents a constant striving to exhibit neighborly love whenever and wherever possible. *Kenosis* and the agapeistic life are intimately related; in fact, kenosis is a necessary condition for agape since, as we have seen, in order to serve others in a way that exhibits neighborly love we must be able to count ourselves as one among many. Commenting on the Philippians passage quoted above, Dana Gioia writes, "The hymn at the center of Philippians articulates the radical change in values offered by Christianity. Jesus provided his followers with a new form of divinity, one based not on power and pride but on self-abasement and compassion."[73] This is a divinity not only for the divine but also one that can be exhibited by us mere mortals.

The life of Jesus is supposed to become our life as well. Sylvia Walsh writes that "The notion of a specifically Christian moral character receives its normative definition and paradigmatic existential expression in Jesus Christ, who is viewed in the New Testament not only as the redeemer of fallen humanity but also as the prototype of or perfect model of human character"[74] Yet these two things— redemption and the moral life—are actually one and the same thing. Often, it is natural to see the crucifixion as the manifestation of God's atonement. It is as if the cross is simply something Jesus did, creating benefits that then get imputed to us just for the asking. Yet atonement is found when our separation is reunited or unified, that is, when we accept our acceptance by God and are reunited with ourselves and our neighbor. But behind this redemption is the death of the self, and this begins with the incarnation, is seen in the life of Jesus, and culminates in the cross. But this is not just a story about Jesus and what he endured; it is a model for us as well. We are called to carry our cross (Matthew 16:24), and we are called to die to self (Luke 9:23). And, as Walsh writes, "To follow Christ thus means to imitate or resemble him by walking alone on the same road that he walked in the lowly form of a servant ... It means to take up one's cross and carry it daily in self-denial, renouncing everything in boundless love for God and the neighbor" (Matthew 16:24).[75] The road to Golgotha is a model for the life we must live as we accept that we are accepted and die daily to our desire to fulfill our own desires at the cost of those in need. Walsh later writes, "The next step is to carry one's cross daily, which means that being a cross-bearer in imitation of Christ is a protracted affair, continuing unto death even if one is not literally put to death on a cross as he was."[76] By crucifying the ego, we are able to put to death the part of us that desires to escape the world, that seeks spiritual materialism in order to be rewarded for all we do, and which looks to domesticate God for our own needs; in a word, we are freed from idolatry.

At the center of the meaning of Christin love, then, is the crucifixion. The death of Jesus was not a sign of the end of sacrifice, but the birth of showing the ongoing need for a living sacrifice. It is the call to die to our ego every day as we are crucified with Christ (Galatians 2:20). The cross is redemptive in that it deals with the root cause of separation, it is salvific in that it offers a new life where we are reconciled to the vicissitudes of life, but it is also a model and picture of what the love of God entails. In our death, we must deal with the forsakenness felt when we give up an idol God who will not rescue us from trials: "My God, my God why hast thou you forsaken me?" (Matthew 27:46 RSV). The rescue is only found in our death as we die while living for others. Walsh, writes, "The moral task in Christianity therefore can essentially be summed up in one word—love properly understood and expressed as unselfish, sacrificial, or self-denying love for God, neighbor and oneself."[77] Yet to love God and oneself is to die to self and to die to the need to appeal to God as a basis for why we love. In this case, love of self and love of God are expressed in the loving of our neighbor. The neighbor is the only Other that is left to serve. The cross is a model of our reality. It is the center of the message of faith standing as a witness not just for something that was done for us but as something that must happen within us. Bonhoeffer writes, "The cross means sharing the suffering of Christ to the last and to the fullest, only a [human] thus totally committed in discipleship can experience the meaning of the cross. The cross is there, right from the beginning, he [she] has only got to pick it up."[78] The cross is at the center because love is at the center, and without the death of self, agape becomes a chimera.

An Atheistic-Theism or a Theistic-Atheism?

In *With Heart and Mind*, Richard Taylor writes:

> True religion is the absolute love of God, and its natural expression is singing, dancing and loving, for nothing provides sweeter rejoicing. False religion is fear, and its expression is reserve, sobriety, rigid moralizing and aloofness. When the love of God is lost, these things are always put in its place, and for a very simple reason: they provide a pathetic kind of security in place of the total security of love.[79]

To forfeit the security of a false and idolatrous God for the freedom to be able to give our lives to love those in need is not to lose God, but rather to relocate the divine. To worry that love of others may not be enough to ground the meaning of faith, and to ask where God is in all of this, is to already have missed the point. This sort of question shows that love is not enough, which places the questioner to the left side of the Son of Man (with the goats, that is). A similar worry is seen in those who may be concerned with the fact that living agapeistically can be done by those who profess no religious belief (or faith) at all. That, however, is to require faith to contain more than love. In I John, however, we see that anyone who loves is a candidate to be befriended by God: "Beloved, let us love one another; for love is of God, and he who loves is born of God and knows God. He who does not love does not know God; for God is love" (I John 4:7–8 RSV).

When Simone Weil writes that "earthly things are the criteria of the spiritual,"[80] or when Levinas states that "Through my relation with the other I am in touch with God,"[81] or when Jesus tells the story of those who are welcomed into the Kingdom when *all* they did was help those in need, or even when Bonhoeffer writes that "Before God and with God we live without God,"[82] none of these individuals are trivializing God or reducing God to ethics. Rather, in each case, these individuals are trying to make sense of what it means to love God in the world without idolatry or hope for recompense. In the end, the only way to do this is by worshipping the God who is not *there* by loving the neighbor who is perpetually *here*.

Part Two

"There—Like Our Life": Religious Practice without Metaphysics

Robert C. Coburn

You must bear in mind that the language-game is so to say something unpredictable. I mean: it is not based on grounds. It is not reasonable (or unreasonable). It is there—like our life.

Ludwig Wittgenstein

Introduction to Part Two

Robert Bolger

There is a sense that without an introduction to Part Two, someone may think they are in possession of two radically different books with very little in common. But this, of course, would be mistaken. Part One was an attempt to free religion from a way of thinking that was essentially anti-religious in nature. In the end, the hope was that faith could be reconceptualized as a way of being in the world, of learning to love others sacrificially, and of looking on life with gratitude and hope.

These themes, however, are not themes that are only discussed in the stodgy language of philosophy. These are themes that are part of the warp and woof of everyday life; they are themes that are found in literature and in the very motifs that the poet and preacher try to convey with precision and wit. In a way, there was no way to get to Part Two without the work of Part One being completed. This is not because Part Two is not able to stand on its own, but rather because many who think that theology is best done in academic language would never waste their time trying to learn something about faith by reading essays that appear more in the language of the sermon than in the language of a philosophical or theological argument. Yet the language of sermons, literature, and poetry is really where, for some at least, faith comes alive. It is where religious concepts can bump up against the real world. It is where the language of faith can find its residence in life rather than being isolated and forced to speak a language which distorts its importance and thwarts its purpose.

In *Love's Knowledge*, Martha Nussbaum writes, "Style itself makes its claims, expresses its own sense of what matters. Literary form is not separable from philosophical content, but is, itself, a part of content—an integral part, then, of the search for and the statement of truth."[1] Compare what Nussbaum says with what the philosopher Richard Taylor writes at the beginning of his book *With Heart and Mind: A Philosopher Looks at Faith, Love and Death*. Taylor writes,

"These thoughts, although of a philosophical character, contain no philosophical dialect. They seek instead to convey a certain vision and so might appropriately be called a collage or a montage, were such words not pretentious. Let us simply say they are a picture."[2] Both Nussbaum and Taylor have important things to say to us when it comes to the contents of Part Two. First, pace Nussbaum, style can be a great aid in the philosophical search for truth. Some ways of writing are more conducive to getting across certain ideas than are others. In writing about faith in a style more indicative of a sermon than a philosophy paper, words are placed in the flow of life where meaning is more easily discernable. If the meaning of religious language is seen in how such language is used, then writing in a style that allows religious concepts to be placed together with nonreligious aspects of life is the best way to meander (or slouch) toward something called religious truth. This is not because religion is more poetry than philosophy, but rather because poetry is a style as conducive to philosophical discovery (as is literature, art, and, dare I say, even the sermon) as philosophy is itself.

Second, Taylor, himself a wonderful philosopher, calls his meditations "pictures," and in the end, I think that is what we get in Part Two from Coburn (i.e., pictures of faith). We see in the essays of Coburn pictures of what the religious life looks like when it is a live option. We see such things as the importance of models and mentors, how faith appears different when viewed from within and without the practice of religion, how laughter can be seen as a sacrament, how we can be blind to certain important aspects of life and faith, how paradoxical language can hold important truth, and how we all, in one way or another, must deal with a world that is ever-changing. In all of these themes, we see pictures of faith that are embedded in pictures of life. Life and faith get mingled together in such a way that one becomes indiscernible from the other. That is how religious language should be presented, but without the philosophical stodginess of Part One, many of us would never come to appreciate, or even be bothered with, the linguistic pictures painted in Part Two: pictures which vividly reinforce the claim that the meaning of words are intricately tied to the way they are used.

6

The Church from without and from Within

A number of years ago, a British anthropologist by the name of E.E. Evans-Pritchard wrote an influential and fascinating book on an African tribe called the Azande.[1] In it, he describes a number of Zande beliefs and practices, including the belief that certain people have an extraordinary power in virtue of which they are able to exert harmful influences on others by just thinking about them in certain ways. This is a power that, they also believe, is rooted in an organic condition (in just the way we all think that our power to recall our own telephone numbers, the faces of our friends, and a vast number of facts about our own past experiences is rooted in an organic condition, specifically a condition of our brains). He also tells of a conviction that the best way of detecting the existence of such malignant influences being directed at one and also of identifying the sources of this influence—the "witches" from whom they emanate—is by appealing to the revelations of oracles. One of the ways they do this is to get hold of a certain kind of bird that is common in their villages and administer to it a dose of a ritualistically prepared poison to which they all have access. Then they ask a question like, "Is Ubangu a witch?" and if the bird dies from the poison, the answer is "yes," and if it lives, the answer is "no." Evans-Pritchard also notes that it is generally believed that one can counteract the influence of a witch or protect oneself from the harm directed at one by a witch by performing certain rites, using certain ritualistically prepared medicines, etc.

When most educated members of modern, Western cultures learn about beliefs and practices like these, they are inclined to view such people as just wildly mistaken about the way the world is, and accordingly as engaging in practices that are at best just a waste of time and energy, and at worst irrational, if not insane.

After all, there just is no way of bringing it about that another tribe member falls deathly ill or is trampled to death by an elephant just by someone sitting in one's hut, thinking evil thoughts about that person, by sticking pins in dolls that look like the person, or by doing anything analogous to such things. The world isn't constructed in that way, and we know it isn't, if we know anything at all. Nor can one gain reliable information about whose liver looks like what by killing birds with ritualistically prepared poisons. That's not a good way to find out about the bodily conditions of others, and we know it isn't, if we know anything at all. One achieves absolutely nothing by way of warding off harm by engaging in odd rituals inside the privacy of one's hut or by smearing one's body with foul-smelling concoctions after reciting some prescribed strings of words, and we know that this is true, if we know anything at all. And we surely do know lots of things about the world, and furthermore, we know that we do.

Anyway, that's the way many educated members of modern, highly technological, science-imbued societies are, I think, inclined to view such beliefs and practices as those of the Azande that I have just described. Looking at their practices from the outside, it appears that their primitive beliefs lack the rational thought possessed by those of us "enriched" by a scientific point of view.

Now the church, it seems to me, is viewed by many in our society, and by modern societies generally, in the way that some view the aspects of Azande culture that I have just been describing. That is, many people in our society are not participating members of the church; in consequence, they view the church from the outside in something like the way anthropologists, at least in the not-too-distant past, often viewed the societies they studied. And many who view the church from outside in this way see it as an institution that is (a) filled with people whose beliefs about the world, about the way things are, are as far from the truth, as poorly supported by the evidence, and even in some instances, as much at odds with the facts, as Zande beliefs about witches and witchcraft. They also see it as (b) filled with people who engage in practices—especially during worship—that are as useless, and as disconnected from reality, as the practices the Zande engage in in order to identify witches or ward off their malignant influences.

If your children go to a typical college or university, they will encounter this attitude in a particularly articulate and vigorous form, though they doubtless already have encountered it in some form in their reading, their contacts with peers and teachers, in the media, etc. An especially strong statement of such an attitude appears in a book entitled *Life Itself*[2] by a famous Nobel-Prize winner who is sometimes described as the greatest theoretical biologist since Darwin, namely, Francis Crick. But it isn't far beneath the surface in the writings of Richard Feynman and Carl Sagan, among publicly well-known scientists, and not beneath the surface at all in the writings of countless philosophers and other scholars in humanities.

Sometimes such an attitude toward the church in general, and believers in particular, is coupled with a kind of bemused indifference (such folks are, after all, relatively innocuous, though occasionally a nuisance [e.g., when they try to get creationism taught as viable science in the public schools]). Others, who are a bit more militant in their atheism, couple this attitude with a (more or less fervent) desire to rid society of such beliefs (after all, such madness cannot very well serve the best interests of those afflicted with it).

The problem, however, may not be the beliefs themselves but rather the perspective from which religious beliefs are looked upon. Viewed from within, the practice of religion, the institution of the church, and the people who participate in its ongoing life look rather different. There is, of course, a great deal of variety among the different Christian churches—not only among the major Christian bodies (Roman Catholic, Eastern Orthodox, and Protestant) but also within these larger groupings themselves, and especially among the Protestant churches. But in spite of such variety, at least this is true: that not infrequently—especially in Protestant churches within the major denominational structures—what one finds in the churches are not collections of superstitious fanatics engaged in weird practices that rest on these antiscientific beliefs. One doesn't find blind acceptance of dogmas that come down from the dark recesses of the past, for which there is no evidence of a kind that would move an unbiased mind. There is no blind acceptance of the values these dogmas embody, dogmas that aim at manipulation of hidden powers for personal gain—a kind of rain-making magic. Certainly, this sort of crass acceptance of anti-scientific superstition is part and parcel of what some call religious belief, but often believers have no interest in this way of looking at religion.

Many years ago, a book was published entitled *A Field Guide to the Little People* by Nancy Arrowsmith.[3] In it, Arrowsmith gives detailed accounts of the Quiet Folk, Drakes, Nixen, Brownies, Hobgoblins, Sirens, Pixies, and Faeries, among others. Arrowsmith notes their habits and dispositions, as well as what angers or insults them, how to perceive them, and what to do to derive benefits from them or to protect oneself and one's property from their ire. The most effective protection against Faeries, it turns out, is iron, though salt is also useful. Wearing a four-leafed clover in one's hat makes it possible to see them. If you happen to see a Drake, you should get safely undercover for they leave behind them an unbearable odor of burning sulfur. Hobgoblins are almost extinct these days. Pixies are tiny, often hairy, and frequently naked (though sometimes they wear red hats). They are often cross-eyed. And so on.

According to some accounts, America is awash in folklore and superstitions of less ancient vintage. There are stories about alligators in the sewers, tales of Devil worship at the Proctor and Gamble Co.,[4] a story of a snake found in the sleeve of clothing manufactured in Taiwan,[5] etc. We might also think of beliefs about broken mirrors and spilling salt bringing bad luck, and the way putting a peeled onion in one's sock will cure cystitis. We may often balk at the silliness of superstition while being unaware of the way we participate in these sorts of practices ourselves.

Now Christian people are not, in a vast number of cases anyway—though not of course invariably—like those who sincerely believe in Hobgoblins, Sirens, Drakes, and the rest. They are not like those who believe weird tales about the goings on at Proctor & Gamble. They are not like those who are busily engaged in avoiding the anger of the Faeries and seeking the good offices of the Quiet Folk.

A former member of the House of Representatives from Georgia, in a speech awhile back, told the following story of one of his last cases before leaving his law practice and going to Congress:

> There was a lady that came to my office who wanted a divorce, but before I talked with her about the divorce I decided that it might be helpful if I found out if she had grounds for divorce. So I asked her if in fact she had grounds, and she looked at me and said, "Yes, as a matter of fact, about an acre and a half." I looked at her and I said, "Perhaps I am not communicating well. Let me try again." I then asked her if she had a grudge, and she looked at me and said, no, she did not have a grudge but she did have a double carport. I said, "Let me try this one more time a little bit more to the point." I said, "Does your husband beat you up in the morning?" She said, "No. Generally I get up earlier than he does." At that point I began to recognize I was going to have to try a different tack entirely, and I said, "Ma'am, let me ask you, are you sure you really want a divorce?" She said, "No. Actually I don't want a divorce at all. It's my husband who wants a divorce. He contends that we have difficulty communicating."[6]

It may be that part of the reason religious folk are assimilated to those with superstitions and wild views of various kinds springs from a difficulty church people have in communicating what brings them to the church and what they find there. It's certainly true that many church people feel an inability to explain why church is so important to them. They feel that in speaking about faith they, as T.S. Eliot put it, are making a "raid on the inarticulate/With shabby equipment always deteriorating."[7]

But whatever the case, the fact remains that many outside the church fail to understand what the church and church people are often really like. The fact remains that the church is, to a large extent, as different from what it is often seen to be, viewed from without, as the proverbial elephant is from the pictures of it gleaned by blindfolded individuals who each touched a different part of its anatomy. The picture from without is partial, incomplete, and lacking in practical details.

What does one find when one views the church from within? Often, I suggest, one finds people for whom a life centered on their own private pleasures and the attempt to secure themselves against losing the means to pursue these pleasures in the future is felt, perhaps dimly, to lack the quality of spirituality or grace. One even finds people who are (or were), from time to time, full of the kind of emptiness and meaninglessness of which the author of Ecclesiastes wrote and who have discovered in the life of the church a path out of what the philosopher George Santayana once referred to as "the burning city of our vanity."[8] They have discovered in the life of the church at least the hint of a direction that might lead to such a path, as well as a community with which to share the journey.

One finds, when one views the church from within, people for whom the words from Paul's letter to the Romans strike a responsive chord; I mean the words: "I do not do what I want, but I do the very thing I hate ... I delight in the law of God, in my inmost self, but I see in my members another law at war with the law of the mind" (Romans 7:15, 22–23 RSV). And one often finds people who again have found, in that historic community which seeks to embody the Spirit of Christ, a power that releases them from the bondage they sometimes feel, a power which keeps them from sinking even deeper into what St. Augustine referred to as "a mass of perdition."[9]

One often finds people who not only have experienced the whips and scorns of time—people to whom experiences of the kind that afflicted Job are not wholly foreign—but, more important, are keenly aware of the fact that "there is no hiding place in the wide world where trouble may not find [one]."[10] People who realize, as Kierkegaard put it, that no one is immune to, or secure against, a fate like Job's. These are those who recognize that (again, adapting more thoughts of Kierkegaard) there has never been a person who was able to say she knew when sorrow would visit her home, that no man knows the time and the hour when the messengers will come to them, as they came to Job, each one more terrifying than the last.[11] That is, even within the church, there are those who recognize that the believer is not immune to immense suffering and pain. But, often simultaneously, one also finds people who experience in the liturgy and beliefs of the church resources that enable them from becoming enslaved by tribulations and crippled by fears and imaginings of worse that may yet come. These are those who find that participation in the corporate life of the church that is shaped and nourished by that tradition catalyzes within them a sense of peace and joy despite the ills that flesh is heir to. They find in worship and community a sense that, as a character in one of Frederick Buechner's novels put it, "What's lost is nothing to what's found and all the death that ever was, set next to life, would scarcely fill a cup."[12]

In T.S. Eliot's play *The Cocktail Party*, the character Reilly says concerning human life: "The best of a bad job is all that any of us make of it—/except, of course, the saints."[13] Then, later on, he says:

> There *is* another way, if you have the courage.
> The first I could describe in familiar terms
> Because you have seen it, as we have all seen it,
> Illustrated, more or less, in the lives of those about us.
> The second is unknown, and so requires faith—
> The kind of faith that issues from despair.
> The destination cannot be described;
> You will know very little until you get there;
> You will journey blind. But the way leads towards possession
> Of what you have sought for in the wrong place.[14]

Viewed from within, one finds people who have at least intimations of the existence of such "another way" and who, in many cases, have even begun to embark on it as best they can, given the light they have; and people who find guidance and support for this endeavor in the church.

Putting it slightly differently, what one finds when one views the church from within, at least what one often finds, are people who are struggling toward faith, where faith is understood as the state of being healed, being whole. The symptoms of such a state include, perhaps among others, a sense of deep security, an attitude of hopefulness in every situation of life, a sense of joy and gratitude and celebration, an effective desire to love one's neighbor as oneself, to participate in public and private worship, and to share the sense of blessing to which this worship and this love give rise with those outside the circle of faith.

It should also be said that church people are often not fanatically wedded to particular dogmatic formulations of religious truth and that they often have no inclination at all to repudiate in the name of religion those views about human beings, society, history, the biological world, or the world of inanimate nature that the best evidence we currently have supports. (Though they are equally disinclined to swallow whoppers that those who speak with the authority of science occasionally urge upon us when the evidence for these theories is not much better than that for the existence of Faeries and Drakes.) A liberal view of religion requires neither credulity nor abandonment of intellectual integrity. The attitude of these church people to their religious tradition is rather like the attitude that Arthur Waskow describes of the Jewish community called Fabrangen in his book *God-Wrestling*. In this community, he writes:

> people come together around the effort, the hope—sometimes bright, sometimes flickering—to create a modern path of life that draws authentically from Jewish tradition but is expressed in new ways. A path of life that reconnects what have become separate areas of our lives: work, leisure, politics, sex, family life, that infuses them with a sense of awe and celebration.[15]

He continues, "We do not, simply accept the tradition, but we do not reject it either. We wrestle it: fighting it and making love to it at the same time. We try to touch it with our lives."[16] Such people, in short, are like those who are deeply moved by the fact that the very words that will be used as a Benediction at the close of a service of worship have been found on recently discovered pieces of silver rolled into scrolls and apparently worn as amulets around the seventh century BCE.[17] But they view the tradition as a rudder and not as an anchor. And they seek to find its relevance to the world we live in—a world of nuclear weapons and sociobiology and operant conditioning; a world of disease, massive hunger and vast disparities of wealth; a world of drugs and overpopulation, and growing holes in the ozone layer and steadily increasing pollution of the oceans; and a world of computers, mass illiteracy, pornography, political upheaval, and terrorism.

Philip Larkin, a famous English poet who died in 1985, once wrote: "In everyone there sleeps/A sense of life according to love."[18] The church, viewed from within, contains large numbers of people in whom this sense is no longer asleep and who insofar are, as one might put it, in the process of descending into God. Larkin also wrote a wonderful poem called "Church Going." In it he writes about entering a church and, while aspects of it seemed old and obsolete, there was also a hint that it was a place where individuals sought out a more serious life or "[a] hunger in himself to be more serious, And gravitating with it to this ground [the church]."[19] Perhaps this puts it best. What one finds when one views the church from within are people who find a pang of hunger in themselves to be more serious, and who have, in consequence, gravitated to this ground.

7

The Turning World

That we live in a turning world is a truism; perhaps it is such a truism that no more obvious one can be imagined.[1] From the subatomic level of protons, mesons, neutrons, etc.—and their quirky constituents—to the galactic level, change is pervasive and continuous. For better or worse, objects like us and our planetary home, somewhere in between the very small and the very large, are not exempt from the pervasive changes wrought by the turning world. The Earth rotates and revolves. The continents alter their shapes and sizes and relative positions. The thin envelope surrounding the Earth that contains all its living creatures is a theater of ceaseless activity in which both individuals and species come and go. Nations and empires wax and wane. Languages, economic systems, scientific theories, legal structures, religious organizations, and ideas develop, alter through time, and disappear from the scene altogether. And, of course, the changes that permeate our individual lives both reflect and influence these larger geological, ecological, and historical changes, too.

Some of the changes that take place in history and that occur in our individual lives are, of course, quite welcome. Most of us are quite glad that there are washing machines, refrigerators, central heating, computers, cell phones, modern means of transportation and communication, mobile coronary care units, aspirin, and even, from time to time, TV. We're also glad to be the beneficiaries of a tradition of thought and experience that has led to the development of institutions that protect, to an impressive degree, a vast array of rights and liberties. And, if we've had an occasion to read anything like Barbara Tuchman's book *A Distant Mirror*,[2] then we're overjoyed to be alive at a time when bubonic plague is (more or less) understood and (more or less) under control.

We also welcome the changes of the seasons and the summer vacations that provide opportunities to get out of our ruts and to see new places and do different things. We're glad (if we think about it) that we don't remain relatively helpless small children for decades, that we grow in strength and size and develop our knowledge and skills and understanding of ourselves and others, and that we grow in an understanding of the way the world works. We welcome, too, spontaneous recovery from debilitating illnesses, we delight in developing new friends and love relationships, and so on.

On the other hand, as we are all painfully aware, not all the changes which affect or characterize us, and the larger social and ecological systems of which we are a part, are as pleasant or happy as those just mentioned. Oppressive—even monstrous—governments all too commonly arise. War and unjust violence of all kinds break out with distressing frequency. Horrendous population growth in the last few hundred years has led, and continues to lead, to tragedy on a massive scale—given the sorts of economic and political conditions that have obtained during this period, and continue to obtain, throughout the world. Environmental deterioration and the depletion of nonrenewable resources have already adversely affected us and may well lead to quite drastic alterations of our lives, or the lives of those we love, in the future. And the emergence of massive arsenals of nuclear weapons may still one day do us all in.

Then, too, we all eventually lose our physical strength and mental faculties, if we don't lose our lives first. We fall ill, we step into crevices, we have cranes fall on us, we suffer whiplash effects, and we get mugged. Our loves sometimes fade and our friendships sometimes sour. Our projects get derailed, the spiritual resources from which we once drew strength and wholeness dry up, and it sometimes happens that those we care about—even those around whom our lives revolve—die, leaving in the wake of their lives an aching void.

So it's a turning world—a world containing a baffling mixture of complexly interwoven changes, some law-governed, some perhaps not; some welcome, even wonderful, and some on the face of it pretty awful—with lots of the gray and the humdrum in between. Question: Does the Christian faith bear in a helpful way on the issue of how we should orient ourselves in such a turning world? Does it speak to the question of how we should comport ourselves in order to best participate in the transforming, healing work to which the church, as the body of Christ, witnesses and which it seeks to facilitate? Of course. Indeed, that's what it's mainly all about, insofar the answer it provides is as long as life itself. So, you'll be happy to hear that I won't try to give it all here, even if I had it all to give, which, of course, I don't. But I'd like briefly to indicate for your consideration three thoughts that strike me as important in this connection. They're not original thoughts, of course; if they were, they'd doubtless be false. But even old truths can be illuminating and helpful when put in a way or in a context that enables us to perceive them afresh.

The first thought to which I would draw your attention, then, is that we need to learn the art of "letting go." This is obvious enough, but it's hard to keep the importance of this art always in mind, and harder still to practice it. The author of Ecclesiastes says that there is a time for everything: "a time to be born and a time to die; a time to plant, and a time to pluck up what is planted; a time to break down and a time to build up; a time to weep and a time to laugh; a time to mourn and a time to dance" (Ecclesiastes 3:1–4 RSV). (We have no single word in English for the idea of the right time to do something or for something to happen; but in Greek there is such a word, *kairos*—a word that plays an important role in the New Testament. That his *kairos* had not yet come is said of Jesus at one point; and then again at another that it had come.)

Sometimes, for example, we need to let relationships go. Every parent, of course, experiences this. There comes a time when one's child is no longer a child, no longer needs the kind of paternalistic care it needed—that is, the kind of care that involves restricting its liberty to do as it wishes in its own best interests. The time comes when the child needs its independence, needs to be able to go its own way, "come hell or high water," as we say. When that time comes, it's time to let go. (Putting it in this way is an oversimplification, to be sure. "Letting go" in this way is almost a continuous process.) And, of course, when the child is no longer a child, the parent not only has to let go in the sense of giving the child its freedom "to pursue its own good in its own way"[3] (to paraphrase John Stuart Mill's famous phrase) but also—and perhaps even harder—the parent must let go of many other patterns of relating to the child too, for the child when it's grown up becomes a very different person, with different needs and interests and perceptions and ideas, and one has to work at discovering who this new person is, and one has to be able to give up all the ways of relating to it that were appropriate only when it was a child.

Sometimes what we need to let go of is the way that we think and feel about ourselves, about who we are, and about our relationship to the world. This is obvious when we've reached fifty or sixty and still like to pretend that we are as spry as when we were only twenty or thirty. If we don't let go of this feeling, we risk life and limb, as many of us have learned on the tennis courts or the mountain trails. But sometimes we also need to stop thinking and feeling about ourselves in the light of models or images that were once appropriate but have since ceased to be so as we and our relations to the world have changed. We might, for example, need to stop viewing ourselves as passive recipients of the loving care of others and objects the world acts upon, and begin thinking of ourselves instead as agents who can initiate changes, initiate new relationships, or enact changes in old ones, taking charge of our own development and responsibility for what happens in the part of the world in which we live. All of this, of course, takes some letting go of a view of self that is no longer efficacious.

Sometimes what we need to let go of are ideas about the way the world is, including theological ideas that we developed, or had inculcated into us, when we were children. Oftentimes this is because we are simply no longer able to harmoniously put these ideas together with everything else we've learned since childhood, and so we can continue to harbor these ideas only on pain of not possessing intellectual integrity and spiritual wholeness. A number of years ago, a book appeared containing recipes for various dishes by young children. The book was called *Smashed Potatoes*—some of you may have come across it. Here's one of my favorites—a recipe for "Basketti with macaronis and noodles":

> 1 whole pack of long sticks—get them the size you want them
> Orangey-red spicy stuff for topping (2 little kinds and 2 big kinds)
> 1 half of a quarter of water
> Many purple onions with the paper off
> Use red meat balls and the soapy kind of cheese that tastes a little bit rotten.
>
> For the cooking get a stove, and pots, and bowls, and spoons and gloves with pink flowers.
> Cook for quite a while.
> The only thing is—when you have it, your father has to stay home for the day because he takes the basketti out of the pan and squeezes out the water.
> Serves all 4 of us—but not Freddy.[4]

I suspect many of the theological views we have as children bear about the same relation to the theological views of the deepest and most reflective religious thinkers as this recipe bears to the standard recipes for spaghetti. (And, of course, these sophisticated theological views may well bear the same relation to the truth, too.) We need to let go of some of our beliefs that we once thought were unshakable.

Sometimes what we need to let go of is a job or a pattern of life because it no longer fits us (or suits what we have become); it no longer releases our creativity or creates a feeling that we are living a life of value and worth.

Sometimes we need to let go of our loves who have died, where "letting go" here means not "forgetting or ceasing to love and cherish in memory," but rather "saying goodbye and meaning it"—in order that the aching grief can be transmuted into joy, and a sense of blessing for having been able to share in another's life in the rich way we did.

And, eventually, we have to let go of our very lives, commend our spirits to their mysterious source, and listen with all our hearts and minds to the One who says, "Run on. I will carry you. I will bring you to the end of your journey and there also will I carry you." (We die in any case, to be sure, but only if we let go of our lives in some such way as this, then when the time comes do we die at peace and with a sense of blessing.)

And, of course, in some sense—a sense that's hard to articulate in detail, but that we all at least dimly grasp, I suspect—we have to let go of our lives each day (we have to "die daily," as St. Paul put it), if we are to walk in the Spirit rather than in the Flesh. Luther put it this way: "All our life should be baptism, and the fulfilling of the sign, or sacrament, of baptism; we have been set free from all else and wholly given over to baptism alone, that is, to death and resurrection."[5]

All our lives should be given over to death and resurrection. That's really "letting go." And it's not easy—for reasons that are suggested in part by the story of the rabbi and the cantor and the humble synagogue cleaner who were preparing for the Day of Atonement. The rabbi beat his breast and said: "I am nothing, I am nothing." Then the cantor beat his breast and said: "I am nothing, I am nothing." Then the cleaner beat his breast and said: "I am nothing, I am nothing." Then the rabbi said to the cantor: "Look who thinks he's nothing."[6]

In addition to learning the art of letting go, it's also important to keep in mind when contemplating the turning world and all the ways in which our lives are ever-changing, an idea which has been stressed by Christian thinkers from very early on—the idea that we live in a sacramental universe. In other words, the idea that everything that exists or happens, every change that takes place in our lives, despite its disquieting, fearful, or tragic aspects, can become a vehicle of grace, a source of new life and deepened spirituality, and a way of becoming more open to others and to the peace of God. (No doubt this is at least part of what St. Paul had in mind when he said in his letter to the church at Rome that "in everything God works for good with those who love him … [Roman 8:28 RSV]" and, "neither death, nor life, nor angels nor principalities, nor things present, nor things to come, nor powers, nor height, nor depth, nor anything else in all creation, will be able to separate us from the love of God in Christ Jesus our Lord" [Romans 8:38–39 RSV].)

It's not easy, of course, to view the really awful things that happen to us as potential sources of grace—and it would certainly be wrong to pursue them because they are. The story is told that when Winston Churchill was thrown out of office in the election of 1945, his wife said to him, "It may be a blessing in disguise," to which Churchill allegedly replied, "Well, at the moment it's certainly very well disguised."[7] I would be among the last to say that such disguises are easy to penetrate. The myriad frustrations and irritations of life we can often handle with a moderate degree of poise—if we work at it. But finding blessings in calamities, and grace in horror, is another matter. (And put in this way, the very idea sounds crazy.) But it's surely nonetheless quite central to the Christian orientation to life (though in a sense paradoxical, i.e., an idea that runs counter to the natural view) that the death and destruction that really matter, the death and destruction that consist in or involve our alienation from the peace of God, come only from our shutting our hearts to God's healing presence and not from the outward changes to which we are subject. And the lives of countless people whose souls are radiant despite suffering some of the more shattering ills that flesh is heir to give testimony to the truth of (or anyhow the truth in) this strange idea.

A number of years ago, a talented woman by the name of Magda Bogin, a successful poet and translator, had an experience she described as follows:

> I first began to experience intense pain in the fall of 1977. I consider myself a strong, resourceful person, but in retrospect I can see how totally unprepared I was for the experience that lay in store for me. In October 1977 my legs suddenly became weak and unsteady and I began to have difficulty going up and down stairs. My gait became a lurch and my legs felt as if they had lead weights attached to them. I was twenty-seven years old and felt seventy-five. After a week my legs were aching so much I couldn't sleep—I who had never had insomnia, who had always slept like a log. I called a friend with a thirty-year history of arthritis, who told me to take aspirin around the clock. I did. Nothing happened. Ten days after the onset of the first symptoms the aches turned into full-blown, agonizing pain. I was terrified.[8]
>
> In the early stages of my illness the pain would come and go, building steadily for about ten days and then suddenly disappearing.[9] ... [Then] later in December 1978, my pain pattern suddenly changed. No more ten days on, ten days off. The pain went through the ceiling. Nothing seemed to stop it. The slightest walking, even standing up to cook, became excruciating. The painkillers I had carefully kept as a last resort (for when I had to capitulate) weren't strong enough. I started doubling the doses, cutting the "every four hours" to three, then two, and spent a good part of the month in bed. This time I had no choice; I was forced to listen. I had my first glimpse of real incapacity which was terrifying. I also realized, for the first time, what it means to heed the body. I had to ...
>
> After a year and a half of trying to free myself of pain I was in more pain than ever.[10]

A gift of grace? One recoils from such a description. But she struggled to cope and reflected on her struggles and struggled some more, and the result was a valuable book entitled *The Path to Pain Control*, which has been a real help—and even an inspiration—to some people who live day in and day out with similar problems. So perhaps her trials were (in some respects) a vehicle for grace.

Albert Schweitzer said that one of the things suffering does for a person is to make him or her a member of "the community of suffering."[11] And if you reflect on it, it's not difficult to see the importance of the existence of such a community; imagine what it would be like to be a sufferer in a world of people who have never experienced this sort of thing, who have never felt deep grief, or who have never had a profound sense of not being at home in the world, who have never experienced nagging, awful pain that just won't go away—a world of healthy teenagers, say, with all their wonderful vitality, curiosity, and zest, but also the kind of shallowness that comes from not understanding, "from the inside," these sorts of things.

I might just mention, too, that some of the deepest thinkers in the Christian tradition have even suggested that apart from certain kinds of calamity (or the recognition of their possibility), the religious life (the life that involves a right relationship to what is [in some sense] at the heart of existence) is difficult or even impossible to achieve. This was apparently Luther's view—dark as it is. Kierkegaard, the nineteenth-century Danish theologian who has had such a powerful influence on twentieth-century Protestant thought, writes at one point:

> To lead a really spiritual life while physically and psychically healthy is altogether impossible. One's sense of immediate well-being at once runs away with one. If one suffers every day, if one is so frail that the thought of death is quite naturally and immediately to hand, then it is just possible to succeed a little; to be conscious that one needs God. Good health, an immediate sense of wellbeing, is a far greater danger than riches, power, and position.[12]

And Simone Weil, the extraordinary French religious thinker who lived and worked in Europe before and through most of the Second World War, wrote:

> To acknowledge the reality of affliction means saying to oneself: "I may lose at any moment through the play of circumstance over which I have no control anything whatsoever I possess, including those things which are so intimately mine that I consider them as being myself. There is nothing that I might not lose." ... To be aware of this in the depths of one's soul is to experience non-being. It is the state of extreme and total truth.[13]

I suspect there may well be some truth in even these apparently extreme—and certainly paradoxical—views, truth over and above the fact that one does not have a deep understanding of a religion like Christianity without an understanding rooted in personal experience of the profound spiritual problems to which it provides a certain kind of response or answer. At any rate, the views of Luther and these words of Kierkegaard and Weil strike me as well worth pondering in the present connection.

Finally, besides letting go in the appropriate ways when the changes of life call for it, and keeping vividly alive our sense that nothing that happens to us is incapable of attaining sacramental status, we do well also, of course, to shun that frame of mind Shakespeare expressed so wonderfully in the sonnet many of us learned in high school that runs in part:

> When, in disgrace with fortune and men's eyes,
> I all alone beweep my outcast state,
> And trouble deaf heaven with my bootless cries,
> And look upon myself and curse my fate,
> Wishing me like to one more rich in hope,
> Featured like him, like him with friends possessed,
> Desiring this man's art and that man's scope.[14]

This disposition to compare the positions of some in the scheme of things with others can, of course, be an engine of justice and thus an important element in the pursuit of the Kingdom of God. It can also help us to perceive the places in the human world of greatest need. But when this tendency to make comparisons leads us to focus on the relative positions of ourselves to others, it often issues in self-pity and envy and possibly under certain circumstances even a feeling that the world is in the hands of a cosmic sadist, to whom the only appropriate response is a combination of depression and defiance. And these are conditions—self-pity, envy, depression, and defiance—that poison our spirits, strangle our joy, and (I suspect) frequently make us less available to others whose burdens we are called upon to share.

So instead of concentrating our thoughts on ourselves and our fates in comparison with others and their fates, we need to keep in the forefront of our minds the big miracle—the miracle of creation itself, of which we are but a tiny fragment, and the great mystery which this miracle embodies or to which it bears witness, and we need to think about ourselves primarily as pieces of the world that we have the power to make into more fitting instruments of that mystery's redemptive work in nature and in history.

8

Markel's Paradoxes

Dostoevsky's novel *The Brothers Karamazov* is not only one of the masterpieces of Western literature; it is one of the greatest Christian novels we have. It's about faith and rebellion, the power of goodness and the self-destructive character of evil, spirituality and worldliness, pride and guilt, saintliness and miracle, the intellect and the heart, murder and love, mystery and authority, Christ and the church—all these themes intricately woven into a gripping story, filled with fascinating characters, and told with the artistry of a genius.

At one point in the novel, some biographical notes are presented on the life of the novel's central representative of the church and the Christian faith, the priest and monk, Father Zossima. According to these notes, Father Zossima had an elder brother, Markel, who was of hasty and irritable temperament and very silent at home. He didn't get on with his schoolfellows, though he was kindhearted and never quarreled. When he was seventeen, he became friends with the young "free thinker" from Moscow, who had gained considerable distinction in philosophy at the university. They spent much time together that winter.

Then, at the beginning of Lent, Markel would not fast. "That's all silly twaddle and there is no God," he said, "horrifying my mother ... and me too,"[1] Zossima reports (he was then only nine). In the sixth week of Lent, Markel was taken seriously ill. He was diagnosed as having "galloping consumption,"[2] and his mother was told he wouldn't live through the spring. She, of course, entreated him to go to church, to confess, and to take the sacrament, which just made Markel angry. But finally, during Holy Week, he began going to church. "'I am doing this simply for your sake, Mother, to please and comfort you,' he said."[3] He soon took to his bed.

Then, rather suddenly, a great change passed over him; his spirit seemed transformed. His face became sweet and gentle, bright and joyous, in spite of coughing all night and sleeping poorly. And he would say very strange things, like: "Don't cry, Mother ... life is paradise, and we are all in paradise, but we won't see it,"[4] and, "every one of us has sinned against all men, and I more than any."[5]

Markel's mother smiled, and through tears asked, "Why, how could you have sinned against all men, more than all? Robbers and murderers have done that, but what sin have you committed yet, that you hold yourself more guilty than all?"[6]

Then Markel said, "Mother, little heart of mine … my joy, believe me, everyone is really responsible to all men for all men and for everything. I don't know how to explain it to you, but I feel it so, painfully even. And how is it we went on then living, getting angry and not knowing?"[7]

When the doctor visited, Markel would say, "'Well, doctor, have I another day in the world?' … 'You'll live many days yet,' the doctor would answer, 'and months and years too.'"[8]

"'Months and years!' he would then exclaim. 'Why reckon the days? One day is enough for a man to know all happiness. My dear ones, why do we quarrel, try to outshine each other and keep grudges against each other? Let's go straight into the garden, walk and play there, love, appreciate, and kiss each other, and glorify life.'"[9]

"'Your son cannot last long,' the doctor told my mother,"[10] Zossima reports. "The disease is affecting his brain."[11]

There's more to the account, but I shall cut it off here, merely noting that Markel died in the third week after Easter, his eyes beaming with joy, so the story goes, right up to the very end.

Now it's clear from what we know of Dostoyevsky's life and work that he would not be inclined to say that a person who had the loving affections, the sense of joy and peace, and the feelings of guilt that Markel had, and who talked as Markel did, subsequent to an extraordinary change within him soon after contracting a fatal illness, is best viewed as merely exhibiting the symptoms of a diseased brain. The remarks ascribed to Markel that "life is paradise" and we are all responsible for (or guilty of) everything are statements that Dostoyevsky would probably have said are true in some important sense. On the face of it, though, it is hard to see how such claims could be true. Horrible things, after all, do sometimes happen to people. Was life a paradise for the Jews who ended up in Auschwitz? For the children born with Tay-Sachs disease or Lesch-Nyham disease? For those who, owing to hormonal or neurochemical disorders, suffer severe and unremitting depression or anhedonia? And how could you and I be guilty of the Goldmark murders, the Holocaust, or the horrors of the Gulag? Each of us is responsible, no doubt, for some of the bad things that happen, but if anything is clear, it's clear that we are not all responsible for (or guilty of) everything terrible that happens.

Though this seems right—and that is why these remarks ascribed to Markel are properly described as paradoxical—Markel's words are worth reflecting on because there are some ideas in their vicinity that may well be true (or at least close to the truth). Furthermore, reflecting on these closely related ideas may help us to see how Markel's statements might be a way of speaking about the meaning of such classical doctrines as the Creation and the Fall, doctrines that receive mythological expression in the early parts of Genesis. In order to see this, however, we must first be able to make some sense of Markel's paradoxes.

Suppose Harry has a little too much to drink after work, and as he drives home, a child darts out into the street from between two parked cars, and because Harry's reactions have been adversely affected by the alcohol in his system, he hits and kills the child. Then Harry is guilty of the child's death. But now what of Mary who does just what Harry does but is lucky in not having a child dart out in front of her as she drives home? Is she really any less blameworthy than Harry, even though she kills no one? After all, that she doesn't is just a matter of good luck.

Suppose Gilbert plans and executes a murder for personal gain. And suppose Violet is in very similar circumstances and makes the same plan but decides not to execute the murder he's planned—but only for fear of getting caught. Is Violet really less morally culpable than Gilbert, even though Gilbert is a murderer and Violet kills no one?

Suppose Kelly injects curare into a recently born infant with an incurable defect in order to end its life. She too is then guilty of murder. But is Kelly any guiltier than Sullivan if he refrains from feeding such an infant and does so with the intention that it die?

Suppose Charlie plans and executes a robbery for reasons that hardly exculpate. Not good. But what about Tom, who draws a map for him? And Celeste, who lets him stay in her apartment after the robbery. And Sarah, who hears of the robbery and is bribed into silence. In the law, they too are all guilty of the crime—though not all equally culpable—and the law here reflects widespread moral convictions.

Finally, suppose Lila, for personal gain, bears false witness against Auburn, who in consequence is convicted of a serious crime of which he is in fact innocent. Very, very bad. And suppose Ellie would have done exactly the same thing if she had grown up in Lila's circumstances or had had Lila's parents or had just been given the opportunity. Also bad? As bad?

Well, there's much, much more to say about these matters, but perhaps even this brief account of these few imaginable cases will suggest something of what might be said by way of finding an element of truth in (or near) the thesis that we are all responsible for (or guilty of) everything. One might, I suggest, express at least part of the truth these words adumbrate (or gesture toward) by saying something like this: In thinking about whether we are (relatively) unblemished from a moral point of view, or the extent to which we stand in need of forgiveness, it's easy to forget or overlook certain kinds of facts. In particular, it's easy to forget or overlook the extent to which we are often similar to people whose culpability is obvious and profound and the fact that, sometimes at least (perhaps more often than we care to concede), we have managed to avoid being the direct cause of really serious harm to another only by virtue of luck (the child wasn't in front of the car when we were so careless or distracted or culpably dysfunctional). It's also easy to forget or overlook the fact that, sometimes at least, we have refrained from actions that would cause really serious harm to another for reasons that are not at all morally creditable—it is, after all, difficult often to be really sure exactly why we did or didn't do something. It's also easy to forget or overlook the fact that it is possible to harm others by acts of omission, as well as by acts of commission—that is, by not engaging in certain courses of action, as well as by engaging in certain courses of action. (This is part of the burden of the Parable of the Good Samaritan.) It's also easy to forget or overlook the fact that we often cause harm by our membership in groups all or many of the members of which make fairly small contributions to the creation of what may be a very great harm indeed. Think here of pollution and the wasteful squandering of nonrenewable resources, and the anti-Semitism that contributed to the atmosphere that made the Holocaust possible, and the widespread social attitudes that nourish racist practices, both North and South. It's also easy to forget or overlook the fact that we are often accomplices in the creation of evil by acts of omission, that is, members of co-responsible harm-causing groups by virtue of what we fail to do as well as by what we do. For example, we don't engage in acts of protest that would cost us little to engage in or we don't take the trouble to find out about certain awful things that are happening, knowledge of which things would put us in a position to take remedial actions or actions that would make a difference if enough others did likewise.

If we really think about ourselves and our lives in the light of facts like these, it's not difficult, I suggest, to begin to feel some attraction, if not to the precise view Markel's words seem to express, at least to the view that we are all guilty, and more seriously guilty than we ordinarily believe.

There is a further thought worth considering here, too. Suppose we were able to convince ourselves that so-and-so is having done some hideous thing rather than us is essentially adventitious; that is, if things had been different in certain ways that we can easily imagine, it would have been you or I that did that hideous thing. Then we would come even closer (I think) to believing true just the view Markel seems to be expressing. Indeed, it may be that it is in large part just this thought about the adventitious character of the fact that so-and-so did some horrible deed rather than someone else that lies behind his strange and paradoxical words, words which Father Zossima later uses to express one of his own deepest convictions, and words which no doubt resonate in the heart of Dostoyevsky, too.

As I have mentioned, Markel's remark that "life is paradise, and we are all in paradise, but we won't see it" is on the face of it no less paradoxical than his claim about our responsibility for evil and the magnitude of our guilt. But again, there are some thoughts that are quite commonly expressed in one form or another by Christian thinkers that may well have something to them and which lie, once again, at least close to the idea Markel's words appear to express.

Here is one way these thoughts are sometimes put. For the most part, each of us is at the center of his or her world. This is so, first, in the sense that we view the objects and events that exist or take place in the world from the midst of them (so to speak), and more specifically, from the point of view of one of these objects (i.e., us) that, taken together, make up the world. But each of us is at the center of his or her world also in the sense that our well-being, from the perspective of which we view everything, is at the center of our concerns (even if not our sole concern). Moreover, equally striking is the fact that we are prone to anxieties that reflect our awareness that things may not, and often don't, go well for us, and indeed we realize that we will sooner or later cease to be part of the familiar world of objects and events that constitute the framework of our lives. We are also prone to feelings of guilt and shame and even self-disgust as we fail to live up to our own personal ideals and internalized standards of right conduct. And we are prone to a feeling of futility about our lives, a sense that all our achievements are ultimately of little or no significance.

But, this line of thinking continues: there is a way of viewing life, a perspective on ourselves and the larger scene in which our lives are lived, that does not involve putting ourselves at the center of our world and that is (relatively) free from these tendencies toward anxiety, self-rejection, and a sense of the vanity of all things and the futility of all action. It involves viewing the world from nowhere in it, or coming to possess (in some measure)—perhaps by grace—the perspective of eternity, which, to the extent that we manage it, issues, in a sense of the inexpressible beauty of creation, deep and even unconditional love for all things, and the replacement of the feeling of the emptiness of life with a sense of its blessedness, a sense that "the world is charged with the grandeur of God."[12]

In its most plausible version, this line of thought also contains the idea that the perspective of eternity is never achieved in an unambiguous way; its presence is always fragmentary or limited and temporary. But the existence of this perspective, and our responsibility, in some obscure way, for not occupying it in our daily lives, is what gives purchase to Markel's paradoxical claim that "life is paradise ... but we won't see it."

The ideas that perhaps lie behind Markel's paradoxes and which they perhaps gesture toward are not unconnected either. For it's our putting (or finding) ourselves at the center of our world, it is often thought anyhow, that ultimately lies behind and explains our guilt, and it's our recognition of our guilt that enables us to be receptive to the perspective from which, or metamorphosis on the basis of which, the paradisal character of existence becomes luminously clear.

The connection of all these ideas with classical Christianity is pretty obvious, upon reflection. I have in mind especially the idea of the goodness of the created order ("God saw everything that he [God] had made and, behold, it was very good" Genesis 1:31 RSV); the idea of the distortion of existence brought about by the Fall, and the connection of the Fall with self-centeredness; the idea of the need of *metanoia*—badly translated "repentance" in the AV (authorized version)—if one is to enter the Kingdom of God and partake of eternal life; and the idea expressed in the Gospel of Thomas, and at least adumbrated in the Fourth Gospel, that the Kingdom of God "is spread out upon the earth, and men do not see it."[13]

While Markel's statements may have appeared odd to those around him (part of a diseased brain or an incurable sickness), they might also be seen as one way of expressing a commitment to certain long-held church doctrines like those of Creation and the Fall. Markel's paradoxes are, or might be, a verbal confession of faith, the expressions of a life committed to the possibility of Grace. The paradoxical statements that Markel uttered on his sick bed were, or could be seen as, commentary on the goodness of creation, the fallen nature of humanness, and the possibility that we are all interconnected in ways not readily visible.[14]

9

Laughter, Love, and Christian Living

Humans were made in the image of God, says Genesis. Usually the features that are singled out in this connection as defining humankind's special status among the living creatures of the earth are features like rationality, freedom, self-consciousness, and self-transcendence—that is, the capacity to develop highly reticulate, reasoned systems of belief about both matters of fact and matters of value; the capacity to act on the basis of such reasoned judgments; the capacity we all have to be aware of and to reflect upon our own mental states and processes; and the capacity to occupy in imagination different points of view, including points of view that abstract from such contingencies as spatial position, position in time, and our peculiar ways of perceiving the world. But as Genesis 17 indicates, humankind's uniqueness among the Earth's creatures is also reflected in our possession of that strange capacity we call a "sense of humor"—the capacity to see and find humor in situations and events, a capacity that manifests itself in a diverse collection of behaviors organisms like cats and dogs never exhibit (but primates probably do) and which we subsume under the heading "laughter."

It may be that this capacity—like the others I've mentioned—is not altogether unique; but in any case, it appears to be possessed by human beings to an unusual degree, and we certainly don't know of any other creatures who have it in anything like the highly developed form in which we have it. Also, it seems plausible to suppose that possession of a sense of humor is intimately connected with these other capacities when they're properly understood. If this is so, then to have created a creature with the kind of dignity and stature that human beings have is *eo ipso* to have created a creature—ironically enough—that is, as one might put it, prone to the giggles. In any event, that proneness is part of any normal human being's repertoire of dispositions. Seeing the funny sides of things and laughing at them is as natural to us as breathing; talking; exploring the world; making music, pictures, and imaginative stories; and—from time to time—reacting to life and the world with awe and reverence.

Ubiquitous as laughter is, however, it's easy, I think, to overlook its importance. We tend to think of the really important things in life as very serious—as indeed they are. But thinking this is quite compatible with acknowledging the importance of laughter in life, with acknowledging a crucial place in life for the zany, the silly, the raucous, the mirthful, the dopey, the wacky, and the uproarious. Indeed, it may be that without a healthy dose of these, we've much less chance of living the kind of life to which we are called, a life "in the Spirit." A life permeated by the charismata: peace, joy, and love.

Part of the reason that this may be so is the role of laughter in maintaining our physical well-being. Many years ago, a woman by the name of Dionisia Perez celebrated her 116th birthday.[1] She was then blind and hard of hearing (not surprisingly), and, when not in bed, she spent all of her time in a wheelchair (also not surprisingly). She lived in a nursing home, and one of the nurses who knew her very well said of her: "She never cries, never complains. Everything about her is laughter."[2] Of course, I don't mean to suggest that she reached 116 because she managed to find lots of things quite laughable—and that you will too if you work hard at keeping your sense of humor alive and well. But in view of various studies of the way our emotional states affect our body chemistry, finding the humor in life may well play a nontrivial role in keeping us fit and even extending our lives. Some of these studies were reported on by Jane Brody, who has written extensively on developments in health and medicine for *The New York Times*. In particular, she gave some of the details on experimental work suggesting that the emotions, acting through the brain, can affect a variety of nervous system functions, hormone levels, and immunological responsiveness. "Depending on circumstances," she writes, "animal and human studies have revealed that emotional reactions can suppress or stimulate disease-fighting white blood cells and trigger the releases of adrenal gland hormones and neurotransmitters, including endorphins, that in turn affect dozens of body processes."[3] Indeed, she says, "new studies strongly indicate ... that virtually every ill that can befall the body—from the common cold to cancer and heart disease—can be influenced, positively or negatively, by a person's mental state."[4]

So it may well be that a life that is regularly lightened and smoothed and relaxed and de-stressed by periodic bouts of laughter will be a healthier and a longer one than otherwise.

Or as Emily Dickenson put it, "A little madness in the spring/Is wholesome even for the king."[5]

And it may be that Lincoln was not exaggerating when he said, "With the fearful strain that is upon me night and day, if I did not laugh I should die."[6]

The positive role of laughter in bodily healing, in particular, is suggested by Norman Cousins's well-known and quite successful self-prescribed therapy for what had every appearance of being an almost certainly fatal ailment. Cousins, who died in 1990, was for many years the editor of *The Saturday Review of Literature*. Some may recall his account as it was later published in what became a widely read book entitled *Anatomy of an Illness*.[7] He had attended a conference in Leningrad as chairman of an American delegation to consider cultural exchanges. The hotel he was put up in was in a residential area, and his room was on the second floor. Each night, diesel trucks went back and forth to a nearby housing project in the process of round-the-clock construction. It was summer, and the windows were open all night. He recalled that during the time he was there, he slept poorly and often felt nauseated upon awakening in the morning. Then on leaving Moscow airport, he caught the exhaust spew of a jet at close range as it swung around near where he was standing. He may, as a consequence, have been subjected to heavy-metal poisoning, especially since he was (he conjectured anyhow) in a state of adrenal exhaustion at the time caused by a number of highly stressful incidents leading up to and during the conference. In any case, whatever the cause, shortly thereafter, he came down with a disease of the connective tissue which binds all the cells of the body together, a disease which one specialist gave him 1 chance in 500 of surviving.

However, he was a firm believer in the power of the emotions, so he decided to pursue the salutary ones with as much vigor as he could muster. He had films of some *Candid Camera* classics brought into his hotel room as well as Marx Brothers' movies. He also had some E.B. White read to him, etc. And he discovered that ten minutes of genuine belly laughter had a powerful anesthetic effect—giving him as much as two hours of pain-free sleep. And he also discovered that each time he had such a laughter episode, his sedimentation rate, which is increased by a variety of infections, dropped by five points and that these drops were cumulative. "I was greatly elated," he writes, "by the discovery that there is a physiological basis for the ancient theory that laughter is good medicine."[8]

It looks, then, as though a lively sense of humor and an easily triggered capacity for laughter may have a significant role to play in maintaining our physical well-being. But I suspect its role in maintaining our spiritual well-being may be just as great or even greater. Of course, like all our talents and capacities, the capacity to appreciate and produce humor is double-edged. It can be used to hurt or to punish—as is often the case when we use ridicule and sarcasm. Thus, we speak of someone's "savage wit" and "cutting humor." It can also be used as a means of self-glorification, building oneself up at the expense of others. And it can be used to poison our spirits as well as uplift them. Think, for example, of the humor that purveys cynicism or contempt, or that assimilates the sublime to the trashy. Some cases in point are Jonathan Swift's famous recommendation for the solution of Ireland's food and population problems—too horrible even to repeat—and Mark Twain's cynical quip that we ought to be very grateful to Adam because he brought death into the world. (Despite his greatness, there's probably no one whose outlook on the human scene is darker than Mark Twain's in his old age.)

Indeed, I suspect that it's often true that the nature or style of a person's sense of humor—the kind of jokes he or she makes and the sorts of situations he or she finds funny—is a pretty reliable indicator of his or her basic orientation to life and other people. And, of course, we learn not just about others in this way. By looking at our own funny bones—what we find uproariously funny and the kind of wit we display—we can gain important self-knowledge, too.

Despite its "ambiguity," however, humor and the laughter it elicits can be genuinely sacramental—and its use can be among the more important ways in which love of neighbor is manifested. Everyone recognizes that it can serve, as they say, to "break the ice" in social situations. The expression "break the ice" is a fine metaphor; a dead one, of course, but thinking about it brings it momentarily to life. How often have we found ourselves with others we know only slightly and our brains are immobilized and a sense of coldness seems to emanate from both ourselves and the others—until someone makes a quip, tells a joke, or relates seeing a cartoon showing a physicist on the telephone saying, "I won? I didn't even know that there was a Nobel Booby Prize."[9]

But humor can "break the ice" in a more significant way than by just making conversation between relative strangers easier and more relaxed (not to mention conversation between strangers who are also relatives). My relationship with my father was mainly made of ice—cold and rigid. (There are lots of possible explanations. He was a troubled man, struggling to make his way during a deep economic depression, stuck in an unsatisfying marriage, in a job that brought him home only a few days a month, with a couple of boys to support who were probably quite unplanned. I might have been a difficult kid to relate to, too. (I have no idea.) In any case, as I thought about the place of laughter in our lives, I made a startling discovery—I recalled, for the first time, that some warmth did spring up between my father and me from time to time as a result of certain very funny radio programs that the family all regularly listened to. He even began to call me by the name of one of the characters in the program called *Henry*

Aldrich[10] that some of you may recall. And I believe I felt a kind of reaching out towards me; at any rate, a slight melting of the ice. Laughing together was one of the ways—perhaps the only way—we could relate to one another positively and warmly, it seems.

But laughter can not only break the ice between people and thereby open them to others, helping people become available to one another at deeper levels and in more significant ways. It can also serve a "healing" function. It can, as Cabot and Dicks say in their classic book *The Art of Ministering to the Sick*, "lift us for the moment above the wounding surface of our road."[11] We all know, sooner or later, that the road can be really rough at times—and, of course, can even cause wounds that are almost (or more than almost) fatal to our spirits.

We all know these to some degree or other: depression, loneliness, inability to love, a sense of missed opportunities, or a wasted life. These are the sort of things that William James somewhere calls "zerissenheit" (torn-apart-ness), and the two kinds of winter that John Crowe Ransom wrote so movingly of in *Winter Remembered* ("Two evils, monstrous either one apart"[12]).

Sometimes, of course, we can't be reached by humor; even the springs of laughter absent our hearts for a time. But often we can be reached—despite the wounding surface of the road. Depressed, we look at Roz Chast's cartoon of an "Unholy Cow," in which she shows a cow in the field with captions saying, "Goddamn this feed," "Nature is overrated," and "I hate being a cow"[13]—and lo and behold, we feel much, much better. Feeling at war with ourselves for reasons we can't quite fathom, or feeling, again for unknown reasons, that we are like a volcano about to erupt, we immerse ourselves in a perfectly zany movie like *The Gods Must Be Crazy* or *The Life of Brian* and again we sometimes find that the inner turbulence has subsided.

Humor isn't always just a catalyst of laughter, a device for perking up our immunological capacities, smoothing out our troubled spirits, or relaxing our instinctive but perhaps quite inappropriate defenses; it can also be a valuable source of insight. Indeed, it can even contain quite profound truths. Lewis Carroll, for example, often illumines via humor interesting features of our everyday conceptual apparatus:

> "I'm sure [my memory] only works one way," Alice remarked. "I can't remember things before they happen."
> "It's a poor sort of memory that only works backwards," the Queen remarked.[14]

Reflecting on wasted time, Lady Muriel says:

> "All one knows is that it is gone—past recall!"

"Well, in my—I mean in a country I have visited," said the old man, "they store it up: and it comes in very useful, years afterwards! ... By a short and simple process ... they store up the useless hours: and, on some other occasion, when they happen to need extra time, they get them out again."[15]

Or think of the way that the contemporary sitcom throws light on creative ways of handling conflict between husbands and wives and between parents and teenage children.

Indeed, humor can even be an instrument through which we become able to hear the Word of God. I always recall a cartoon I saw a number of years ago that shows a group of people in a large city standing around doing absolutely nothing while a man is pulled into the sewer by a monster that lives beneath the streets. What could present more forcefully the implication of the Second of the Great Commandments ("Love your neighbor as yourself") that, where our relations with others are concerned, there are sins of omission as well as sins of commission? Or think of that extraordinary passage in *Huckleberry Finn* in which Huck wrestles with his conscience, which tells him to turn in the runaway slave Jim.

> Jim talked out loud all the time while I was talking to myself. He was saying how the first thing he would do when he got to a free state he would go to saving up money and never spend a single cent, and when he got enough he would buy his wife, which was owned on a farm close to where Miss Watson lived; and then they would both work to buy the two children, and if their master wouldn't sell them, they'd get an Ab'litionist to go and steal them.
>
> It most froze me to hear such talk. He wouldn't ever dared to talk such talk in his life before. Just see what a difference it made in him the minute he judged he was about free ...
>
> I was sorry to hear Jim say that, it was such a lowering of him. My conscience got to stirring me up hotter than ever, until at last I says to it, "Let up on me—it ain't too late yet—I'll paddle ashore at the first light and tell [that Jim was a slave]." I felt easy and happy and light as a feather right off.[16]

Then, as they're about to arrive at the shore of a free state, Jim says:

> "Pooty soon I'll be a-shout'n' for joy, en I'll say, it's all on account o' Huck; I's a free man, en I couldn't ever ben free ef it hadn' ben for Huck; Huck done it. Jim won't ever forget you, Huck; you's de bes' fren' Jim's ever had; en you's de only fren' old Jim's got now."
>
> I was paddling off, all in a sweat to tell on him; but when he says this, it seemed to kind of take the tuck all out of me. I went along slow then, and I warn't right down certain whether I was glad I started or whether I warn't. When I was fifty yards off, Jim says:

> "Dah you goes, de ole true Huck; de on'y white gentleman dat ever kep' his promise to old Jim."
>
> Well, I just felt sick. But I says, I got to do it—I can't get out of it. Right then along comes a skiff with two men in it with guns, and they stopped and I stopped. One of them says:
>
> "What's that yonder?"
>
> "A piece of a raft," I says.
>
> "Do you belong on it?"
>
> "Yes, sir."
>
> "Any men on it?"
>
> "Only one, sir."
>
> "Well, there's five niggers run off tonight up yonder, above the head of the bend. Is your man white or black?"
>
> I didn't answer up prompt. I tried to, but the words wouldn't come. I tried for a second or two to brace up and out with it, but I warn't man enough—hadn't the spunk of a rabbit. I see I was weakening; so I just give up trying, and up and says:
>
> "He's white."[17]

After fooling the slave-hunters into not looking into his raft by feigning that it held his sick family members, Huck began to wrestle with the decision he made not to give up Jim:

> They went off and I got aboard the raft, feeling bad and low, because I knowed very well I had done wrong and I see it warn't no use for me to try to learn to do right; a body that don't get started right when he's little ain't got no show—when the pinch comes there ain't nothing to back him up and keep him to his work, and so he gets beat. Then I thought a minute, and says to myself, hold on; s'pose you'd "a" done right and give Jim up, would you felt better than what you do now? No, says I, I'd feel bad—I'd feel just the same way I do now. Well, then, what's the use you learning to do right when it's troublesome to do right and ain't no trouble to do wrong, and the wages is just the same? I was stuck. I couldn't answer that. So I reckoned I wouldn't bother no more about it, but after this always do whichever come handiest at the time.[18]

What could present more powerfully the idea that is absolutely fundamental to the Christian faith than that there is a distinction to be drawn between the morality that happens to obtain in a given society and the correct (or best justified) system of moral principles? What could present more forcefully the idea that a person could act in accordance with the dictates of his conscience and still do wrong, and thus that there is such a thing as a malformed (or erroneous) conscience?

Humor, it seems, is not always concerned with the frivolous and superficial. It can be genuinely prophetic in the Old Testament sense of the word; it can be a powerful weapon in the struggle for justice and the kind of truth that sets us free. Perhaps, there's even some truth in Emily Dickenson's remark that "unless we become as Rogues, we cannot enter the kingdom of heaven."[19]

Sometimes, too, oddly enough, humor can function to put us in a better position to face facts that we find ourselves strongly inclined to forget and that we need to face if we are to bear the kind of witness in the world we're called upon as Christians to bear. One of the greatest concerns in the world today are those that surround the existence of the horrendous nuclear arsenals, and we as Christians stand under the demand that we give these issues prayerful consideration and think about actions we can take as citizens to move the world away from the unimaginable horror and tragedy that a large-scale nuclear war would entail. Many years ago, the United Methodist Council of Bishops authorized a two-year program of study and action on "the nuclear crisis," which was designed to inspire Methodists to study and reflect upon these difficult issues. Yet many people—probably all of us some of the time—find the current situation so disturbing whenever we read about it or reflect on it in any depth that we're powerfully motivated to avert our eyes and give our time and energy to various of the other matters that are always clamoring for our attention.

I suspect that humorous treatments of this area may well, for some people at least, help to keep the crippling emotions at bay by putting some of our worst fears in a context of laughter and thereby make it easier to think about some of these matters that we must think about if we are to do what we ought to do. Here I think, of course, of movies like *Dr. Strangelove* (1964) and *The Russians Are Coming, the Russians Are Coming* (1966). Satire and irony can be good antidotes to our propensity to avoid the serious.

No doubt humor's role is even more various than these brief hints suggest; but, in any case, I hope I've said enough to indicate something of the significance of its place in our lives. I hope, too, that I've at least hinted at the ways in which it can be genuinely sacramental and thus why it is probably a mistake when we think about those creative spirits who have made significant contributions to the quality of our lives, not to include the people who make us smile, guffaw, giggle, and sometimes erupt into contagious and exhausting laughter—people like Charlie Chaplin, Peter Sellers, Allen Funt, Lucille Ball, John Cleese, Michael Palin, James Thurber, Moms Mabley, Minnie Pearl, Bob Hope, S.J. Perelman, W.C. Fields, Carol Burnett, Gilda Radner, George Burns, and Charles Schulz among scores of others.

Moreover, given its power to edify, to break down the barriers that separate us from others, to undercut our pretenses, to reveal us to ourselves, I certainly have wanted to suggest that its use can be among "the works of love"[20] that we are called upon to do as Christians and that the development of our abilities to use it for these purposes is one of the matters we wrongly neglect but may want to reconsider. Laughter as a sacrament of faith!

10

Blind as a Bat

"Blind as a bat," we say. It's a familiar expression. We might say it of someone with tunnel vision or cataracts that haven't been removed. But more frequently we say it of the normally sighted, of people who just miss things, things that are—as we say—right in front of their noses. "You didn't see what was depicted on his tie?" "You didn't notice that her hair was orange on one side and purple in the back?" Of course, more often what's missed is not something that's visually perceivable like the picture on a tie or the color of someone's hair. We say he's blind because he couldn't see her insecurity or her anxiety or that she's blind because she couldn't see his reticence to talk about his trip or his obvious loss of short-term memory.

Of course, there are people who miss a lot but of whom we don't say they're blind as a bat. We don't expect them to see lots of the things that the rest of us see. The people I have in mind are children. Indeed, part of the charm of children, and one of the sources of the delight they give us, lies in their failures to see things properly. "Who is the good Mrs. Murphy who will follow us all the days of our lives?" ("Surely Goodness and Mercy shall follow me all the days of my life" [Psalm 23:6 RSV]).[1] "Why do we say, 'Lead us not into Penn station'?" ("Lead us not into temptation" [Mark 6:13 RSV]).[2] These are things children ask in their blindness, to our amusement and delight.

Sure, children miss a lot. They're quite blind to much that goes on around them. But, then, so are we all—really—aren't we? A striking example of our blindness to others was brought out in an article by the late Oliver Sacks, the well-known professor of neurology who served at the Albert Einstein College of Medicine until 2007. Sacks writes about the famous twins, John and Michael, who, at the time, had been institutionalized for thirty-one years—from the age of seven on.[3] They had been institutionalized because they'd been diagnosed as autistic, psychotic, and severely cognitively impaired. And they certainly were seriously impacted. They couldn't do simple addition and subtraction with any accuracy, nor comprehend what multiplication and division involved. But early on, it was discovered that they had some extraordinary powers. Given a date anywhere in the next 40,000 years—for example, December 21 of the year 38,472 CE—they could almost immediately tell you what day of the week it would fall on. They also had an extraordinary memory for digits. Given a series of five or even seven digits, most of us can repeat the series with ease. They could do it for a series of 300 digits with equal ease. They could also accurately report the weather, as well as the details of what they did, on every day of their lives from the age of four on. These facts about the twins were discovered quite early. But Sacks, by putting "aside the urge to limit and test,"[4] and by just getting to know them better, by observing them "quietly, without presuppositions, but with a full and sympathetic phenomenological openness,"[5] as he put it, learned that those around them had been blind to the full range and depth of the powers the twins possessed. One day a box of matches fell off their table and spilled out on the floor. They both said simultaneously, "111."

"How could you count the matches so quickly,"[6] Sacks asked.

"We didn't count," they said. "We saw the 111."[7]

Another time, they were seated in a corner together, with a "secret" smile on their faces that was unlike any Sacks had seen before. Sacks snuck up quietly in order to not disturb them and listened. John would speak out a six-digit number. Michael would savor it appreciatively. Then he would respond with another. And so on. They struck Sacks as like wine connoisseurs—tasting, appreciating, savoring their mutual offerings, offerings of six-figure numbers. Subsequently, Sacks discovered what they were doing. They were presenting to each other prime numbers. They were somehow picking out and tossing to each other huge numbers of the kind that are evenly divisible only by themselves and the number one. After making this discovery, Sacks decided to join them in such a "game." Using a crib sheet containing eight-figure prime numbers, he joined in at one point with such a number. John and Michael both became very quiet; wonder appeared on their faces—and intense concentration. Thirty seconds passed. Then they both broke into smiles. Apparently, they had both "seen" that the number Sacks had mentioned was prime.

Well, the story continues, but even this much of it can't help but make us wonder how often we are blind to what's going on in the lives of others around us, and especially to those aspects of their lives that give them their deepest contentment and joy—or perhaps their deepest pain and most paralyzing fear. It may well be that such blindness affects us all much of the time and perhaps is the curse of some of us all of the time. Indeed, such blindness can sometimes, tragically, even prevent us from appreciating important aspects of the lives of those closest to us. Helmer, in Ibsen's play *A Doll's House*,[8] clearly cherishes his wife, Nora. But he sees only her gaiety, affection, and eagerness to please. He sees her as his lovely "featherbrain," as he puts it. But that's blindness on his part. She's a capable, responsible, deep person. In consequence of this blindness to some of Nora's most important features, Helmer's sense of how he can best act so as to serve her best interests is quite inadequate—as is also his understanding of how he himself might be benefited, deepened, and enlarged by their relationship. So his love for Nora, genuine as it is, is profoundly defective—defective because, where she's concerned, he's blind as a bat.

We are not only blind to others, of course. Each of us is, if you wish, blind also to one person to whom we bear a very special closeness, namely ourselves. Everyone has had the experience of hearing his or her own voice on tape and being quite shocked, and perhaps quite disturbed too. "I sound like *that*?" Several years ago, I had one of my classes at the University of Washington videotaped. (The university made this opportunity available so the concerned faculty could take steps to improve their teaching.) I was quite amazed when I later saw the tape. A number of the wonderfully crafted, incisive sentences I thought I was uttering turned out to be ungrammatical mush. I also found myself early on in the lecture doing things with my body in general and my hands in particular that suggested that I was expecting one of those Monty Python ten-ton weights to come crashing down on me at any moment. Or perhaps that I would very much like to have a high, thick wall (or a broad, deep moat) between the class and me. (Fortunately, this suggestion was only strongly present, I think, at the outset, before I'd begun to feel I was among friends—well, quasi-friends—and so had begun to relax a bit.)

Of course, it's a truism that we rarely see our face and bodies as others see them or hear our voices as others hear them. But once again this is a relatively trivial aspect of the blindness to ourselves from which we all tend to suffer. Much more serious is the fact that we often miss facts about what's going on inside our minds and hearts. We don't see that the anger we direct at our spouses or kids is displaced anger, anger whose real cause and appropriate target is someone (or something) else. We don't see that our depression is not caused by the state of the world or our own continual failures, but by the fact that we're not getting enough full-spectrum light—as would be shown by the fact that as soon as we get it, the depression lifts. We don't see the hostility we sometimes feel toward those we're expected to love, and that we expect ourselves to love—hostility that, as Freud taught us, creeps out sometimes in most surprising ways, like slips of the tongue or pen. Recall the story of the man who, while on vacation in Hawaii, sent his mother a telegram which read, "Having a wonderful time, wish you were dead." We don't even notice our own compulsive, or in other ways bizarre, behavior; the character of our dreams; even the persistent themes of our daydreams—the theme of conquest or power over others, perhaps; or the theme of sudden wealth or the return to a secure and carefree childhood.

Sometimes people even build their lives on a foundation of self-deception. Casaubon in George Eliot's *Middlemarch*[9] is a beautifully articulated fictional example of a person who has done just this. His life is, to all appearances, built around the value of scholarship. He seems wholly committed to it and is so seen by his neighbors and acquaintances. And this is the way he sees himself, too—as the devoted scholar. But it's all a fiction, one he has created and which he believes—or half-believes (self-deception is a strange business). Of course, to maintain his vision of himself, he has to isolate himself from other scholars in his field and remain ignorant of their work. He has to constantly find support from others to keep his false self-image intact. Indeed, his marriage is undertaken just to serve this purpose. His wife, Dorothea, is brought into his life because she so admirably functions to keep his badly distorted picture of himself from crumbling.

We even tend, more often than we like to think, not to see our own real values, to be blind to our own deepest sense of what is most important in our lives. Paul Tsongas retired from the US Senate at the young age of forty-two upon learning that he had cancer and that he probably had only about 8–12 years to live. At the time, Tsongas told of receiving a letter from a close friend shortly after he'd announced he was leaving the Senate. It said, "No one on his death bed ever said, I wish I had spent more time on my business."[10]

Then, too, we are blind to many aspects of the natural and cultural world that surrounds us. Most of us know almost nothing about the various national command, control, communication, and intelligence systems that have grown up with the world's nuclear arsenals, and only a select few of us, apparently, know how all of these systems work in any detail. And the same is true of the international economic system, the character and extent of the global environmental degradation that is occurring owing to the continuous pollution of land, air, and water worldwide, and so on *ad infinitum*. And when it comes to the world of nature, it may be that our blindness is ineluctable and not just due to practical limits that could in principle be overcome. Bats, for example—which, incidentally, are not blind—perceive the world primarily by echolocation. They send out rapid series of subtly modulated high-frequency shrieks and detect the reflections of these sounds from objects within range. Their brains are designed to correlate the outgoing impulses with the subsequent echoes, and this information enables them to discriminate the distances, sizes, shapes, motions, and textures of the things in their immediate surroundings. Now when we ask ourselves what it is like to be a bat perceiving the world in this way, what it feels like, what the character of the sort of experience they must have when they perceive in this way is we, of course, have absolutely no idea. Furthermore, we have absolutely no idea how we might conceivably find out. (It may, to be sure, be an illusion that there is something it is like to have this batty kind of experience. Perhaps once we know how their nervous systems work in sufficient detail, we'll know all there is to know about what it's like to be a bat. But if it is an illusion, it's a stubborn one and one we will relinquish only in the face of argument that is even harder to relinquish.)

So we're all among the blind. We're blind to others, blind to ourselves, and blind to many aspects of the world that surround us. But, of course, you will say, "How could it be otherwise?" This is what it is to be a creature—a limited, finite piece of the natural order. Yet, central in the cluster of ideas that are part of our Judeo-Christian heritage is the idea that we have a deep-lying tendency to forget or mask or deny our creatureliness, to pretend that we are not as limited as we obviously are. Central to this tradition in which so many, in different ways, still find nurture, strength, insight, and direction is the thought that we have a deep-lying tendency to be blind to our blindness.

Thus we tend to forget that those around us are hidden, that there is always more to learn about them—and that the things we don't see may well be among the most important things. We tend to forget (or mask from ourselves the fact) that we are to a large extent hidden from ourselves. So we become lax and lazy when it comes to self-scrutiny; we take the way we appear to ourselves as the way we really are. We tend to forget how much there is about what's going on in the world that we don't grasp and so think it's perfectly obvious—or even absolutely certain—that the tax policies, defense strategy, approach to handling the deficit, etc. that we favor is the correct one. We tend to oversimplify, to forget the endless and disconcerting complexity of things: the highly reticulate feedback loops in social systems, the fundamental rule of ecology—which applies in the political, economic, and social realms as well—that "one cannot change just one thing." Indeed, this tendency to forget our limits, to be blind to our own blindness, may well be at the center of the classical Christian doctrine of the Fall, the doctrine that seeks—perhaps among other things—to connect our estrangement from the deepest sources of our health and wholeness with our deep-lying inclinations to pretend to deeper virtue, insight, and spiritual depth than we actually possess.

If this is right, then perhaps the revolution in our hearts and minds the gospels present Jesus as calling for, and perhaps the special way of life that Paul referred to as "walking in the Spirit" (Galatians 5:16) and that he speaks of as following from our putting on "the mind of Christ" (Philippians 2:5), a way of life that the Christian tradition has witnessed to by taking the cross as the dominant symbol of Christianity—perhaps that revolution of mind and heart, and that way of life, consists (at least in part) in coming to see clearly and face squarely the fact that we are blind as bats, that all our views and insights tend to be infected with our creatureliness, tend to lack finality and completeness.

And perhaps the church—insofar anyway as it approximates to what it ideally is—is properly thought of (in part at least) as a community of those who struggle to face up to their blindness and thereby to open themselves to the power and grace and the transformations of mind and heart such openness involves, a community of those animated by faith in a God who stands in judgment upon all the faiths that blind creatures create and try to live by, and so a faith that makes room for doubt concerning all our attempts—even our profoundly inspired attempts—to articulate saving truth in final form.

"Today also my complaint is bitter," said Job (23:2 RSV), before being confronted by the Voice out of the whirlwind. "Oh that I knew where I might find him, That I might come even to his seat! I would lay my case before him and fill my mouth with arguments" (Job 23:3–4 RSV), he says. Poor Job. Resting confidently on the age-old faith of his genuinely inspired ancestors, he was "blind as a bat."

"God, I thank thee, that I am not like other men, extortioners, unjust ... like this tax collector" (Luke 18:11 RSV), said the Pharisee in the temple. "I fast twice a week, I give tithes of all that I get" (Luke 18:12 RSV). How good a man he was, how upright, a solid citizen if ever there was one, no doubt a pillar of his religious community. And yet, how complacent and how boastful. "Blind as a bat," is Jesus' radical and deeply disturbing comment (in effect).

"We know that God has spoken to Moses, but as for this man, we do not know where he comes from" (John 9:29 RSV), say the Pharisees in John 9 to the man whose eyes have just been opened by the power of God present in the young prophet from Nazareth, whose words were so startling and amazing, and in whose presence men's hearts burned within them. They said confidently, "We see," and Jesus said of them (in effect): "Blind as a bat."

11

Models and Mentors

In a short article that came to my attention a while back, a woman by the name of Susan Schnur wrote:

> My earliest memory pertaining to ethics ... date[s] to kindergarten and to a ritual we had at the school water fountain called "frontsies and backsies."
>
> Frontsies meant that you let a kid cut in front of you as you stood in line for a drink. Backsies meant you let a kid cut behind you.
>
> A complex moral microcosm presented itself in the world of frontsies and backsies, with a wide range of available moral responses.
>
> There were, for example, those kids who always asked for frontsies (ethical hedonists); others who generally went for backsies (immoralists—requesting permission to infringe on others from someone who was not, himself, affected); those who gave backsies (collaborationists), and those who manipulated the water fountain line into a political opportunity (Machiavellians) ...
>
> And then there was my first ethical mentor, Judy Simon ... who, one day in line, refused frontsies to Buzzy Chateau. "You should stand where you end up Buzzy, like the rest of us," she said, with great probity, I thought. Another time she gave frontsies to Corinne who, probably in her whole life, had never been given frontsies by anyone. Judy then went to stand, herself, at the back of the line (Christian ethicist).[1]

Ms. Schnur describes Judy Simon as a mentor—an ethical mentor. But, of course, it may not have been Judy's intention to instruct those observing her behavior. In that case, the term "model" might be more apt. Mentors, I take it, teach intending to do so; others shape us by providing us with models of behavior or attitudes.

Models and mentors pervade our lives. We are surrounded by them from birth on. And our beliefs, our values, our attitudes, our emotional lives, and the thoughts that fill our minds (both conscious and unconscious) are, to a large extent, formed by those who functioned for us as models or mentors in the past or so function now.

No doubt for the majority of us, the most important models and mentors in our early years are our parents and older siblings—though sometimes a younger sibling or an aunt, uncle, or a grandparent is an even more powerful influence. I recall, for example, that my brother and I used to pretend to be my father and various of his business associates; we'd imagine the circumstances of their adult lives as best we could and then go through the motions and carry on the conversations in these imagined circumstances that we took to be those that they would engage in. You probably have analogous memories.

I once read that in 1938 there were some 80 million movie admissions every week—a figure representing about 65 percent of the US population at the time! Now a lot of the movie tickets sold in that era must have been mine since I seem to be familiar with a distressingly large number of the films produced in Hollywood's golden age, the period from 1930 to the end of the Second World War. And it's somewhat frightening to contemplate how enormous an influence on my mind and heart all those silver-screen models may have had—Captain Blood, Dr. Kildare, Zorro (who made that famous mark), Mr. Deeds (who went to Washington), the Man in the Iron Mask, Robin Hood and Little John, and, yes, the Gipper.

Family and movies are, of course, only a couple of the sources of the models and mentors that shape us. Friends, teachers, ministers, sports figures, politicians, journalists, business and professional associates, the characters in the TV sitcoms and soaps and masterpiece theater productions, and the characters of novels and plays, among others, can also be significant models or mentors for us.

A former student of mine took Elizabeth Bennet of Jane Austin's *Pride and Prejudice* as a model. One could do a lot worse. I always suspected that an acquaintance of my college days did; for he seems to have been captivated by Dostoyevsky's Raskolnikov, who as you may recall murdered two women in order to show something about himself and also perhaps to conform his behavior to his considered views about what kinds of conduct are legitimate. And who teaches us more about ourselves and those around us than Charles Schulz? In one comic strip, Linus sits reading, a little blond girl next to him listening politely. "In those days a decree went out from Caesar Augustus that all the world should be enrolled,"[2] he reads. Then he says:

> Caesar Augustus was the Emperor of Rome and the most powerful person on Earth! One night, in the little town of Bethlehem, a child was born, but no one paid attention. After all, he was born in a common stable ... Who would have thought that this child would someday be revered by millions while Caesar Augustus would be almost forgotten?[3]

Then the little girl says: "No one paid any attention when I was born either, but now everyone loves me, and I'm gonna get so many presents for Christmas, it'll make your head swim."[4] As Linus walks off with a sad look on his face, she then says: "Hey, aren't you gonna finish the story?" He says: "I think you finished it."[5] Don't we see ourselves in her?

Who have been your most important teachers, the people who have taught you the most, or what you now think to be the most important things you've been taught? What figures—real or otherwise—have been significant models for you, models who have, for good or ill, played a large role in shaping your beliefs, attitudes, and values?

Once we think about who the important models and mentors in our lives were, it's easy to be struck by this fact, namely, that it is largely a matter of luck—anyhow from the perspective of common sense that most of us occupy most of the time—if our models and mentors were positive and healthful in their effects upon us rather than the reverse.

We certainly don't choose our parents or our siblings; if they taught us well and gave us healthful models, what wonderful good fortune was ours.

For all its faults, the Hollywood that produced the movies I saw as a child drew a line between the good guys and the bad guys that was clear and firm, and by and large, the bad guys did not appear in very attractive colors. The models presented by other films are sometimes rather different; they include Clyde Barrow and his lovely friend Bonnie, and Butch Cassidy and his sidekick the Sundance Kid—characters who are charming, witty, handsome, brave, and loving—but also bank robbers and murderers. In some ways, I feel rather fortunate that I grew up with the movies I did.

Also, the main athletic hero I remember from the days of my youth was not routinely shot full of steroids, doused with amphetamines, or addicted to cocaine. He was "Whizzer" White, a University of Colorado All-American football player, and a straight-A student who went on to sit on the Supreme Court, one of John Kennedy's appointees. Not a bad model.

Realizing the element of luck involved in the formative influences upon us should make us quite receptive to the New Testament theme expressed in the Gospels and in the letters of Paul about the importance of not standing in judgment on others, a theme Solzhenitsyn powerfully expresses in *The Gulag Archipelago* with these words: "the line dividing good and evil cuts through the heart of every human being ... Confronted by the pit into which we are about to toss those who have done us harm, we halt, stricken dumb; it is after all only because of the way things worked out that they were the executioners and we weren't."[6]

It's also important to bear in mind that sometimes coming to realize in a fully conscious way that we are under the influence of a certain model can be liberating. We watch the TV and Internet ads—probably many thousands of them in the course of the years—and wonder why we feel so vaguely disconnected, why we feel so eaten up by envy, or why we feel so left out by life. Then we realize that we've got a picture of how we and the world should be that is formed by all those ads of the beautiful, young, healthy people, with loving partners, happy children, backyard swimming pools, vacations in Hawaii, frequent trips to other exotic places through the friendly skies, etc. But when we bring clearly to mind what the source of our feelings are, we are helped to be free of it. We see that these models are not the ones we want to shape our minds and hearts at all; they are too far from those provided by Scripture and the parts of the history of the Church that clearly manifest the Spirit of Christ.

Think, for example, of the model of the suffering servant that one finds in the book of Isaiah. Think, too and especially, of the model which the life of Christ as pictured in the Gospels presents, a life that may well have taken the form it did partly because of the presence in the tradition of the suffering servant model. The shortest and yet perhaps most moving sentence in Paul's letters is the sentence which is translated in the Authorized Version as "I die daily" (I Corinthians 15:31). When we think of what depths of experience must have been behind that sentence and the spiritual power that Paul's life exhibited, the disquietude caused by the world of the TV ads tends to vanish.

It may seem odd that realizing that some model or another is the cause of our disquiet should free us from its clutches. But we do seem to work that way, at least often. I remember being struck by this phenomenon when I was in college. I had the feeling that things weren't right, that my life wasn't the way it should be. Then it came to me that my model of college life had been formed to a certain extent by the movies, a model according to which college life consisted largely of parties and pretty girls and fast cars and fur coats and football games. It didn't involve long hours of study, and difficult and seemingly endless struggles with words and ideas, and the profound and often deeply disturbing reorganization of the mind and the emotions that liberal education characteristically involves, and the perplexing and painful task of finding the right path for oneself, finding who one is. The movie model didn't contain any of this. And once I realized the source of my discontent, I felt much better—oddly enough. I was freed by the realization that I'd been haunted by a fiction, a picture of the way things should be that was quite inappropriate—even kind of silly.

Coming to see the sort of models and mentors that have shaped others can be a source of valuable insight too. It can help us to understand why others are as they are, why they see things in what seems to us such strange ways, why they respond to events and persons so differently from the ways we do, and why they suffer from the kind of inner turmoil from which we are perhaps free.

I recall how much of the behavior of a friend of mine fell into place when he let it out one day that he'd taken Machiavelli and de Gaulle as his mentors when it came to the exercise of political leadership. "So that's why his words sometimes failed to match his behavior." "So that's why such effort was made to befriend X, and so little concern was shown about alienating Y." "So that's why, knowing he could at most only wound, he preferred not to strike at the king at all."

In his horrifying and revealing *Letter to His Father*, the incomparable Franz Kafka wrote:

> From your armchair you ruled the world. Your opinion was correct, every other was mad, wild ... not normal. Your self-confidence indeed was so great that you had no need to be consistent at all and yet never ceased to be in the right. It did sometimes happen that you had no opinion whatsoever about a matter and as a result all opinions that were at all possible with respect to the matter were necessarily wrong, without exception. You were capable, for instance of running down the Czechs, and then the Germans, and then the Jews, and what is more, not only selectively but in every respect, and finally nobody was left except yourself.[7]

He then continues:

> in all my thinking I was ... under the heavy pressure of your personality ... All these thoughts, seemingly independent of you, were from the beginning burdened with your belittling judgements ....[8] Courage, resolution, confidence, delight in this and that, could not last when you were against it or even if your opposition was merely to be assumed; and it was to be assumed in almost everything I did.[9]

If we suppose that this account is even roughly accurate—and there is much, much more, all of a kind that breaks one's heart—it's easier to understand why Kafka was the tormented and crippled soul throughout his entire life. To use a figure that the philosopher Wittgenstein used, he walked in that ostensibly bizarre way because he was walking against a strong wind, and, after we realize this, we are no longer puzzled by the very strange way of walking that we see from within the house looking out.[10] (Of course, it should also be said that we probably would not have *The Trial* and *The Castle* and much, much more if Kafka hadn't had the father he did.)

But perhaps the most important thought that reflection on the pervasiveness and power of models and mentors in our lives gives rise to is the thought that each of us play the roles of model and mentor for others. This is surely a matter that we do well to ponder.

After all, as Christians, we are participants in the new creation of which St. Paul speaks, or the abundant life of which the author of the fourth Gospel speaks—though at best in an anticipatory and fragmentary way, to be sure. And we are such participants insofar as it is given to us to walk in the Spirit, or to put on the mind of Christ, or to follow in the way of the Cross—which again most of us tend to manage only in an ambiguous, halting, and stumbling way at best. But now, what is it to walk in the Spirit, to put on the mind of Christ, to follow the way of the Cross? In part at least, it involves living in such a way as to edify, build up, strengthen, heal, and make whole our neighbors. And one way we can do this is by making our own lives models for others of the sort that have these kinds of consequences—models that edify and strengthen, rather than tear down and weaken.

Martin Buber, in the introduction to his collection of tales of the Hasidim, records the legend of a man who had been in the inner circle of the founder of the Hasidic movement in Judaism, the Baal Shem, a movement which, incidentally, began at the time of Wesley's founding of Methodism. This man, who had been lame, was asked to say something about his mentor, the Baal Shem. So he told of how the Baal Shem was wont to dance while he prayed. And then, carried away by his tale, he himself got up as he spoke and began to dance in order to show how his master had done it. From that hour on, he was cured of his lameness, the legend concludes. Buber recounts this legend to make a point about the power that the telling of stories can have.[11] But we can take it here as defining an exemplar of the sorts of models and mentors we should strive to be for others, models that "heal" when they are followed or imitated, mentors whose words and actions make others whole when they hear and or heed them.

How do you respond to the onset of serious illness? Whatever the answer, you will be a model for those around you—spouse, children, friends, colleagues—a model that edifies or one that undermines their strength and courage. How do you respond to the uncaring, or cruel, or deceitful behavior of others? How do you react to missed opportunities, a situation that calls for a really big decision in your life, a wonderful piece of good fortune? Whatever the answer, you will be a model for those around you, whether you desire to be or not, a model that inspires and heals or wilts and weakens. How do you respond to the early signs of middle age, to the shock (e.g.,) of going to a physician who seems not much older than one of your recently adolescent children? How do you respond to success and to failure, to triumph and to deep disappointment, to the ingratitude of those for whom you have made really significant sacrifices, to the onset of old age and the painful losses it often brings in its train—in addition perhaps to a sense of liberation, an enlarged perspective on life, and a deep sense of peace? Whatever the answers, you will be a model for those around you, whether you intend it or not, a model that will build them up or tear them down, give a home within them to the power of death or be a ministry of healing and a "work of love" that gives to their hearts a home for the Spirit of Christ.

Notes

Preface

1 Richard Taylor, *With Heart and Mind: A Philosopher Looks at the Nature of Love and Death* (New York: St. Martin's Press, 1973) 1.
2 See, D.T. Max, *Every Love Story Is a Ghost Story: A Life of David Foster Wallace* (New York: Penguin Books, 2013). For a discussion of Wallace's use of the phrase, see "D.T. Max, D.F.W.: Tracing the Ghostly Origins of a Phrase," *The New Yorker*, December 11, 2012, https://www.newyorker.com/books/page-turner/d-f-w-tracing-the-ghostly-origins-of-a-phrase.

Introduction to Part One

1 Ludwig Wittgenstein, *Philosophical Investigations*, trans. G.E.M. Anscombe (Oxford: Blackwell Publishing, 2003), §109.
2 Kevin W. Hector, *Theology without Metaphysics* (Cambridge: Cambridge University Press, 2011), 28. Kindle Edition.

Chapter 1

1 Shalom Auslander, *Foreskin's Lament: A Memoir* (New York: Penguin Publishing Group, 2007), Kindle Locations 118–124. Kindle Edition.
2 Quoted in, Richard Dawkins, *The God Delusion* (New York: Houghton Mifflin Company, 2006), 40.
3 Dawkins, *The God Delusion*, 40. Emphasis added.
4 Dawkins, *The God Delusion*, 40.
5 For a look at scientism in and out of religion, see my *Kneeling at the Altar of Science: The Mistaken Path of Contemporary Religious Scientism* (Eugene, OR: Pickwick Publications, 2012).
6 Mark Johnston, *Saving God* (Princeton, NJ: Princeton University Press, 2009), 40.
7 Dawkins, *The God Delusion*, 39. Emphasis in the original.
8 Dawkins, *The God Delusion*, 52.

9 Brian Davies, "The New Atheism: Its Virtues and Its Vices," *New Blackfriars* 92 (2011): 23. Comments in the brackets have been added by me and are not in the original quote.
10 Quoted in Johnston, *Saving God*, 46.
11 Richard Dawkins, *River out of Eden: A Darwinian View of Life* (New York: Basic Books, 1995), 133. Quoted in Eric Reitan, *Is God a Delusion? A Reply to Religion's Cultured Despisers* (Malden, MA: Wiley-Blackwell, 2009), 36.
12 Victor J. Stenger, *God: The Failed Hypothesis* (Amherst, NY: Prometheus Books, 2007).
13 Terry Eagleton, "Lunging, Flailing, Mispunching," *London Review of Books* 28, no. 20 (2006), https://www.lrb.co.uk/v28/n20/terry-eagleton/lunging-flailing-mispunching.
14 Alvin Plantinga, "The Dawkins Confusion: Naturalism 'ad absurdum,'" *Books and Culture: A Christian Review*, March/April 2007, http://www.booksandculture.com/articles/2007/marapr/1.21.html?paging=off.
15 Denys Turner, *Faith Seeking* (London: SCM Press, 2002), 7.
16 Quoted in D.Z. Phillips, *The Problem of Evil & the Problem of God* (Minneapolis: Fortress Press, 2004), Kindle Locations 1948–1949. Kindle Edition.
17 Alvin Plantinga and Michael Tooley, *Knowledge of God* (Malden, MA: Blackwell Publishing, 2008), 2. For a philosophical critique of construing the divine as a "person without a body," see David Bentley Hart's discussion of "monopolytheism," in *The Experience of God* (New Haven, CT: Yale University Press, 2013), chapter 3, part 6, and Brian Davies's discussion of "Theistic Personalism," in *An Introduction to the Philosophy of Religion*, 3rd ed. (Oxford: Oxford University Press, 2004), chapter 1.
18 Phillips, *The Problem of Evil*. Kindle Locations 1950–1951. Kindle Edition.
19 Ludwig Feuerbach, *Principles for the Philosophy of the Future*. Quoted in Jeffery L. Koskey, "The Birth of the Modern Philosophy of Religion and the Death of Transcendence," in *Transcendence: Philosophy, Literature, and Theology Approach the Beyond*, ed. Regina Schwartz (New York: Routledge, 2004), 22.
20 William Watson, *The Hope of the World and Other Poems* (New York: John Lane, 1898), 18.
21 Abraham Joshua Heschel, *God in Search of Man: A Philosophy of Judaism* (New York: Farrar, Straus and Giroux, 1976), 9. Kindle Edition.
22 Johnston, *Saving God*, 14.
23 Johnston, *Saving God*, 23.
24 Johnston, *Saving God*, 23.
25 Peter Rollins, *How (Not) to Speak of God* (Brewster, MA: Paraclete Press, 2006), 12.
26 Simone Weil, *First and Last Notebooks*, trans. Richard Rees (London: Oxford University Press, 1970), 147. Quoted in Rebecca A. Rozelle-Stone, *Simone Weil and Theology* (New York: Bloomsbury Publishing), 5. Kindle Edition.

27 For a good discussion on the difference between idols and icons, see Jean-Luc Marion, *God without Being* (Chicago: University of Chicago Press, 1991).
28 See Rollins, *How (Not) to Speak of God*, 12. See also, Marion, *God without Being*.
29 Johnston, *Saving God*, 14.
30 Johnston, *Saving God*, 14.
31 Johnston, *Saving God*, 16.
32 Johnston, *Saving God*, 15.
33 Johnston, *Saving God*, 15.
34 Phillips, *The Problem of Evil and the Problem of God*, Kindle Location 2371. Kindle Edition.
35 Johnston, *Saving God*, 23.
36 Robert C. Coburn, *The Strangeness of the Ordinary: Problems and Issues in Contemporary Metaphysics* (Savage, MD: Rowman & Littlefield, 1990), 34.
37 Abraham Joshua Heschel, *God in Search of Man: A Philosophy of Judaism* (New York: Farrar, Straus and Giroux, 1955), 117. Kindle Edition.
38 Phillips, *The Problem of Evil & the Problem of God*, Kindle Location 3053. Kindle Edition.
39 Johnston, *Saving God*, 23.
40 Jeffrey C. Pugh, *Religionless Christianity: Dietrich Bonhoeffer in Troubled Times* (New York: T&T Clark, 2008), 98.
41 Ludwig Feuerbach, *The Essence of Christianity*, trans. George Elliot (Amherst, NY: Prometheus Books, 1989), 14.
42 Paul Ricoeur, "Religion, Atheism and Faith," in *The Religious Significance of Atheism*, ed. Alasdair Macintyre and Paul Ricoeur (New York: Columbia University Press, 1969), 60.
43 Johnston, *Saving God*, 23.
44 William Placher, *The Domestication of Transcendence: How Modern Thinking about God Went Wrong* (Louisville, KY: Westminster John Knox Press, 1996), 75. Emphasis in the original.
45 Placher, *The Domestication of Transcendence*, 75.
46 Karen Armstrong, *The Case for God* (New York: Knopf Doubleday Publishing Group, 2009), 145. Kindle Edition.
47 Armstrong, *The Case for God*, 149. Emphasis in the original.
48 Placher, *The Domestication of Transcendence*, 75.
49 René Descartes, *Meditations on First Philosophy: With Selections from the Objections and Replies (Cambridge Texts in the History of Philosophy)*, ed. John Cottingham (Cambridge: Cambridge University Press, 1996), 31.
50 William P. Alston, "Functionalism and Theological Language," in *Divine Nature and Human Language: Essays in Philosophical Theology* (Ithaca, NY: Cornell University Press, 1989), 79.

51 Placher, *The Domestication of Transcendence*, 87.
52 Rollins, *How (Not) to Speak of God*, 7–8.
53 Rollins, *How (Not) to Speak of God*, 8. Emphasis in the original.
54 D.Z. Phillips, *Faith after Foundationalism: Critiques and Alternatives* (Oxford: Westview Press, 1995), 3.
55 D.Z. Phillips, *Wittgenstein and Religion* (New York: Saint Martin's Press, 1993), 1. Emphasis in the original.
56 Simone Weil, *Gravity and Grace* (Routledge, 2002), xxi, quoted in Richard Bell, *Simone Weil's Philosophy of Culture, Readings towards a Divine Humanity*, ed. Richard H. Bell (Cambridge: Cambridge University Press, 1993), 85.
57 Bell, *Simone Weil's Philosophy of Culture*, 85.

Chapter 2

1 Owen Barfield, *Saving the Appearances: A Study in Idolatry*, 2nd ed. (Middletown, CT: Wesleyan University Press, 1988), 11. Emphasis in the original.
2 Robert C. Coburn, "A Neglected Use of Theological Language," in *New Essays on Religious Language*, ed. Dallas M. High (New York: Oxford University Press, 1969), 218.
3 Coburn, "A Neglected Use of Theological Language," 219.
4 Coburn, "A Neglected Use of Theological Language," 220.
5 Wittgenstein, *Philosophical Investigations*, 580.
6 Coburn, "A Neglected Use of Theological Language," 221.
7 Coburn, "A Neglected Use of Theological Language," 221.
8 William Brenner, "D.Z. Phillips and Classical Theism," *New Blackfriars* 90, no. 1025 (2009): 34. Emphasis in the original.
9 Coburn, "A Neglected Use of Theological Language," 224.
10 Coburn, "A Neglected Use of Theological Language," 228.
11 Coburn, "A Neglected Use of Theological Language," 227.
12 Ludwig Wittgenstein, *Culture and Value*, trans. Peter Winch (Chicago: The University of Chicago Press, 1980), 64.
13 John Cottingham, *Philosophy of Religion: Towards a More Humane Approach* (Cambridge: Cambridge University Press, 2014), 63. Kindle Edition.
14 Charles Taylor, *A Secular Age* (Cambridge, MA: The Belknap Press of Harvard University Press, 2007), 20.
15 Taylor, *A Secular Age*, 20.
16 Taylor, *A Secular Age*, 20.
17 Quoted in Maurice O'Connor Drury, *The Selected Writing of Maurice O'Connor Drury: On Wittgenstein, Philosophy, Religion, Psychiatry*, ed. John Hayes (London: Bloomsbury Academic, 2017), 100.

18 Simone Weil, *The Notebooks of Simone Weil Volume 1*, trans. Arthur Wills (New York: Routledge, 2004), 238.
19 Simone Weil, *Gravity and Grace* (Lincoln, NE: Bison Books, 1997) 19–20.
20 Denys Turner, *The Darkness of God: Negativity in Christian Mysticism* (Cambridge: Cambridge University Press, 1995) 20. Emphasis in the original.
21 Ludwig Wittgenstein, *Tractatus Logico-Philosophicus* (New York: Harcourt Brace & Co, 1922), 7.
22 D.Z. Phillips, *Faith after Foundationalism* (Boulder, CO: Westview Press, 1995), 264. Emphasis in the original.
23 Wittgenstein, *Philosophical Investigations*, 373.
24 Phillips, *Faith after Foundationalism*, 279. For a detailed and interesting account of how language can refer to God, which is related to the work of Wittgenstein but sufficiently different from what Phillips writes, see Hector, *Theology without Metaphysics*.
25 Phillips, *Faith after Foundationalism*, 289.
26 Jean Luc Marion, "In the Name: How to Avoid Speaking of 'Negative Theology,'" in *God, the Gift and Postmodernism*, ed. John D. Caputo and Michael J. Scanlon (Bloomington: Indiana University Press, 1999), 34.
27 Paul Tillich, *Systematic Theology, Volume 1* (Chicago: University of Chicago Press), 108. Kindle Edition.
28 Tillich, *Systematic Theology, Volume 1*, 109. Kindle Edition.
29 Denys Turner, "Apophaticism, Idolatry and the Claims of Reason," in *Silence and the Word: Negative Theology and Incarnation*, ed. Oliver Davis and Denys Turner (Cambridge: Cambridge University Press), 17.
30 Walter Chalmers Smith, "Immortal, Invisible, God Only Wise," quoted in C. Michael Hawn, "History of Hymns: 'Immortal, Invisible, God Only Wise,'" Discipleship Ministries, accessed July 11, 2018, https://www.umcdiscipleship.org/resources/history-of-hymns-immortal-invisible-god-only-wise.
31 See, Phillips, *Faith after Foundationalism*, 279.
32 Dietrich Bonhoeffer, *Letters and Papers from Prison*, ed. Eberhard Bethge (New York: Touchstone, 1997), 360.
33 What the grammar of the concept of God shows us is that not all concepts function by pointing to objects. The concept of God is such that it functions by showing how language breaks when it comes to referring to God, but it is in this brokenness of language that God is seen. For an expanded and nuanced account of the different ways that concepts function in relation to talk about God, see Hector, *Theology without Metaphysics*. Cambridge: Cambridge University Press, 2011. Hector recognizes the ill effects of applying concepts to God when he writes, "since God is infinite, boundless, measureless, and so on, which means that concepts cannot possibly be applied to God without cutting God down to their size—without turning God into 'God,' in other words" (49). Hector then goes on to show that there is a different way to think about

the function of concepts that is indeed more conducive to speaking about God without linguistically restricting the divine nature.

34 Bishop Kallistos Ware, *The Orthodox Way* (Crestwood, NY: St. Vladimir's Seminary Press, 1979), 13.
35 Quoted in Jules Evans, "The New Atheists Are Actually Transcendentalists," Philosophy for Life, posted January 24, 2014, accessed January 6, 2018, http://philosophyforlife.org/the-new-atheists-are-actually-transcendentalists.
36 Laura Sheahen, "Christopher Hitchens: 'Why Religion Poisons Everything,'" *SoMA Review*, accessed July 11, 2018, http://www.somareview.com/christopherhitchens.cfm.
37 Ludwig Wittgenstein, *Philosophical Occasions: 1912–1951*, ed. James Klagge and Alfred Nordmann (Indianapolis, IN: Hackett Publishing Company, 1996), 41.
38 Wittgenstein, *Philosophical Occasions*, 42. Emphasis added.
39 Coburn, *The Strangeness of the Ordinary*, 128.
40 David Foster Wallace, *This Is Water: Some Thoughts, Delivered on a Significant Occasion, about Living a Compassionate Life* (New York: Little, Brown and Company, 2009), 93. Kindle Edition.
41 Cottingham, *Philosophy of Religion*, 60. Kindle Edition.
42 Ludwig Wittgenstein, *Tractatus Logico-Philosophicus*, trans. C.K. Ogden (Mineola, NY: Dover Publications Inc., 1999), §6.4321. Emphasis in the original.
43 J.R. Jones, "Love as Perception of Meaning," in *Religion and Understanding*, ed. D.Z. Phillips (Oxford: Basil Blackwell, 1967), 143.
44 Jones, "Love as Perception of Meaning," 145. Emphasis in the original.
45 Wallace, *This Is Water*, 36–37. Kindle Edition.
46 Johnston, *Saving God*, 19.
47 John D. Caputo, *The Folly of God: A Theology of the Unconditional* (Salem, OR: Polebridge Press, 2016), Kindle Location 1764. Kindle Edition.
48 Ludwig Wittgenstein, *Culture and Value*, trans. Peter Winch (Chicago: The University of Chicago Press, 1980), 47.
49 This isn't to deny that people sometimes rationally present arguments for why they believe in God, but these arguments may be best seen as forms of self-reassurance rather than as an objective rational argument whose conclusion all reasonable people should agree on. In *Culture and Value*, Wittgenstein writes, "A proof of God's existence ought really to be something by means of which one could convince oneself that God exists. But I think that what believers who have furnished such proofs have wanted to do is give their 'belief' an intellectual analysis and foundation, although they themselves would never have come to believe as a result of such proofs" (*Culture and Value*, 85).
50 For another recent account of the diversity of fideism and the acceptability of some aspects of what it claims for religious belief, see Mikel Burley, "Wittgenstein and the Study of Religion: Beyond Fideism and Atheism," in *Wittgenstein, Religion and*

Ethics: New Perspectives from Philosophy and Theology, ed. Mikel Burley (London: Bloomsbury Press, 2018), 49–75.
51 Hilary Putnam, *The Many Faces of Realism* (LaSalle, IL: Open Court, 1987), 18.
52 Kai Nielsen, "Wittgensteinian Fideism," *Philosophy* 42, no. 161 (1967): 191–209.
53 See Kai Nielsen and D.Z. Phillips, *Wittgensteinian Fideism?* (London: SCM Press, 2005).
54 Of course, a "form of life" that only involves counting objects is not much of a form of life at all since it excludes most of what we mean when we speak of a life. In real life, people share numerous ways of assessing the value of life, and a great overlap exists in thinking ethically about how others should be treated. It is this ethical agreement that generally allows us to apply ethical principles across context and condemn certain practices as morally wrong. It should also be mentioned that from within certain practices, we can come to believe that our way of assessing life is justified and would be beneficial as a universal maxim, but this can only occur if there is an overlap between the internal claims that are being universalized and the ethical lives of those in diverse cultures (I think something like the religious command to "love your neighbor" is just such a command). Philosophical fideism does not entail relativism, although working out an ethical view that is common (or should be common) to something called the "human form of life"—the life which all of us share—would take some work. For a good read that is at least somewhat related to my discussion, see James D. Wallace, *Norms and Practices* (Ithaca, NY: Cornell University Press, 2008). For a defense of the fact that there are interrelated language games, see Rush Rhees, *Wittgenstein and the Possibility of Discourse*, ed. D.Z. Phillips (Oxford: Blackwell Publishing, 2006).
55 Kai Nielsen, *An Introduction to the Philosophy of Religion* (New York: Macmillan Press, 1982), 65.
56 Ludwig Wittgenstein, *Vermischte Bemerkungen* (Frankfurt, Germany: Suhrkamp Verlag, 1977), 46. Quoted in Norman Malcolm, *Wittgenstein: A Religious Point of View?*, ed. Peter Winch (Ithaca, NY: Cornell University Press, 1993), 17.
57 Nielsen, "Wittgensteinian Fideism," 193.
58 Nielsen, *An Introduction to the Philosophy of Religion*, 66.
59 Nielsen, *An Introduction to the Philosophy of Religion*, 66–67.
60 Rush Rhees, *Wittgenstein and the Possibility of Discourse*, ed. D.Z. Phillips (Cambridge: Cambridge University Press, 1998).
61 Bolger, *Kneeling at the Altar of Science*.
62 D.Z. Phillips, "Philosophy, Theology and the Reality of God," in *Wittgenstein and Religion* (New York: St. Martin's Press, 1993), 2.
63 Phillips, "Philosophy, Theology and the Reality of God," 2. Emphasis in the original.
64 D.Z. Phillips, *Death and Immortality* (London: Macmillan, 1970), 55. Emphasis in the original.
65 Phillips, "Philosophy, Theology and the Reality of God," 3.
66 William H. Brenner, "D.Z. Phillips and Classical Theism," New BlackFriars, December 2008, 18.

67 Ludwig Wittgenstein, *On Certainty*, ed. G.E.M. Anscombe and G.H. von Wright (New York: Harper & Row Publishers, 1969), 110.
68 Wittgenstein, *On Certainty*, 205.
69 John H. Whittaker, "At the End of Reason Comes Persuasion," in *The Possibilities of Sense*, ed. John H. Whittaker. (New York: Palgrave, 2002), 142. Emphasis in the original.
70 Wittgenstein, *Culture and Value*, 64.
71 Wittgenstein, *On Certainty*, 559.

Chapter 3

1 Flannery O'Connor, "Parker's Back," in *The Complete Stories* (New York: Farrar, Straus and Giroux, 1971), 510. Kindle Edition.
2 O'Connor, "Parker's Back," 510. Kindle Edition.
3 O'Connor, "Parker's Back," 514. Kindle Edition.
4 O'Connor, "Parker's Back," 520. Kindle Edition.
5 O'Connor, "Parker's Back," 520. Kindle Edition.
6 O'Connor, "Parker's Back," 521. Kindle Edition.
7 O'Connor, "Parker's Back," 522. Kindle Edition. Emphasis added.
8 O'Connor, "Parker's Back," 525–526. Kindle Edition.
9 O'Connor, "Parker's Back," 527. Kindle Edition.
10 O'Connor, "Parker's Back," 528. Kindle Edition.
11 O'Connor, "Parker's Back," 529. Kindle Edition.
12 O'Connor, "Parker's Back," 530. Kindle Edition.
13 Nicholas Lash, *Easter in Ordinary: Reflections on Human Experience and the Knowledge of God* (Notre Dame, IN: University of Notre Dame Press, 1990), 180.
14 Friedrich Nietzsche, *The Will to Power* quoted in Walter Kaufmann, *Nietzsche: Philosopher, Psychologist, Antichrist* (Princeton, NJ: Princeton University Press, 1974), 343.
15 Joel Osteen, "The Power of Forgiveness," Joel Osteen Ministries, accessed August 3, 2018, https://www.joelosteen.com/Pages/Blog.aspx?blogid=13347.
16 Daniel L. Migliore, *Faith Seeking Understanding: An Introduction to Christian Theology* (Grand Rapids, MI: Eerdmans Publishing Co., 1991), 182. Kindle Edition.
17 The fact that human beings stand in need of forgiveness might also be taken as part of the objective side of atonement.
18 Dietrich Bonhoeffer, *The Cost of Discipleship* (New York: Touchstone, 1995), 43.
19 Bonhoeffer, *The Cost of Discipleship*, 43.
20 Bonhoeffer, *The Cost of Discipleship*, 43–44.
21 Bonhoeffer, *The Cost of Discipleship*, 45. Emphasis in the original.
22 Paul Tillich, *Systematic Theology, Volume 2* (Chicago: University of Chicago Press, 1957), 66. Kindle Edition.

23 See, Ernest Becker, *The Denial of Death* (New York: Free Press Paperbacks, 1973).
24 Simone Weil, *Gravity and Grace*, trans. Emma Crawford and Mario von der Ruhr (New York: Routledge, 2004), 16.
25 See Paul Tillich, *The Courage to Be* (New Haven, CT: Yale University Press, 2000).
26 Patrick Horn, "D.Z. Phillips on Christian Immortality," *International Journal for Philosophy of Religion* 71 (2012): 45.
27 Weil, *Gravity and Grace*, 30.
28 Weil, *Gravity and Grace*, 26.
29 Simone Weil, *Waiting on God* (New York: Routledge, 2009), 87–88.
30 These sorts of phrases need not be taken to posit the existence of a "place" where the recompense will be meted out, but they often are taken that way.
31 Rush Rhees, "Natural Theology," in *Without Answers* (London: Routledge, 1969).
32 Horn, "D.Z. Phillips on Christian Immortality," 45.
33 Wittgenstein, *Tractatus Logico-Philosophicus*, § 6.4312. Quoted in D.Z. Phillips, *Recovering Religious Concepts: Closing Epistemic Divides* (New York: Saint Martin's Press, 2000), 151. Emphasis in the original.
34 Weil, *Gravity and Grace*. Quoted in Phillips, *Death and Immortality*, 53.
35 Phillips, *Death and Immortality*, 53.
36 Wittgenstein, *Tractatus Logico-Philosophicus*, § 6.4312.
37 Weil, *Gravity and Grace*, 37.
38 Marcus Borg, *Days of Awe and Wonder: How to Be a Christian in the 21st Century* (New York: HarperCollins), 244.
39 David Hume, *Writings on Religion*, ed. Antony Flew (Chicago: Open Court, 1992), 261.
40 Hume, *Writings on Religion*, 266.
41 Phillips, *The Problem of Evil and the Problem of God*.
42 John Hick, "An Irenaean Theodicy," in *Encountering Evil: Live Options in Theodicy*, ed. Stephen T. Davis (Louisville, KY: Westminster John Knox Press, 2001), 50.
43 Quoted in Howard Wettstein, *The Significance of Religious Experience* (Oxford: Oxford University Press, 2012), 160. Kindle Edition.
44 Blaise Pascal, *Pensées*, trans. A.J. Krailsheimer (London: Penguin Books, 1995).Quoted in Rozelle-Stone, *Simone Weil and Theology*, 75.
45 Rozelle-Stone, *Simone Weil and Theology*, 75.
46 Phillips, *The Problem of Evil & the Problem of God*, Kindle Locations 880–881. Kindle Edition.
47 Johnston, *Saving God*, 115. Kindle Edition. Emphasis in the original.
48 Wettstein, *The Significance of Religious Experience*, 152.
49 Wettstein, *The Significance of Religious Experience*, 155.
50 Albert Camus, *The Plague* (New York: Vintage Press, 1991), 218.
51 Fyodor Dostoyevsky, *The Brothers Karamazov*, trans. David McDuff (London: Penguin, 1993), 274. Quoted in Nick Trakakis, *The End of Philosophy of Religion* (London: Continuum, 2008), 20–21. Kindle Edition.

52 Dostoyevsky, *The Brothers Karamazov*, 281. Quoted in Trakakis, *The End of Philosophy of Religion*, 21–22. Kindle Edition.
53 Dostoyevsky, *The Brothers Karamazov*, 282. Quoted in Trakakis, *The End of Philosophy of Religion*, 22–23. Kindle Edition. Emphasis in the original.
54 D.Z. Phillips, *Religion and Friendly Fire: Examining Assumptions in Contemporary Philosophy of Religion* (New York: Taylor and Francis), 59. Kindle Edition.
55 Cottingham, *Philosophy of Religion*, 5–6. Kindle Edition.
56 Johnston, *Saving God*, 16. Kindle Edition.
57 Phillips, *Death and Immortality*, 55. Emphasis in the original.
58 Ludwig Wittgenstein, *Lectures and Conversations on Aesthetics, Psychology and Religious Belief*, ed. Cyril Barrett (Berkeley: University of California Press, 1966), 66. Brackets appear in the original.
59 Wittgenstein, *Lectures and Conversations*, 59.
60 Wittgenstein, *Lectures and Conversations*, 59.
61 Wittgenstein, *Philosophical Investigations*, 522.
62 Wittgenstein, *Philosophical Investigations*, 522. Emphasis in the original.
63 Wittgenstein, *Lectures and Conversations*, 72. Emphasis in the original.
64 Wittgenstein, *Lectures and Conversations*, 63.
65 Wittgenstein, *Lectures and Conversations*, 56.
66 Lissa McCullough, *The Religious Philosophy of Simone Weil: An Introduction* (Library of Modern Religion) (New York: I.B.Tauris & Co Ltd, 2014), 171. Kindle Edition.
67 Rozelle-Stone, *Simone Weil and Theology* (Philosophy and Theology), 81. Kindle Edition.
68 Phillips, *Death and Immortality*, 54.
69 Phillips, *Death and Immortality*, 54–55.
70 Phillips, *Recovering Religious Concepts*, 154.
71 Phillips, *Recovering Religious Concepts*, 154.
72 Phillips, *Recovering Religious Concepts*, 148.
73 Phillips, *Recovering Religious Concepts*, 155.
74 Phillips, *The Problem of Evil & the Problem of God*, Kindle Locations 2370–2373. Kindle Edition. Emphasis in the original.
75 Phillips. *The Problem of Evil & the Problem of God*, Kindle Location 2384–2386. Kindle Edition.
76 Wettstein, *The Significance of Religious Experience*, 155.
77 Phillips, *The Problem of Evil & the Problem of God*, Kindle Locations 2403–2404. Kindle Edition.

Chapter 4

1 See, D.Z. Phillips, *Religion and the Hermeneutics of Contemplation* (Cambridge: Cambridge University Press, 2001).

2   D.Z. Phillips, *Philosophy's Cool Place* (Ithaca, NY: Cornell University Press, 1999), 11.
3   Phillips, *Philosophy's Cool Place*, 11.
4   Phillips, *Philosophy's Cool Place*, 10.
5   Much of what I say here about the search for a univocal concept of truth as well as my outline of a basic deflationary theory of truth is indebted to the writing of Paul Horwich, especially his *Truth-Meaning-Reality* (Oxford: Oxford University Press, 2010) and *Truth* (Oxford: Oxford University Press, 1998). Horwich's work is very well-argued and quite detailed, so any mistakes I have made in trying to simplify things he might have said are purely my own fault.
6   Horwich, *Truth*, 2. Emphasis in the original.
7   Pascal Engel, *Truth* (New York: Routledge, 2014), 10. Kindle Edition.
8   Gottlob Frege, "The Thought: A Logical Inquiry," trans. A.M. Quinton and Marcelle Quinton, in *Readings in the Philosophy of Language*, ed. Peter Ludlow (Cambridge, MA: The MIT Press, 1997), 12.
9   F.P. Ramsey, "Facts and Propositions," in *F.P. Ramsey: Critical Reassessments*, ed. Maria J. Fr Frápolli (London: Continuum Press, 2005), 56.
10 Alfred Tarski, "The Semantic Conception of Truth and the Foundation of Semantics," in *Semantics and the Philosophy of Language: A Collection of Readings*, ed. Leonard Linsky (Chicago: University of Illinois Press, 1970), 15.
11 Wittgenstein, *Philosophical Investigations*, §136.
12 Horwich, *Truth*, 5. Emphasis in the original.
13 Horwich, *Truth*, 6. Emphasis in the original.
14 Simon Blackburn, *Truth: A Guide* (Oxford: Oxford University Press, 2005), 60.
15 Engel, *Truth*, 10. Emphasis in the original.
16 Phillips, "Philosophy, Theology and the Reality of God," 3.
17 Peter Winch, *The Idea of a Social Science* (London: Routledge, 1958). Quoted in Phillips, *Wittgenstein and Religion*, 5.
18 Paul Horwich, "A Defense of Minimalism," in *Principles of Truth*, ed. Volker Halbach and Leon Horsten (Frankfurt: Verlag, 2003), 57.
19 Michael Dummett, *Thought and Reality* (Oxford: Clarendon Press, 2006), Kindle Location 447–448. Kindle Edition.
20 Horwich, *Truth*, 70. Emphasis in the original.
21 Sara Ellenbogen, *Wittgenstein's Account of Truth* (Albany: State University of New York Press, 2003), 6.
22 Ellenbogen, *Wittgenstein's Account of Truth*, 2.
23 Ludwig Wittgenstein, *The Blue and Brown Books* (Oxford: Oxford University Press, 1958), 24. Quoted in Rogers Albritton, "On Wittgenstein's Use of the Term 'Criterion,'" in *Wittgenstein: The Philosophical Investigations*, ed. George Pitcher (New York: Anchor Books, 1966), 231.
24 Albritton, "On Wittgenstein's Use of the Term 'Criterion,'" 249.

25 D.Z. Phillips, "Introduction: On Reading Wittgenstein on Religion," in *Religion and Wittgenstein's Legacy*, ed. D.Z. Phillips and Mario von der Ruhr (New York: Routledge, 2005), 5.
26 For a different account of the importance of recognizing a competent speaker, which sees the Holy Spirit as (at least partly) responsible for maintaining the sense of God talk from person to person, see Kevin Hector, *Theology without Metaphysics: God, Language, and the Spirit of Recognition* (Cambridge: Cambridge University Press, 2011).
27 Ellenbogen, *Wittgenstein's Account of Truth*, 6. Emphasis added.
28 Stanley Cavell, *The Claim of Reason: Wittgenstein, Skepticism, Morality and Tragedy* (Oxford: Oxford University Press, 1979), 9.
29 Cavell, *The Claim of Reason*, 47.
30 Stanley Cavell argues that there is some sense in which humans agree to participate in upholding criteria and which they can also choose to cease to participate (in some sense). See Part I and II of *The Claim of Reason* for Cavell's account of criteria. For a response to some of what Cavell has to say, see Phillips, *Philosophy's Cool Place*, chapter 5.
31 Wittgenstein, *Philosophical Investigations*, §241–242. Emphasis in the original.
32 Cavell, *The Claim of Reason*, 110. Emphasis in the original.
33 Espen Hammer, *Stanley Cavell: Skepticism, Subjectivity, and the Ordinary* (Oxford: Polity Press, 2002), 36.
34 Wittgenstein, *Philosophical Investigations*, §217.
35 Wittgenstein writes, "[T]he questions that we raise and our doubts depend on the fact that some propositions are exempt from doubt, are as it were like hinges on which those turn." Ludwig Wittgenstein, *On Certainty*, ed. G.E.M. Anscombe and G.H. von Wright, trans. G.E.M. Anscombe and D. Paul (Oxford: Blackwell, 1969), 341.
36 Michael Williams, "Wittgenstein, Truth and Certainty," in *Wittgenstein's Lasting Significance*, ed. Max Kölbel and Bernhard Weiss (London: Routledge, 2004), 250. Emphasis in the original.
37 Wittgenstein, *The Blue and Brown Books*, 24–25. Quoted in Anthony Kenny, *The Wittgenstein Reader*, 2nd ed. (Oxford: Blackwell Publishing, 2006), 127. Emphasis added.
38 John V. Canfield, *Wittgenstein: Language and the World* (Amherst: University of Massachusetts Press, 1981), 36.
39 Canfield, *Wittgenstein: Language and the World*, 36.
40 Wittgenstein, *The Blue and Brown Books*, 24. Quoted in, Albritton, "On Wittgenstein's Use of the Term 'Criterion,'" 231.
41 D.Z. Phillips, *Introducing Philosophy* (Cambridge, MA: Blackwell Publishers, 1996), 67.
42 Phillips, *Philosophy's Cool Place*, 91.

43 Cavell, *The Claim of Reason*, 45. Emphasis in the original.
44 Hammer, *Stanley Cavell*, 32. Emphasis in the original.
45 Cavell, *The Claim of Reason*, 47. Emphasis in the original. Part of the problem in what Cavell writes here is his statement that criteria are "only human." Cavell knows that putting "only" in front of "human" is not a philosophical argument. The fact that criteria are part of the human form of life (or "human life form") means that there is already a complexity built into the existence of criteria so much so that using "only" is a bit of a sophomoric trick that should be dismissed.
46 Phillips, *Introducing Philosophy*, 66.
47 Phillips, *Introducing Philosophy*, 66. Emphasis in the original.
48 Cavell, *The Claim of Reason*, 178–179.
49 D.Z. Phillips, *Faith and Philosophical Enquiry* (New York: Routledge, 1970), 4. Kindle Edition.
50 For a different, but in some way related, view to what I have presented here, see, Hector, *Theology without Metaphysics*, and Kevin M. Cahill, *The Fate of Wonder: Wittgenstein's Critique of Metaphysics and Modernity* (New York: Columbia University Press, 2011).
51 Tillich, *Systematic Theology, Volume 1*, 163. Kindle Edition.
52 For the most detailed discussion of Tillich's view on God, see Tillich, *System Theology Volume 1*. Especially part II, "Being and God."
53 Tillich, *Systematic Theology, Volume 1*, 60.
54 Tillich, *Systematic Theology, Volume 1*, 64.
55 Tillich, *Systematic Theology, Volume 1*, 61–62.
56 Paul Tillich, *The Courage to Be* (New Haven, CT: Yale University Press, 1980), 155. Kindle Edition.
57 Tillich, *Systematic Theology, Volume 1*, 113.
58 Tillich, *The Courage to Be*, 43. Kindle Edition.
59 Tillich, *The Courage to Be*, 155.
60 Tillich, *Systematic Theology, Volume 1*, 211.
61 Tillich, *Systematic Theology, Volume 1*, 235.
62 Tillich, *Systematic Theology, Volume 1*, 166.
63 Tillich, *Systematic Theology, Volume 1*, 64. For a nice discussion of Tillich's philosophical background relating to his use of the concept of Being-itself, see George Pattison, *Paul Tillich's Philosophical Theology: A Fifty-Year Reappraisal* (New York: Palgrave, 2015).
64 Pattison, *Paul Tillich's Philosophical Theology*, 6. Kindle Edition.
65 Tillich, *Systematic Theology, Volume 1*, 238–239. The idea that God described as Being-itself is nonsymbolic is not without some controversy, even in the writings of Tillich himself. For example, in *The Courage to Be*, 179, Tillich writes, "(and every assertion about being-itself is either metaphorical or symbolic)."

For a discussion of this topic, see Martin Leiner, "Tillich on God," in *The Cambridge Companion to Paul Tillich* (Cambridge: Cambridge University Press, 2008), chapter 3. Also see, Robert C. Coburn, "God, Revelation and Religious Truth: Some Themes and Problems in the Theology of Paul Tillich," *Faith and Philosophy* 13, no. 1 (1996): 3–33.

66 Tillich, *Systematic Theology, Volume 1*, 235.
67 Tillich, *Systematic Theology, Volume 1*, 236.
68 Tillich, *Systematic Theology, Volume 1*, 205.
69 Simone Weil, *Gravity and Grace*, trans. Emma Crawford and Mario van der Ruhr (New York: Routledge Classics, 2004), 115.
70 Weil, *Gravity and Grace*, 55.
71 Rozelle-Stone, *Weil and Theology*, 15. Kindle Edition.
72 Weil, *Gravity and Grace*, 9.
73 Weil, *Gravity and Grace*, 13.
74 Alexander Nava, *The Mystical and Prophetic Thought of Simone Weil and Gustavo Gutiérrez: Reflections on the Mystery and Hiddenness of God* (Albany: State University of New York Press, 2001), 45.
75 Weil, *Gravity and Grace*, 10. Quoted in Simone Weil, *Love in the Void*, ed. Laurie Gagne (Walden, NY: Plough Publishing House, 2018), 75.
76 Weil, *Gravity and Grace*, 110.
77 Simone Weil, *Waiting on God* (New York: Routledge, 2010), 48.
78 Weil, *Gravity and Grace*, 30.
79 Weil, *Gravity and Grace*, 32.
80 Stephen Plant, *Simone Weil: A Brief Introduction* (Maryknoll, NY: Orbis Books, 2007), 42.
81 Weil, *Gravity and Grace*, 34. Emphasis in the original.
82 Ludwig Wittgenstein, *Tractatus Logico-Philosophicus*, trans. C.K. Ogden (Mineola, NY: Dover Publications Inc., 1999), 33.
83 Wittgenstein, *Tractatus*, 33.
84 For a more complete view of the *Tractatus*, you may want to refer to H.O. Mounce, *Wittgenstein's Tractatus: An Introduction* (Chicago: University of Chicago Press, 1981). For a good look at how Wittgenstein's work in the *Tractatus* relates to his later philosophy, see John Koethe, *The Continuity of Wittgenstein's Thought* (Ithaca, NY: Cornell University Press, 1996).
85 Avrum Stroll, *Wittgenstein* (Oxford: One World Publications, 2007).
86 Wittgenstein, *Tractatus*, 51.
87 Wittgenstein, *Tractatus*, 107–108.
88 Wittgenstein, *Tractatus*, 88. Emphasis in the original.
89 Wittgenstein, *Tractatus*, 108.
90 For a discussion of scientism and religion, see my *Kneeling at the Altar of Science*.
91 Jones, "Love as Perception of Meaning," 144. Emphasis in the original.

92 Wittgenstein, *Tractatus*, 105–107. Emphasis in the original.
93 For a discussion of Wittgenstein's idea of the mystical, see James R. Atkinson, *The Mystical in Wittgenstein's Early Writings* (New York: Routledge, 2009),' and Russell Nieli, *Wittgenstein: From Mysticism to Ordinary Language* (Albany: State University of New York Press, 1987). This also raises a lot of questions about just what sort of nonsense Wittgenstein meant to present in the *Tractatus*. Some take it that Wittgenstein meant that all the things he wrote leading up to the end of the *Tractatus* were literally good old-fashion nonsense that had no deeper meaning. I think this view is both unwarranted and, frankly, silly. Since I have to leave my comments there for now, here are a few of the many available resources on this topic: D.Z. Phillips, *Philosophy's Cool Place*. *The New Wittgenstein*, ed. Alice Crary and Rupert Read (London: Routledge, 2000). Kevin Cahill, *The Fate of Wonder*, New York: Columbia University Press, 2011.
94 Jones, "Love as Perception of Meaning," 145. Emphasis in the original.
95 John Whittaker, "D.Z. Phillips and Reasonable Belief," *International Journal for Philosophy of Religion* 63 (2008): 124. Emphasis in the original.
96 Whittaker, "D.Z. Phillips and Reasonable Belief," 119.
97 R.B. Braithwaite, *An Empiricist's View of the Nature of Religious Belief* (Cambridge: Cambridge University Press, 1955), 15.
98 Braithwaite, *An Empiricist's View of the Nature of Religious Belief*, 16.
99 Braithwaite, *An Empiricist's View of the Nature of Religious Belief*, 18.
100 Braithwaite, *An Empiricist's View of the Nature of Religious Belief*, 21. Emphasis in the original.
101 Braithwaite, *An Empiricist's View of the Nature of Religious Belief*, 19.
102 D.Z. Phillips. *Religion without Explanation* (Oxford: Basil Blackwell, 1976), 144.
103 Whittaker, "D.Z. Phillips and Reasonable Belief," 123.

Chapter 5

1 Leo Tolstoy, *War and Peace*, trans. Constance Garnett (New York: The Modern Library, 2002), 1050.
2 Leo Tolstoy, *The Death of Ivan Ilyich*, trans. Rosemary Edmonds (London: Penguin Books, 1960), 160.
3 Weil, *First and Last Notebooks*, 147.
4 Mark Johnston, *Surviving Death* (Princeton, NJ: Princeton University Press, 2010), 4210–4213. Kindle Edition.
5 The best works on the subject of *agape*, for my money at least, are Anders Nygren, *Agape and Eros* (Philadelphia, PA: Westminster Press, 1953); Gene Outka, *Agape: An Ethical Analysis* (New Haven, CT: Yale University Press, 1972); and Nicholas

Wolterstorff, *Justice in Love* (Grand Rapids, MI: William B. Eerdmans Publishing, 2011).

6   Emmanuel Levinas, *Totality and Infinity*, trans. Alphonso Lingis (Dordrecht: Kluwer Academic Publishers, 1991), 78.

7   Leo Tolstoy, *The Gospel in Tolstoy: Selections from His Short Stories, Spiritual Writings & Novels* (Walden, NY: Plough Publishing House, 2015), Kindle Locations 735–736. Kindle Edition.

8   Tolstoy, *The Gospel in Tolstoy*, Kindle Location 764–765. Kindle Edition.

9   Tolstoy, *The Gospel in Tolstoy*, Kindle Location 780–781. Kindle Edition.

10 Tolstoy, *The Gospel in Tolstoy*, Kindle Location 787–788. Kindle Edition.

11 Tolstoy, *The Gospel in Tolstoy*, Kindle Location 791–792. Kindle Edition.

12 Tolstoy, *The Gospel in Tolstoy*, Kindle Location 793–794. Kindle Edition.

13 Tolstoy, *The Gospel in Tolstoy*, Kindle Location 794–796. Kindle Edition.

14 Simone Weil, letter to Joë Bousquet, April 13, 1942. Quoted in Simone Pétrement, *Simone Weil: A Life*, trans. Raymond Rosenthal (New York: Pantheon Books, 1976), 462.

15 Susan Salter Reynolds, "A Time for Us," Los Angeles Times (Los Angeles, CA), January 06, 2008.

16 Nel Noddings, *Caring: A Feminine Approach to Ethics and Moral Education*, 2nd ed. (Berkeley: University of California Press, 2003), Kindle Locations 510. Kindle Edition.

17 Noddings, *Caring*, Kindle Locations 512–514. Kindle Edition.

18 Miklos Vetö, *The Religious Metaphysics of Simone Weil*, trans. Joan Dargan (Albany: State University of New York Press, 1994), 45.

19 Paul Ramsey, *Basic Christian Ethics* (Louisville, KY: Westminster/John Knox Press, 1950), 92.

20 Ramsey, *Basic Christian Ethics*, 92.

21 Tolstoy, *War and Peace*, 1050.

22 See Peter Singer, "Famine, Affluence, and Morality," *Philosophy and Public Affairs* 1, no. 1 (1972): 229–243. Also see Peter Singer, "The Drowning Child and the Expanding Circle," *New Internationalist*, 1997, https://www.utilitarian.net/singer/by/199704-.htm and Peter Singer, *Practical Ethics*, 3rd ed. (Cambridge: Cambridge University Press, 2011), especially chapter 8.

23 Peter Singer, *The Life You Can Save* (New York: Random House, 2010), 3.

24 Singer, *Practical Ethics*, 199. Kindle Edition.

25 Singer, *Practical Ethics*, 199. Kindle Edition.

26 Singer, *Practical Ethics*, 191. Kindle Edition.

27 Singer, *The Life You Can Save*, 15–16. A similar argument, though worded slightly differently, can be found in Singer, *Practical Ethics*, 200.

28 Singer, *Practical Ethics*, 194. For a fuller explanation of these arguments, as well as answers to a variety of objections, you may want to refer to the following: Singer,

The Life You Can Save; Peter Singer, *The Most Good You Can Do: How Effective Altruism Is Changing Ideas about Living Ethically* (New Haven, CT: Yale University Press, 2015); and Singer, *Practical Ethics*, chapter 8. Peter Unger, *Living High and Letting Die: Our Illusion of Innocence* (Oxford: Oxford University Press, 1996). Also, for an example of Singer's work placed in dialogue with Christian Theology and Ethics, see Camosy, *Peter Singer and Christian Ethics* (Cambridge: Cambridge University Press, 2012).

29 Johnston, *Surviving Death*, Kindle Locations 2847–2849. Kindle Edition.
30 Wallace, *This Is Water*, 33. Kindle Edition.
31 Wallace, *This Is Water*, 36.
32 Wallace, *This Is Water*, 38.
33 Johnston, *Surviving Death*, Kindle Locations 2503–2507. Kindle Edition.
34 Richard Taylor, *With Heart and with Mind: A Philosopher Looks at Nature, Love and Death* (New York: Saint Martin's Press, 1973), 28.
35 Johnston, *Surviving Death*, Kindle Locations 3389–3390. Kindle Edition.
36 Johnston, *Surviving Death*, Kindle Locations 3390–3391. Kindle Edition.
37 Johnston, *Surviving Death*, Kindle Locations 3402. Kindle Edition.
38 Johnston, *Surviving Death*, Kindle Locations 3396–3399. Kindle Edition.
39 Johnston, *Surviving Death*, Kindle Locations 3405–3407. Kindle Edition.
40 Johnston, *Surviving Death*, Kindle Locations 3410–3411. Kindle Edition.
41 Johnston, *Surviving Death*, Kindle Locations 3423–3424. Kindle Edition.
42 Johnston, *Surviving Death*, Kindle Locations 3440–3441. Kindle Edition.
43 Leo Tolstoy, *The Death of Ivan Ilyich and Other Stories*, trans. Rosemary Edmonds (New York: Penguin, 1960), 137.
44 Johnston, *Surviving Death*, Kindle Locations 3434–3436. Kindle Edition.
45 Johnston, *Surviving Death*, Kindle Locations 3445–3447. Kindle Edition.
46 Wallace, *This is Water*, 36.
47 Johnston, *Surviving Death*, Kindle Locations 2506–2507. Kindle Edition.
48 This example comes from Alcoholics Anonymous, *Alcoholics Anonymous,* 4th Edition (New York: A.A. World Services, 2001). See chapter 5.
49 Ryan Holiday, *Ego Is the Enemy* (New York: Penguin Publishing Group, 2016), 2–3.
50 Tillich offers a longer discussion of this topic referring to "separation" as "estrangement" in Tillich, *Systematic Theology, Volume 2*. Here Tillich relates the condition of estrangement to unbelief, hubris, and concupiscence.
51 Paul Tillich, "You Are Accepted," in *The Shaking of the Foundations* (New York: Charles Scribner's Sons, 1948), 154. Emphasis in the original.
52 Tillich, "You Are Accepted," 155.
53 Tillich, "You Are Accepted," 157.
54 Taylor, *With Heart and with Mind*, 8.
55 Tillich, "You Are Accepted," 157.

56 Tillich, "You Are Accepted," 158.
57 Tillich, "You Are Accepted," 158.
58 Tillich, "You Are Accepted," 158.
59 Tillich, "You Are Accepted," 159.
60 Terry Eagleton, *Radical Sacrifice* (New Haven, CT: Yale University Press, 2018), 47.
61 Tillich, "You Are Accepted," 159.
62 Tillich, "You Are Accepted," 159.
63 Paul Tillich, *Dynamics of Faith* (New York: HarperCollins, 1957), 130. Kindle Edition.
64 Tillich, "You Are Accepted," 159.
65 Tillich, "You Are Accepted," 162. Emphasis in the original.
66 Eberhard Jüngel, *God as the Mystery of the World* (Grand Rapids, MI: Eerdmans Publishing Co., 1983), 314.
67 Alain Boublil and Claude-Michel Schönberg, *Les Misérables: The Complete Libretto*, accessed July 30, 2018, http://point11.tripod.com/lmlyric1.htm.
68 Feuerbach, *The Essence of Christianity*, 52.
69 Feuerbach, *The Essence of Christianity*, 53.
70 Caputo, *The Folly of God*, Kindle Locations 1759–1761. Kindle Edition.
71 Lissa McCullough, *The Religious Philosophy of Simone Weil: An Introduction* (London: I.B. Tauris, 2007), 7. Kindle Edition.
72 Frederick Buechner, *Beyond Words: Daily Readings in the ABC's of Faith* (New York: HarperCollins, 2004), 169.
73 Dana Gioia, "The Epistle of Paul to the Philippians," in *Incarnation: Contemporary Writer's on the New Testament*, ed. Alfred Corn (New York: Viking Penguin, 1990), 186.
74 Sylvia Walsh, "Moral Character and Temptation," in *The Wisdom of the Christian Faith*, ed. Paul Moser and Michael T. McFall (Cambridge: Cambridge University Press, 2012), 121.
75 Walsh, "Moral Character and Temptation," 132.
76 Walsh, "Moral Character and Temptation," 133.
77 Walsh, "Moral Character and Temptation," 133.
78 Bonhoeffer, *The Cost of Discipleship*, 89.
79 Taylor, *With Heart and with Mind*, 67.
80 *Totality and Infinity*. See note 6.
81 Emmanuel Levinas, "A Religion for Adults," in *Difficult Freedom: Essays on Judaism*, trans. Sean Hand (Baltimore: The John Hopkins University Press, 1997), 17. Quoted in, Fiona Ellis, "Murdoch and Levinas on God and Good," *European Journal for Philosophy of Religion* 1, no. 2 (2009): 63–87, 78.
82 Dietrich Bonhoeffer, *Letters and Papers from Prison*, ed. Eberhard Bethge, trans. R.H. Fuller (New York: Macmillan, 1972), 360.

Introduction to Part Two

1   Martha Nussbaum, *Love's Knowledge: Essays on Philosophy and Literature* (Oxford: Oxford University Press, 1990), 3.
2   *With Heart and Mind: A Philosopher Looks at Faith, Love and Death* (New York: St. Martin's Press, 1973), Quote is from section titled "Proem." No Page number given.

Chapter 6

1   E.E. Evans-Pritchard, *Witchcraft, Oracles, and Magic among the Azande* (Oxford: Clarendon Press, 1976). Azande and Zande are sometimes used interchangeably; at other times, Azande will be used as the plural of Zande.
2   Francis Crick, *Life Itself* (New York: Simon and Schuster, 1982).
3   Nancy Arrowsmith, *Field Guide to the Little People: A Curious Journey into the Hidden Realm of Elves, Faeries, Hobgoblins & Other Not-so-Mythical Creatures* (Woodbury, MN: Llewellyn, 2009).
4   Laura Blumenfeld, "Proctor Gamble's Devil of a Problem," *The Washington Post*, July 15, 1991.
5   See, Gary Alan Fine and Bill Ellis, *The Global Grapevine: Why Rumors of Terrorism, Immigration and Trade Matter* (Oxford: Oxford University Press, 2010), 49–50.
6   "Divorce and the Deficit," *New York Times*, October 9, 1985, accessed August 21, 2018, https://www.nytimes.com/1985/10/09/us/divorce-and-the-deficit.html.
7   T.S. Eliot, *Four Quartets* (New York: Houghton Mifflin Harcourt Publishing, 1943), Kindle Locations 316–317. Kindle Edition.
8   George Santayana, *The Last Puritan: A Memoir in the Form of a Novel* (New York: Charles Scribner's Sons, 1936), 579.
9   Quoted in *Nicene and Post-Nicene Fathers, Vol. V: St. Augustine: Anti-Pelagian Writings*, ed. Philip Schaff (New York: Cosimo Classics, 2007), 482.
10 Soren Kierkegaard, *Eighteen Upbuilding Discourses*, ed. and trans. Howard V. Hong and Edna H. Hong (Princeton, NJ: Princeton University Press, 1990), 124.
11 Soren Kierkegaard, "Edifying Discourses," quoted in Nahum N. Glatzer, *The Dimensions of Job: A Study and Selected Readings* (Eugene, OR: Wipf and Stock Publishers, 2002), 268.
12 Frederick Buechner, *Godric* (New York: HarperCollins, 1980), 196.
13 T.S. Eliot, *The Cocktail Party* (New York: Hardcourt Inc., 1950), 126.
14 Eliot, *The Cocktail Party*, 141. Emphasis in the original.
15 Arthur I. Waskow, *God-Wrestling* (New York: Schocken Books, 1978), 2–3.

16 Waskow, *Godwrestling*, 11.
17 This was discovered in 1979. For a more recent account of the story, see John Noble Wilford, "Solving a Riddle Written in Silver," *New York Times*, September 28, 2004, accessed August 24, 2018, https://www.nytimes.com/2004/09/28/science/solving-a-riddle-written-in-silver.html.
18 Philip Larkin, *Poems: Selected and with an Introduction by Martin Amis* (London: Faber and Faber, 2011). Kindle Location 565. Kindle Edition.
19 Philip Larkin, *Philip Larkin Poems: Selected by Martin Amis* (London: Faber & Faber, 2011), Kindle Locations 374–375. Kindle Edition.

Chapter 7

1 The term "Turning World" comes from T.S. Eliot's "Burnt Norton," the first poem in *The Four Quartets*.
2 Barbara W. Tuchman, *A Distant Mirror: The Calamitous 14th Century* (New York: Random House, 2010).
3 Mill Writes, "The only freedom which deserves the name, is that of pursuing our own good in our own way." John Stuart Mill, *On Liberty*, quoted in Bruce Baum, *Rereading Power and Freedom in J.S. Mill* (Toronto: University of Toronto Press, 2000), 24.
4 *Smashed Potatoes: A Kids-Eye View of the Kitchen*, ed. Jane G. Martell (Boston, MA: Houghton Mifflin Harcourt, 1974), 3.
5 Quoted in, Lane Hall, *Works of Martin Luther: With Introduction and Notes, Vol. 2* (Philadelphia, PA: A.J. Holman Company, 1915).
6 Quoted in, Tom Gordon, *Look Well to This Day: A Year of Daily Reflections* (Glasgow: Wild Goose Publications, 2014), 66.
7 Quoted in, Mary Soames, *Clementine Churchill: The Biography of a Marriage* (New York: Houghton Mifflin Company, 2002), 424.
8 Meg Bogin, *The Path to Pain Control* (Boston, MA: Houghton Mifflin Company, 1982), xv.
9 Bogin, *The Path to Pain Control*, xvii.
10 Bogin, *The Path to Pain Control*, xviii–xix.
11 Quoted in, *Albert Schweitzer an Anthology*, ed. Charles R. Joy (Boston, MA: The Beacon Press, 1960), 120.
12 Soren Kierkegaard, *The Journal of Kierkegaard*, ed. and trans. Alexander Dru (Oxford: Oxford University Press, 1938), 326.
13 Simone Weil, "Human Personality," in *Simone Weil: Selected Works, Selected Essays, 1934–1943: Historical, Political, and Moral Writings*, trans. Richard Rees (Eugene, OR: Wipf & Stock, 2015), 27.

Chapter 8

1. Fyodor Dostoevsky, *The Brothers Karamazov*, trans. Constance Garnett (New York: Macmillan Company, 1922), 302.
2. Dostoevsky, *The Brothers Karamazov*, 303.
3. Dostoevsky, *The Brothers Karamazov*, 303.
4. Dostoevsky, *The Brothers Karamazov*, 304.
5. Dostoevsky, *The Brothers Karamazov*, 304.
6. Dostoevsky, *The Brothers Karamazov*, 304.
7. Dostoevsky, *The Brothers Karamazov*, 304.
8. Dostoevsky, *The Brothers Karamazov*, 304–305.
9. Dostoevsky, *The Brothers Karamazov*, 305.
10. Dostoevsky, *The Brothers Karamazov*, 305.
11. Dostoevsky, *The Brothers Karamazov*, 305.
12. Gerard Manley Hopkins, "God's Grandeur," *Poetry Foundation*, accessed August 22, 2018, https://www.poetryfoundation.org/poems/44395/gods-grandeur.
13. *Gospel of Thomas* saying 113. *Earlychristianwritings.com*, accessed August 22, 2018, http://www.earlychristianwritings.com/thomas/gospelthomas113.html.
14. The discussion of the first of the paradoxes derives, in large part, from Herbert Morris's paper "Shared Guilt," which appears in his book *On Guilt and Innocence* (Berkeley: University of California Press, 1976). The discussion of the second paradox is indebted to J.R. Jones's paper "Love as Perception of Meaning," which appears in Phillips, *Religion and Understanding*.

14. William Shakespeare, "Sonnet 29: When, in Disgrace with Fortunes and Men's Eyes," *Poetry Foundation*, accessed August 22, 2018, https://www.poetryfoundation.org/poems/45090/sonnet-29-when-in-disgrace-with-fortune-and-mens-eyes.

Chapter 9

1. David Vidal, "A 116-Year-Old's Good Advice," *New York Times*, January 1, 1976.
2. Vidal, "A 116-Year-Old's Good Advice."
3. Jane Brody, "Emotions Found to Influence Nearly Every Human Ailment," *New York Times*, 1983, accessed August 22, 2018, https://www.nytimes.com/1983/05/24/science/emotions-found-to-influence-nearly-every-human-ailment.html.
4. Brody, "Emotions Found to Influence Nearly Every Human Ailment."
5. Emily Dickenson, "A Little Madness in the Spring," quoted in Peter Corn, *Literature in America: An Illustrated History* (Cambridge: Cambridge University Press, 1989), 226.

6   Quoted in Merrill D. Peterson, *Lincoln in American Memory* (Oxford: Oxford University Press, 1994), 97.
7   Norman Cousins, *Anatomy of an Illness as Perceived by the Patient: Reflections on Healing and Regeneration* (New York: W.W. Norton & Company, 1979).
8   Cousins, *Anatomy of an Illness*, 44.
9   Sidney Harris, *Chalk Up Another One: The Best of Sidney Harris* (Washington, DC: AAAS Press, 1992), 81.
10 The radio program *The Aldrich Family* ran from the late 1930s to the early 1950s.
11 Richard Clarke Cabot and Russell Leslie Dicks, *The Art of Ministering to the Sick* (New York: The Macmillan Company, 1936), 66.
12 John Crowe Ransom, "Winter Remembered," *The Sewanee Review*, accessed August 25, 2018, https://thesewaneereview.com/john-crowe-ransom-winter-remembered/.
13 Roz Chast, *Theories of Everything: Selected, Collected, Health-inspected* (New York: Bloomsbury Publishing, 2006), no page numbers provided in the book.
14 Lewis Carroll, *Through the Looking-Glass* (Boston, MA: Lothrop Publishing Company, 1898), 150.
15 Lewis Carroll, *Alice's Adventures in Wonderland and Other Tales* (New York: Race Point Publishing, 2015), 423.
16 Mark Twain, *Adventures of Huckleberry Finn* (Clayton, DE: Prestwick House, 2005), 94.
17 Twain, *Adventures of Huckleberry Finn*, 95.
18 Twain, *Adventures of Huckleberry Finn*, 96–97.
19 Quoted in Alfred Habegger, *My Wars Are Laid Away in Books: The Life of Emily Dickenson* (New York: The Modern Library, 2001), 75.
20 The phrase "works of love" is borrowed from Kierkegaard's use of the term. See, Soren Kierkegaard, *Works of Love*, trans. Howard V. Hong and Edna H. Hong (Princeton, NJ: Princeton University Press, 1998).

Chapter 10

1   See, John Hollander, *The Work of Poetry* (New York: Columbia University Press), 114.
2   See, Richard Lederer, *The Revenge of Anguished English: More Accidental Assaults upon Our Language* (New York: St. Martin's Press, 2005), 17.
3   Oliver Sacks, *The Man Who Mistook His Wife for a Hat and Other Clinical Tales* (New York: Harper & Row Publishers, 1985), 195–213.
4   Sacks, *The Man Who Mistook His Wife for a Hat and Other Clinical Tales*, 196.
5   Sacks, *The Man Who Mistook His Wife for a Hat and Other Clinical Tales*, 196.
6   Sacks, *The Man Who Mistook His Wife for a Hat and Other Clinical Tales*, 199.
7   Sacks, *The Man Who Mistook His Wife for a Hat and Other Clinical Tales*, 199.
8   Henrik Ibsen, *A Doll's House* (Mineola, NY: Dover Publications, 1992).

9   George Eliot, *Middlemarch* (New York: Penguin Books, 1994).
10 Quoted in a commencement address given at Villanova by Ann Quindlen. The transcript can be viewed at Aoutschool.com, accessed September 1, 2018, http://www.aboutschool.com/graduation.htm.

Chapter 11

1   Susan Schnur, "Hers," *New York Times*, 1985, accessed August 25, 2018, https://www.nytimes.com/1985/08/15/garden/hers.html.
2   Charles Schultz, *The Complete Peanuts: 1985–1986* (Seattle: Fantagraphics Books, 2012), 153.
3   Schultz, *The Complete Peanuts*, 153.
4   Schultz, *The Complete Peanuts*, 153.
5   Schultz, *The Complete Peanuts*, 153.
6   Quoted in Ari Kohen, *In Defense of Human Rights: A Non-religious Grounding in a Pluralistic World* (New York: Routledge, 2007), 38.
7   Franz Kafka, *Letter to the Father/Brief an den Vater: Bilingual Edition*, trans. Ernst Kaiser and Eithne Wilkins (New York: Schocken Books, 1966), 17. Kindle Edition.
8   Kafka, *Letter to the Father*, 17.
9   Kafka, *Letter to the Father*, 17.
10 The Wittgenstein quote reads, "You remind me of someone who is looking through a closed window and cannot explain to himself the strange movements of a passer-by. He doesn't know what kind of a storm is raging outside and that this person is perhaps only with great effort keeping himself on his feet." Quoted in, Norman Malcolm, "Wittgenstein's Confessions," *London Review of Books* 3, no. 21 (1981): 16–18.
11 Martin Buber, *Tales of the Hasidism: The Early Masters/The Late Masters* (New York: Schocken Books, 1947).

Bibliography

Albritton, Rogers. "On Wittgenstein's Use of the Term 'Criterion.'" In *Wittgenstein: The Philosophical Investigations*, edited by George Pitcher, 231–250. New York: Anchor Books, 1966.

Alston, William P. *Divine Nature and Human Language: Essays in Philosophical Theology*. Ithaca, NY: Cornell University Press, 1989.

Anonymous. *Alcoholics Anonymous*, 4th ed. New York: A.A. World Services, 2001.

Armstrong, Karen. *The Case for God*. New York: Knopf Doubleday Publishing Group, 2009.

Arrowsmith, Nancy. *Field Guide to the Little People: A Curious Journey into the Hidden Realm of Elves, Faeries, Hobgoblins & Other Not-So-Mythical Creatures*. Woodbury, MN: Llewellyn, 2009.

Atkinson James R. *The Mystical in Wittgenstein's Early Writings*. New York: Routledge, 2009.

Auslander, Shalom. *Foreskin's Lament: A Memoir*. New York: Penguin Publishing Group, 2007.

Barfield, Owen. *Saving the Appearances: A Study in Idolatry*, 2nd ed. Middletown, CT: Wesleyan University Press, 1988.

Baum, Bruce. *Rereading Power and Freedom in J.S. Mill*. Toronto: University of Toronto Press, 2000.

Becker, Ernest. *The Denial of Death*. New York: Free Press Paperbacks, 1973.

Bell, Richard, ed. *Simone Weil's Philosophy of Culture, Readings toward a Divine Humanity*. Cambridge: Cambridge University Press, 1993.

Blackburn, Simon. *Truth: A Guide*. Oxford: Oxford University Press, 2005.

Blumenfeld, Laura. "Proctor Gamble's Devil of a Problem." *The Washington Post*, July 15, 1991.

Bogin, Meg. *The Path to Pain Control*. Boston, MA: Houghton Mifflin Company, 1982.

Bolger Robert. *Kneeling at the Altar of Science: The Mistaken Path of Contemporary Religious Scientism*. Eugene, OR: Pickwick Publication, 2012.

Bonhoeffer, Dietrich. *Letters and Papers from Prison*. Edited by Eberhard Bethge. New York: Touchstone, 1997.

Bonhoeffer, Dietrich. *The Cost of Discipleship*. New York: Touchstone, 1995.

Borg, Marcus. *Days of Awe and Wonder: How to Be a Christian in the 21st Century*. New York: HarperCollins, 2017.

Boubil, Alain and Claude-Michel Schönberg. *Les Misérables: The Complete Libretto*, 1980. Accessed July 30, 2018. http://point11.tripod.com/lmlyric1.htm. 68

Braithwaite, R.B. *An Empiricist's View of the Nature of Religious Belief*. Cambridge: Cambridge University Press, 1955.

Brenner, William. "D.Z. Phillips and Classical Theism." *New Blackfriars* 90, no. 1025 (January 2009): 17–37.

Brody, Jane. "Emotions Found to Influence Nearly Every Human Ailment." *New York Times*, 1983. https://www.nytimes.com/1983/05/24/science/emotions-found-to-influence-nearly-every-human-ailment.html.

Buber, Martin. *Tales of the Hasidism: The Early Masters/The Late Masters*. New York: Schocken Books, 1947.

Buechner, Frederick. *Beyond Words: Daily Readings in the ABC's of Faith*. New York: HarperCollins, 2004.

Buechner, Frederick. *Godric*. New York: HarperCollins, 1980.

Burley, Mikel. "Wittgenstein and the Study of Religion: Beyond Fideism and Atheism." In *Wittgenstein, Religion and Ethics: New Perspectives from Philosophy and Theology*, edited by Mikel Burley, 49–75. London: Bloomsbury Press, 2018.

Cabot, Richard C. and Russell Leslie Dicks. *The Art of Ministering to the Sick*. New York: The Macmillan Company, 1936.

Cahill, Kevin M. *The Fate of Wonder: Wittgenstein's Critique of Metaphysics and Modernity*. New York: Columbia University Press, 2011.

Camosy, Charles C. *Peter Singer and Christian Ethics*. Cambridge: Cambridge University Press, 2012.

Camus, Albert. *The Plague*. New York: Vintage Press, 1991.

Canfield, John V. *Wittgenstein: Language and the World*. Amherst: University of Massachusetts Press, 1981.

Caputo, John D. *The Folly of God: A Theology of the Unconditional*. Salem, OR: Polebridge Press, 2016. Kindle Edition.

Carroll, Lewis. *Alice's Adventures in Wonderland and Other Tales*. New York: Race Point Publishing, 2015.

Carroll, Lewis. *Through the Looking-Glass*. Boston, MA: Lothrop Publishing Company, 1898.

Cavell, Stanley. *The Claim of Reason: Wittgenstein, Skepticism, Morality and Tragedy*. Oxford: Oxford University Press, 1979.

Chast, Roz. *Theories of Everything: Selected, Collected, Health-inspected*. New York: Bloomsbury Publishing, 2006.

Coburn, Robert C. "God, Revelation and Religious Truth: Some Themes and Problems in the Theology of Paul Tillich." *Faith and Philosophy* 13, no. 1 (1996): 3–33.

Coburn, Robert C. *The Strangeness of the Ordinary: Problems and Issues in Contemporary Metaphysics*. Savage, MD: Rowman & Littlefield, 1990.

Coburn, Robert C. "A Neglected Use of Theological Language." In *New Essays on Religious Language*, edited by Dallas M. High, 215–235. New York: Oxford University Press, 1969.

Cottingham, John. *Philosophy of Religion: Towards a More Humane Approach*. Cambridge: Cambridge University Press, 2014. Kindle Edition.

Cousins, Norman. *Anatomy of an Illness as Perceived by the Patient: Reflections on Healing and Regeneration*. New York: W.W. Norton & Company, 1979.

Crary, Alice and Rupert Read, eds. *The New Wittgenstein*. London: Routledge, 2000.

Crick, Francis. *Life Itself*. New York: Simon and Schuster, 1982.

Davies, Brian. "The New Atheism: Its Virtues and Its Vices." *New Blackfriars* 92 (2011): 18–34.

Davies, Brian. *An Introduction to the Philosophy of Religion*, 3rd ed. Oxford: Oxford University Press, 2004.

Dawkins, Richard. *The God Delusion*. New York: Houghton Mifflin Company, 2006.

Dawkins, Richard. *River Out of Eden: A Darwinian View of Life*. New York: Basic Books, 1995.

Dostoyevsky, Fyodor. *The Brothers Karamazov*. Translated by David McDuff. London: Penguin, 1993.

Drury, Maurice O'Connor. *The Selected Writing of Maurice O'Connor Drury: On Wittgenstein, Philosophy, Religion, Psychiatry*. Edited by John Hayes. London: Bloomsbury Academic, 2017.

Dummett, Michael. *Thought and Reality*. Oxford: Clarendon Press, 2006. Kindle Edition.

Eagleton, Terry. *Radical Sacrifice*. New Haven, CT: Yale University Press, 2018.

Eagleton, Terry. "Lunging, Flailing, Mispunching." *London Review of Books* 28, no. 20 (2006): 32–34.

Eliot, George. *Middlemarch*. New York: Penguin Books, 1994.

Eliot, T.S. *Four Quartets*. New York: Houghton Mifflin, 1971. Kindle Edition.

Eliot, T.S. *The Cocktail Party*. New York: Hardcourt Inc., 1950.

Ellenbogen, Sara. *Wittgenstein's Account of Truth*. Albany: State University of New York Press, 2003.

Ellis, Fiona. "Murdoch and Levinas on God and Good." *European Journal for Philosophy of Religion* 1, no. 2 (2009): 63–87.

Engel, Pascal. *Truth*. New York: Routledge, 2014.

Evans, Jules. "The New Atheists Are Actually Transcendentalists." *Philosophy for Life*, January 24, 2014: No page numbers. http://www.philosophyforlife.org/the-new-atheists-are-actually-transcendentalists/.

Evans-Pritchard, E.E. *Witchcraft, Oracles, and Magic among the Azande*. Oxford: Clarendon Press, 1976.

Feuerbach, Ludwig. *The Essence of Christianity*. Translated by George Elliot. Amherst, NY: Prometheus Books, 1989.

Feuerbach, Ludwig. *Principles for the Philosophy of the Future*. Translated by Manfred Vogel. Indianapolis: Hackett Publishing, 1986.

Fine, Gary Alan and Bill Ellis. *The Global Grapevine: Why Rumors of Terrorism, Immigration and Trade Matter*. Oxford: Oxford University Press, 2010.

Frappolli, Maria, ed. *F.P. Ramsey: Critical Reassessments*. London: Continuum Press, 2005.

Gioia, Dana. "The Epistle of Paul to the Philippian's." In *Incarnation: Contemporary Writer's on the New Testament*, edited by Alfred Corn. New York: Viking Penguin, 1990.

Glatzer, Nahum N. *The Dimensions of Job: A Study and Selected Readings*. Eugene, OR: Wipf and Stock Publishers, 2002.

Gordon, Tom. *Look Well to This Day: A Year of Daily Reflections*. Glasgow: Wild Goose Publications, 2014.

Habegger, Alfred. *My Wars Are Laid Away in Books: The Life of Emily Dickinson*. New York: The Modern Library, 2001.

Hammer, Espen. *Stanley Cavell: Skepticism, Subjectivity, and the Ordinary*. Oxford: Polity Press, 2002.

Harris, Sidney. *Chalk Up Another One: The Best of Sidney Harris*. Washington, DC: AAAS Press, 1992.

Hart, David Bentley. *The Experience of God: Being, Consciousness, Bliss*. New Haven, CT: Yale University Press, 2013.

Hawn, Michael. "History of Hymns: 'Immortal, Invisible, God Only Wise.'" *Discipleship Ministries*. Accessed July 11, 2018. https://www.umcdiscipleship.org/resources/history-ofhymns-immortal-invisible-god-only-wise.

Heschel, Abraham Joshua. *God in Search of Man: A Philosophy of Judaism*. New York: Farrar, Straus and Giroux, 1976.

Hector, Kevin. *Theology without Metaphysics: God, Language and the Spirit of Recognition*. Cambridge: Cambridge University Press, 2011.

Hick John. "An Irenaean Theodicy." In *Encountering Evil: Live Options in Theodicy*, edited by Stephen T. Davis, 38–72. Louisville, KY: Westminster John Knox Press, 2001.

Holiday, Ryan. *Ego Is the Enemy*. New York: Penguin Publishing Group, 2016.

Hollander, John. *The Work of Poetry*. New York: Columbia University Press.

Hopkins, Gerard Manley. "God's Grandeur." *Poetry Foundation*, 1877. Accessed August 22, 2018. https://www.poetryfoundation.org/poems/44395/gods-grandeur.

Horn, Patrick Horn. "D.Z. Phillips on Christian Immortality." *International Journal for Philosophy of Religion* 71, no. 1 (2012): 39–53.

Horwich, Paul. *Truth-Meaning-Reality*. Oxford: Oxford University Press, 2010.

Horwich, Paul. "A Defense of Minimalism." In *Principles of Truth*, edited by Volker Halbach and Leon Horsten. Franfurt: Verlag, 2003.

Horwich, Paul. *Truth*. Oxford: Oxford University Press, 1998.

Hume, David. *Writings on Religion*. Edited by Antony Flew. Chicago: Open Court, 1992.

Ibsen, Henrik. *A Doll's House*. Mineola, NY: Dover Publications, 1992.

Johnston, Mark. *Surviving Death*. Princeton, NJ: Princeton University Press, 2010. Kindle Edition.

Johnston, Mark. *Saving God: Religion after Idolatry*. Princeton, NJ: Princeton University Press, 2009.

Jones, J.R. "Love as Perception of Meaning." In *Religion and Understanding*, edited by D.Z. Phillips. Oxford: Basil Blackwell, 1967.

Jüngel, Eberhard. *God as the Mystery of the World*. Grand Rapids, MI: Eerdmans Publishing Co., 1983.

Kaufman, Walter. *Nietzsche: Philosopher, Psychologist, Antichrist*. Princeton, NJ: Princeton University Press, 1974.

Kierkegaard, Soren. *Works of Love*. Translated by Howard V. Hong and Edna H. Hong. Princeton, NJ: Princeton University Press, 1998.

Kierkegaard, Soren. *Eighteen Upbuilding Discourses*. Edited and translated by Howard V. Hong and Edna H. Hong. Princeton, NJ: Princeton University Press, 1990.

Kierkegaard, Soren. *The Journal of Kierkegaard*. Edited and translated by Alexander Dru. Oxford: Oxford University Press, 1938.

Koethe, John. *The Continuity of Wittgenstein's Thought*. Ithaca, NY: Cornell University Press, 1996.

Kohen, Ari. *In Defense of Human Rights: A Non-religious Grounding in a Pluralistic World*. New York: Routledge, 2007.

Koskey, Jeffery L. "The Birth of the Modern Philosophy of Religion and the Death of Transcendence." In *Transcendence: Philosophy, Literature, and Theology Approach the Beyond*, edited by Regina Schwartz, 11–26. New York: Routledge, 2004.

Larkin, Philip. *Poems: Selected and with an Introduction by Martin Amis*. London: Faber and Faber, 2011. Kindle Edition.

Larkin, Philip. *Philip Larkin Poems*. Selected by Martin Amis. London: Faber & Faber, 2011. Kindle Edition.

Lash, Nicholas Lash. *Easter in Ordinary: Reflections on Human Experience and the Knowledge of God*. Notre Dame, IN: University of Notre Dame Press, 1990.

Lederer, Richard. *The Revenge of Anguished English: More Accidental Assaults upon Our Language*. New York: St. Martin's Press, 2005.

Leiner, Martin. "Tillich on God." In *The Cambridge Companion to Paul Tillich*, edited by Russell Re Manning. 37–55. Cambridge: Cambridge University Press, 2008.

Levinas, Emmanuel. *Totality and Infinity*. Translated by Alphonso Lingis. Dordrecht: Kluwer Academic Publishers, 1991.

Ludlow, Peter, ed. *Readings in the Philosophy of Language*. Cambridge, MA: The MIT Press, 1997.

Luther, Martin. *Works of Martin Luther: With Introduction and Notes, Vol. 2*. Philadelphia, PA: A.J. Holman Company, 1915.

Malcolm, Norman. *Wittgenstein: A Religious Point of View?* edited by Peter Winch. Ithaca, NY: Cornell University Press, 1993.

Malcolm, Norman "Wittgenstein's Confessions." *London Review of Books* 3, no. 21 (1981): 16–18.

Marion, Jean Luc. "In the Name: How to Avoid Speaking of 'Negative Theology.'" In *God, the Gift and Postmodernism*, edited by John D. Caputo and Michael J. Scanlon. Bloomington: Indiana University Press, 1999.

Marion, Jean-Luc Marion. *God without Being*. Chicago: University of Chicago Press, 1991.

Martell, Jane G., ed. *Smashed Potatoes: A Kids-Eye View of the Kitchen*. Boston, MA: Houghton Mifflin Harcourt, 1974.

Max, D.T. *Every Love Story Is a Ghost Story: A Life of David Foster Wallace*. New York: Penguin Books, 2013.

Max, D.T. "D.F.W.: Tracing the Ghostly Origins of a Phrase." *The New Yorker*, December 11, 2012.

McCullough, Lissa. *The Religious Philosophy of Simone Weil: An Introduction*. London: I.B. Tauris & Co. Ltd, 2014.

Migliore, Daniel L. *Faith Seeking Understanding: An Introduction to Christian Theology*. Grand Rapids, MI: Eerdmans Publishing Co., 1991. Kindle Edition.

Morris, Herbert, *On Guilt and Innocence*. Berkeley: University of California Press, 1976.

Mounce, H.O. *Wittgenstein's Tractatus: An Introduction*. Chicago: University of Chicago Press, 1981.

Nava, Alexander. *The Mystical and Prophetic Thought of Simone Weil and Gustavo Gutiérrez: Reflections on the Mystery and Hiddenness of God*. Albany: State University of New York Press, 2001.

Nieli, Russell. *Wittgenstein: From Mysticism to Ordinary Language*. Albany: State University of New York Press, 1987.

Nielson, Kai and D.Z. Phillips. *Wittgensteinian Fideism?* London: SCM Press, 2005.

Nielson, Kai. *An Introduction to the Philosophy of Religion*. New York: Macmillan Press, 1982.

Nielson, Kai. "Wittgensteinian Fideism." *Philosophy* 161, no. 42 (1967): 191–209.

Noddings, Nel. *Caring: A Feminine Approach to Ethics and Moral Education*, 2nd ed. Berkeley: University of California Press, 2003. Kindle Edition.

Nussbaum, Martha. *Love's Knowledge: Essays on Philosophy and Literature*. Oxford: Oxford University Press, 1990.

Nygren, Anders. *Agape and Eros*. Philadelphia, PA: Westminster Press, 1953.

O'Connor, Flannery. "Parker's Back." In *The Complete Stories*. New York: Farrar, Straus and Giroux, 1971. 510–529. Kindle Edition.

Osteen, Joel. "The Power of Forgiveness." *Joel Osteen Ministries*. Accessed August 3, 2018. https://www.joelosteen.com/Pages/Blog.aspx?blogid=13347.

Outka, Gene. *Agape: An Ethical Analysis*. New Haven, CT: Yale University Press, 1972.

Pattison, George. *Paul Tillich's Philosophical Theology: A Fifty-Year Reappraisal*. New York: Palgrave, 2015.

Peterson, Merrill D. *Lincoln in American Memory*. Oxford: Oxford University Press, 1994.

Pétrement, Simone. *Simone Weil: A Life*. Translated by Raymond Rosenthal. New York: Pantheon Books, 1976.

Phillips, D.Z. and Mario von der Ruhr. *Religion and Wittgenstein's Legacy*. New York: Routledge, 2005.

Phillips, D.Z. *Religion and Friendly Fire: Examining Assumptions in Contemporary Philosophy of Religion*. New York: Taylor and Francis, 2004.

Phillips, D Z. *The Problem of Evil & the Problem of God*. Minneapolis: Fortress Press, 2004.

Phillips, D.Z. *Religion and the Hermeneutics of Contemplation*. Cambridge: Cambridge University Press, 2001.
Phillips, D.Z. *Recovering Religious Concepts: Closing Epistemic Divides*. New York: Saint Martin's Press, 2000.
Phillips, D.Z. *Philosophy's Cool Place*. Ithaca, NY: Cornell University Press, 1999.
Phillips, D.Z. *Introducing Philosophy*. Cambridge, MA: Blackwell Publishers, 1996.
Phillips, D.Z. *Wittgenstein and Religion*. New York: Saint Martin's Press, 1993.
Phillips, D.Z. *Faith after Foundationalism: Critiques and Alternatives*. Boulder, CO: Westview Press, 1985.
Phillips, D.Z. *Religion without Explanation*. Oxford: Basil Blackwell, 1976.
Phillips, D.Z. Phillips, *Death and Immortality*. London: Macmillan, 1970.
Placher, William. *The Domestication of Transcendence: How Modern Thinking about God Went Wrong*. Louisville, KY: Westminster John Knox Press, 1996.
Plant, Stephen. *Simone Weil: A Brief Introduction*. Maryknoll, NY: Orbis Books, 2007.
Plantinga, Alvin and Michael Tooley. *Knowledge of God*. Malden, MA: Blackwell Publishing, 2008.
Plantinga, Alvin. "The Dawkins Confusion: Naturalism 'ad absurdum.'" *Books and Culture: A Christian Review*, March/April 2007. https://www.booksandculture.com/articles/2007/marapr/1.21/html.
Pugh, Jeffrey C. *Religionless Christianity: Dietrich Bonhoeffer in Troubled Times*. New York: T&T Clark, 2008.
Putnam, Hilary. *The Many Faces of Realism*. LaSalle, IL: Open Court, 1987.
Ramsey, Paul. *Basic Christian Ethics*. Louisville, KY: Westminster/John Knox Press, 1950.
Ransom, John Crowe. "Winter Remembered." *The Sewanee Review*. Accessed 25, 2018. https://thesewaneereview.com/john-crowe-ransom-winter-remembered/
Reitan, Eric. *Is God a Delusion? A Reply to Religion's Cultured Despisers*. Malden, MA: Wiley-Blackwell, 2009.
Reynolds, Susan Salter. "A Time for Us." *Los Angeles Times*, January 06, 2008. http://articles.latimes.com/2008/jan/06/books/bk-reynolds6.
Rhees, Rush. *Wittgenstein and the Possibility of Discourse*. Edited by D.Z. Phillips. Oxford: Blackwell Publishing, 2006.
Rhees, Rush. *Without Answers*. London: Routledge, 1969.
Ricoeur, Paul and Alasdair Macinytre. *The Religious Significance of Atheism*. New York: Columbia University Press, 1969.
Rollins, Peter. *How (Not) to Speak of God*. Brewster, MA: Paraclete Press, 2006.
Rozelle-Stone, Rebecca A. *Simone Weil and Theology*. New York: Bloomsbury Publishing, 2013.
Sacks, Oliver. *The Man Who Mistook His Wife for a Hat and Other Clinical Tales*. New York: Harper & Row Publishers, 1985.
Santayana, George. *The Last Puritan: A Memoir in the Form of a Novel*. New York: Charles Scribner's Sons, 1936.

Schaff, Philip, ed. *Nicene and Post-Nicene Fathers, Vol. V: St. Augustine: Anti-Pelagian Writings*. New York: Cosimo Classics, 2007.

Schnur, Susan. "Hers." *New York Times*, 1985. https://www.nytimes.com/1985/08/15/garden/hers.html.

Schultz, Charles. *The Complete Peanuts: 1985–1986*. Seattle: Fantagraphics Books, 2012.

Schweitzer, Albert. *An Anthology*. Edited by Charles R. Joy. Boston, MA: The Beacon Press, 1960.

Shakespeare, William. "Sonnet 29: When, in Disgrace with Fortunes and Men's Eyes." *Poetry Foundation*. Accessed August 22, 2018. https://www.poetryfoundation.org/poems/45090/sonnet29-when-in-disgrace-with-fortune-and-mens-eyes

Sheahen, Laura. "Christopher Hitchens: 'Why Religion Poisons Everything.'" *SoMA Review*, June 15, 2007. http://www.somareview.com/christopherhitchens.cfm.

Singer, Peter. *The Most Good You Can Do: How effective Altruism is Changing Ideas About Living Ethically*. New Haven, CT: Yale University Press, 2015.

Singer, Peter. *Practical Ethics*, 3rd ed. Cambridge: Cambridge University Press, 2011.

Singer, Peter. *The Life You Can Save*. New York: Random House, 2010.

Singer, Peter. "Famine, Affluence, and Morality." *Philosophy and Public Affairs* 1, no. 1 (1972): 229–243.

Soames, Mary. *Clementine Churchill: The Biography of a Marriage*. New York: Houghton Mifflin Company, 2002.

Stenger, Victor J. *God: The Failed Hypothesis*. Amherst, NY: Prometheus Books, 2007.

Stroll, Avrum. *Wittgenstein*. Oxford: One World Publications, 2007.

Tarski, Alfred. "The Semantic Conception of Truth." In *Semantics and the Philosophy of Language: A Collection of Readings*, edited by Leonard Linsky, 13–49. Chicago: University of Illinois Press, 1970.

Taylor, Charles. *A Secular Age*. Cambridge, MA: The Belknap Press of Harvard University Press, 2007.

Taylor, Richard. *With Heart and Mind: A Philosopher Looks at Faith, Love and Death*. New York: St. Martin's Press, 1973.

Tillich, Paul. *The Courage to Be*. New Haven, CT: Yale University Press, 1980. Kindle Edition.

Tillich, Paul. *Dynamics of Faith*. New York: HarperCollins, 1957. Kindle Edition.

Tillich, Paul. *Systematic Theology, Volume 2*. Chicago: University of Chicago Press, 1957. Kindle Edition.

Tillich, Paul. *Systematic Theology, Volume 1*. Chicago: University of Chicago Press, 1951. Kindle Edition.

Tillich, Paul. *The Shaking of the Foundations*. New York: Charles Scribner's Sons, 1948.

Tolstoy, Leo. *The Gospel in Tolstoy: Selections from His Short Stories, Spiritual Writings & Novels*. Walden, NY: Plough Publishing House, 2015. Kindle Edition.

Tolstoy, Leo. *War and Peace*. Translated by Constance Garnett. New York: The Modern Library, 2002.

Tolstoy, Leo. *The Death of Ivan Ilyich*. Translated by Rosemary Edmonds. London: Penguin Books, 1960.

Trakakis, Nick. *The End of Philosophy of Religion*. London: Continuum, 2008. Kindle Edition.

Tuchman, Barbara W. *A Distant Mirror: The Calamitous 14th Century*. New York: Random House, 2010.

Turner, Denys. "Apophaticism, Idolatry and the Claims of Reason." In *Silence and the Word: Negative Theology and Incarnation*, edited by Oliver Davis and Denys Turner. Cambridge: Cambridge University Press, 2008.

Turner, Denys. *Faith Seeking*. London: SCM Press, 2002.

Turner, Denys. *The Darkness of God: Negativity in Christian Mysticism*. Cambridge: Cambridge University Press, 1995.

Twain, Mark. *Adventures of Huckleberry Finn*. Clayton, DE: Prestwick House, 2005.

Unger, Peter. *Living High and Letting Die: Our Illusion of Innocence*. Oxford: Oxford University Press, 1996.

Vetö, Miklos. *The Religious Metaphysics of Simone Weil*. Translated by Joan Dargan. Albany: State University of New York Press, 1994.

Vidal, David. "A 116-Year-Old's Good Advice." *New York Times*, January 1, 1976. https://www.nytimes.com/1976/01/01/archives/a-116yearolds-good-advice-no-more-dancing.html.

Wallace, David Foster. *This Is Water: Some Thoughts, Delivered on a Significant Occasion, about Living a Compassionate Life*. New York: Little, Brown and Company, 2009. Kindle Edition.

Wallace, James D. *Norms and Practices*. Ithaca, NY: Cornell University Press, 2008.

Walsh, Sylvia. "Moral Character and Temptation." In *The Wisdom of the Christian Faith*, edited by Paul Moser and Michael T. McFall. Cambridge: Cambridge University Press, 2012.

Ware, Kallistos. *The Orthodox Way*. Crestwood, NY: St. Vladimir's Seminary Press, 1979.

Waskow, Arthur I. *Godwrestling*. New York: Schocken Books, 1978.

Watson, William. *The Hope of the World and Other Poems*. New York: John Lane, 1898.

Weil, Simone. "Human Personality." In *Simone Weil: Selected Works, Selected Essays, 1934–1943: Historical, Political, and Moral Writings*. Translated by Richard Rees. Eugene, OR: Wipf & Stock, 2015.

Weil, Simone. *Waiting on God*. New York: Routledge, 2009.

Weil, Simone. *Gravity and Grace*. Translated by Emma Crawford and Mario von der Ruhr. New York: Routledge, 2004.

Weil, Simone. *The Notebooks of Simone Weil Volume 1*. Translated by Arthur Wills. New York: Routledge, 2004.

Weil, Simone. *First and Last Notebooks*. Translated by Richard Rees. London: Oxford University Press, 1970.

Wettstein, Howard. *The Significance of Religious Experience*. Oxford: Oxford University Press, 2012. Kindle.

Whittaker, John. "D.Z. Phillips and Reasonable Belief." *International Journal for Philosophy of Religion* 63 (2008): 103–129.

Whittaker, John H. "At the End of Reason Comes Persuasion." In *The Possibilities of Sense*, edited by John H. Whittaker, 133–153. New York: Palgrave, 2002.

Wilford, John Noble. "Solving a Riddle Written in Silver." *New York Times*, September 28, 2004. https://www.nytimes.com/2004/09/28/science/solving-a-riddle-written-in-silver.html.

Williams, Michael. "Wittgenstein, Truth and Certainty." In *Wittgenstein's Lasting Significance*, edited by Max Kölbel and Bernhard Weiss, 249–284. London: Routledge, 2004.

Winch, Peter. *The Idea of a Social Science*. London: Routledge, 1958.

Wittgenstein, Ludwig. *Philosophical Investigations*. Translated by G.E.M. Anscombe. Oxford: Blackwell Publishing, 2003.

Wittgenstein, Ludwig. *Tractatus Logico-Philosophicus*. Translated by C.K. Ogden. Mineola, NY: Dover Publications Inc., 1999.

Wittgenstein, Ludwig. *Philosophical Occasions: 1912–1951*. Edited by James Klagge and Alfred Nordmann. Indianapolis, IN: Hackett Publishing Company, 1996.

Wittgenstein, Ludwig. *Culture and Value*. Translated by Peter Winch. Chicago: The University of Chicago Press, 1980.

Wittgenstein, Ludwig. *On Certainty*. Edited by G.E.M. Anscombe and G.H. von Wright. New York: Harper & Row Publishers, 1969.

Wittgenstein, Ludwig. *Lectures & Conversations on Aesthetics, Psychology and Religious Belief*. Edited by Cyril Barrett. Berkeley: University of California Press, 1966.

Wittgenstein, Ludwig. *The Blue and Brown Books*. Oxford: Oxford University Press, 1958.

Wolterstorff, Nicholas. *Justice in Love*. Grand Rapids, MI: William B. Eerdmans Publishing, 2011.

Index

absolute safety 44–5
acceptance 10, 21, 34–6, 70–1, 73–4, 95, 153, 155–6, 161, 171
active attention 137–41, 144
  importance of 138
  physical need of 145
Aesop's Fables 90
agape 5, 21, 31, 37–8, 93–4, 133–5, 139–40, 152
  acceptance 155–6
  agapeic atheism 156–8
  anecdotal 144–6
  application 145–6
  atheistic theism 162–3
  and care for other 135
  definition of 135, 137–8, 144
  language of 91
  life of 92
  love without reason 158–62
  responsibility 142–4
  self at center 146–52
  sin, separation, and acceptance 153–5
  stories of love 135–42
  theistic-atheism 162–3
  virtue of 140
agapeic atheism 156–8
agapeic love 144
agapeistic triage 142–3
Albritton, Rogers 110
Alston, William 26
ambiguity 76, 88, 194
Andrey, Prince 133, 140
anecdotal agape 144–6
anthropomorphic God 4, 8–9, 22–3, 68, 82, 85, 87
  of supernatural theism 39, 84
anthropomorphism 11–12, 42, 81
apophaticism 218 n.29
Aquinas 25
Armstrong, Karen 25
Arrowsmith, Nancy 171

atheism 5, 8, 14, 23, 28, 39, 87, 157, 171
  ethical 123–6
  forms of 123, 129
  ontological 120–3, 129
  purification of 39
  semantic 126–9
atheistic theism 162–3
atonement 72
  concept of 73
  doctrines of 69–70
  idea of 70–1
  and idolatry 69–70
  impotent 72
  interpretation of 93
  objective side of 71
  theories 70
attention 61–2
  active 138
attentive love 137
Augustus, Caesar 208
Auslander, Shalom 7
autonomy 152–3
  freedom and 157
avoidance 83
Azande 169–70

Barfield, Owen 29
Barrow, Clyde 209
Becker, Ernest 222 n.23
believers 5–6, 8–16, 18, 21, 27, 31–3, 37, 48–9, 53, 55–9, 62–3, 72–3, 76, 79, 82, 87–92, 119, 126, 129–32, 134–5, 146, 157, 160, 171, 174, 193
Bell, Richard 28
Blackburn, Simon 105–6
Blair, Tony 44
Blue and Brown Books (Wittgenstein) 113–14
Bogin, Magda 182
Bonhoeffer, Dietrich 43, 72, 162–3
  analysis of religion 22
  cheap grace 73–5

Borg, Marcus 80
Braithwaite, R.B. 130–1
"break the ice" in social situations 194
Brenner, William 33, 62
Brothers Karamazov, The (Dostoevsky) 185–6
Buber, Martin 68, 212
Buechner, Frederick 160, 174

Camus, Albert 86
Canfield, John V. 114
Caputo, John 49, 159
Carnap, Rudolf 107
Carroll, Lewis 195
Carter, Jimmy 76
Cates, Sarah Ruth 65
Cavell, Stanley 111–12, 116–18, 225 n.30
Chapel, Sistine 91
Charles, Walter 42
Chast, Roz 195
cheap grace 71–5
cheap immortality 75, 77
Christian/Christianity 22, 49, 134, 157, 206
　assertions of 130
　belief 35, 79
　faith 69, 134, 159, 185, 197
　love 161
　tradition 206
Christian Ethics (Ramsey) 140
church 27–9, 72–3, 75, 169–75, 185, 210
　liturgy and beliefs of 174
Churchill, Winston 181
Coburn, Robert C. 21, 30, 32–6, 44–5, 49, 84, 120, 168
Cocktail Party, The (Eliot) 174
cognitive content 30
communication 26, 109, 111, 113, 117, 177, 204
community 17–18, 31, 52, 91, 100, 109, 112, 173–5, 183, 206
conceptual idol 19, 42
conceptual mystery 42
conceptual relativism 107
conceptual relativity 51–3
consciousness 77, 79, 81, 94, 133, 147, 151, 157–8
　human 15
　mystery of 41
　nature of 48

contemplative philosophy 99–100
contemporary idolatry 22
correlation 120
　systematic theology in 122
Cost of Discipleship, The (Bonhoeffer) 72
Cottingham, John 37, 45, 88
Courage to Be, The (Tillich) 121
Cousins, Norman 193
Crick, Francis 170–1
criteria 5, 31, 33, 109–11
　defining 113–15
　groundlessness of 112–13
　justification, and shams 115–18
　and language 109–11
　religious 118–19
　as social conventions 111–12
　for truth and falsity 109
criterial agreement 112–13
criticism 10, 13, 19, 30, 58–61, 88, 131
crucifixion 71, 93, 161
Culture and Value (Wittgenstein) 36, 49, 63
cynicism 155, 194

Davies, Brian 11
Dawkins, Richard 4, 28, 39, 81, 127
　anthropomorphic God of 23
　arguments against 13
　atheism 14
　criticism of 13
　God Delusion, The 9, 12–13
　God hypothesis, definition of 11
　"God" means for 9
　philosophical audience 14
　religion 9–10
　supernatural theism 15–16
　on theology 13
death 77, 83–4, 86, 92–3, 133–4, 143, 150, 160
　dimensions of 22
　existential impact of 56
　fate and 121
　fear of 31, 74, 93
　ineluctable frustration of 33
　of Jesus 71, 74
　life and 78
　religious significance of seeing 80
　and resurrection 181
　of self 93
Death and Immortality (Johnston) 88–9

decreation 125
defiance 184
defining criterion 114–15
deflationary theory of truth 5, 105–6, 108, 118
depression 184, 195
de se reasons 148–52
Dickenson, Emily 192, 198
Distant Mirror, A (Tuchman) 177
divine mystery 41–2, 68
divine reality 27, 37, 61–2
doctrines 87–9, 187, 190
   of atonement 70
   belief in 74
   Christian 23
   religious 28, 68–9
Doll's House, A (Ibsen) 203
domestication 17, 23
   epistemological 27
   of God 24, 26
   ontological 27
Dostoevsky, Fyodor 86, 185
Dummett, Michael 108
Dynamics of Faith, The (Tillich) 155

Eagleton, Terry 13, 154
economic depression 194
egocentrism 149–50
Ego Is the Enemy (Holiday) 152
Einstein, Albert 9–10, 201
Eliot, George 204
Eliot, T.S. 174
Ellenbogen, Sara 109
empathy 56, 137–9, 144
emptiness 83, 124–5, 155, 173
Engel, Pascal 103
Enlightenment concept of revelation 27
environmental deterioration 178
epistemic humility 43–4, 80
epistemological domestication 27
epistemological humility 42, 46
Essence of Christianity, The (Feuerbach) 157
eternal harmony 86–7
eternal life 5, 70, 76–80, 88, 90, 138
   concept of 74–5
   forgiveness of 75
   idolatrous use of 80
   meaning of 77
   philosophical accounts of 77

   thought of 77
   use of 94
eternity 47, 75, 190
ethical atheism 85, 123–6
Evans-Pritchard, E.E. 169
everyday egocentrism 149
evil 84
   deliver me from 84–5
   explanation for 84
   reality of 83–4
   searching for story 82–3
   and supernatural theism 80–2
   trivializing suffering 85

failed hypothesis 12
faith/belief 4, 11, 13, 16, 28, 30, 35, 43, 46, 58–9, 68, 72, 78–81, 92, 124, 129–32, 158–9, 163, 171–3, 219 n.49
   anthropomorphic stage of 8
   Christian/Christianity 69, 134, 159, 185, 197
   confessional language of 131
   in doctrines 74
   dominate form of 30
   forgiveness and 70–1
   genuine 119
   in God 27, 80–1
   justification and truth of 49, 69
   language of 63
   in non-anthropomorphic God 9
   and practices 27, 130, 169
   prayer of 70
   religious (*see* religious belief)
   transcendent God of 38
   transformative 74
   without practice revisited 75–7
falsity 50, 57, 63, 104, 109, 127
Feuerbach, Ludwig 15, 23–4, 42, 157
Feynman, Richard 170–1
fideism 5, 49–51, 55, 60–1
   aspects of 53
   contemporary dispute about 53
   definition of 53
   diversity of 219 n.50
   forms of 30
   justification and truth 57–61
   narrow view of 56
   Nielsen criticism of 60

Nielsen's label of 53
semantic 55–7
senses of 30, 55–61
truth 57–61
types of 53–5
uses of 52
Field Guide to the Little People, A (Arrowsmith) 171
Foreskin's Lament: A Memoir (Auslander) 7
forgiveness 5–6, 71, 73, 136
    and belief 70–1
    of eternal life 75
    magical conception of 72
    real cost of 72–3
    requirement for 72
    of sin 75, 88, 90, 93
    subjective side of 71
freedom, and autonomy 157
Frege, Gottlob 104

genre pictures 90–1
Gioia, Dana 161
global skepticism 117–18
God 78, 123
    adieu to 4, 125
    anthropomorphic (*see* anthropomorphic God)
    atheism 14
    belief in 27
    believer's language about 16
    Christian "conception" of 73
    communication to humanity 26
    concept of 14, 18–19, 24, 84, 218 n.33
    consciousness 15
    description of 7
    domestication of 24, 26
    existence of 24–5, 27, 29, 49
    goodness and attributes of 82
    healing presence 182
    hypothesis of 11–13
    ineffability 40
    mystery of 39–40
    nonexistence of 120
    non-idolatrous picture of 96
    and ontology 122
    pictorial representation 67
    plans and purposes 13
    power of 7
    reality of 27, 61–2, 89
    realization and humanization of 15
    speaking of 42
    of spiritual materialism 85
    supernaturalism 8, 11–12, 81, 85, 119
    tattoo of 66
    transcendence of 17, 37–43
    unknowability of 39
    worship of 42
God as the Mystery of the World (Jungel) 156
God Delusion, The (Dawkins) 9, 12–13
God of Dawkins 16, 22–3
goodness 20–1, 26, 82, 85, 185, 190
Good Samaritan, the 138–41
Gospel of Thomas 190
grace 124, 155, 173, 182–3
    cheap 71–5
    potential sources of 181
    transformative power of 73
grammatical structure, language 3, 32
gratitude 21, 42, 45–6, 87, 95–6, 174, 213
groundlessness of criteria 112–13
Gulag Archipelago, The 209

Hammer, Espen 112, 117
"healing" function 195
Hector, Kevin W. 4
Henry Aldrich program 194–5
Heschel, Abraham Joshua 16, 21
Hick, John 15, 82
hinge propositions 113
Hitchens, Christopher 44
Holiday, Ryan 152
Holy Spirit 225 n.26
Horn, Patrick 78
Horwich, Paul 103–5, 108
Huckleberry Finn 196
human consciousness 15, 77
human finitude 20, 44, 56
human form of life 101, 112, 220 n.54, 226 n.45
human language game 99–100
human social interaction 112

Ibsen, Henrik 203
idol 6, 17–22, 39, 49, 68, 87, 92, 162
    concept of 18
    worship 28
idolatry 4, 31, 40, 77, 94, 125, 148, 155
    atonement and 69–70
    "cheap grace" as 71–4
    claim of 17, 92

components of 68
concept of 22
contemporary 22
definition of 17
identifying 18
and practice 17–19
religious 9, 16
and spiritual materialism 20, 42
and supernatural theism 23–8
temporal immortality and 74–5
and transformative faith 74
"idolatry of mere belief" 77
Ilyich, Ivan 133, 150
immortality
  cheap 75, 77
  religious belief in 94–5
  temporal 74–5, 79–80
  use of 94
incarnation 157–61
independent reality 101
intellectual integrity 175, 180
interactionism with anthropomorphism 11
Introduction to the Philosophy of Religion, An (Nielsen) 55

James, William 33, 43, 195, 198
Jesus 7, 69
  believing in 76
  death of 71, 74
  historical execution of 71
  incarnation of 160
  life of 43, 73, 92
  objective death of 71
  self-emptying of 160
  substitutionary death of 70
Jesus and the Good Samaritan (story) 138–41
Johnston, Mark 10, 17–22, 24, 49, 85, 88–9, 144, 146–8
  account of salvation 21
  agape, definition of 135
  Death and Immortality 88–9
  domestication of God 24
  initial definition of idolatry 19
  Saving God 10, 17
  Surviving Death 135, 148
Jones, J.R. 47, 128
Judaism 212
Jüngel, Eberhard 156

justification 5, 30, 59–62, 119
  by faith 49, 69
  fideism 57
  for religious belief 119
  and truth 49, 51, 57–61

Kafka, Franz 211
kairos 179
Kant, Immanuel 146–7, 151
Karamazov, Ivan 86–7
kenosis 159–61
kenotic theology 159–60
Kierkegaard, Soren 173, 183–4
knowledge 11, 13, 24, 34, 39, 41, 46, 48, 62, 69, 105, 108, 112–13, 183, 188
  and skills 177–8

language 3, 40, 109, 112
  about God 40
  about religious faith 3
  aspects of 113, 118
  brokenness of 218 n.33
  criteria and 110
  of faith 63
  game 109
  limits of 45–6
  meaning of 3
  of religion 49–50
  religious (*see* religious language)
  religious uses of 30, 57
  rules of 110
  of science 127–8
  speaking of 41
  spiritual 3, 20
  theological 34
  thinking of 126
  univocal 26
  use of 4, 55, 100, 111
Larkin, Philip 175
Lash, Nicholas 68
laughter 194
  context of 198
  importance of 191–2
  periodic bouts of 192
  role of 192–3
"letting go," art of 179–81, 184
Lewis, C.S. 29
life. *See also* human form of life
  and actions 18
  of agape 92

and death 78
eternal (*see* eternal life)
forms of 58
interrelatedness of 34
of Jesus 43, 73, 92
kenotic model of 160
pattern of 180
religious (*see* religious life)
spiritual 18–19, 134, 183
value of 220 n.54
Life You Can Save, The (Singer) 141
limiting question 30–6, 49, 56, 63, 100
Lincoln, Abraham 192
linguistic communication 109
linguistic community 100, 109
"logically complete" answers 34–6, 49, 56, 120
loneliness 195
love 20–1, 28–31, 133–4, 137, 140, 145
    agapeic 144
    attentive 137
    and care 137–8
    inability to 195
    self-sacrificial 43, 159
    stories of 135–42
    without reason 158–62

magnetism 102–3
Marion, Jean Luc 40, 102
McCullough, Lissa 93, 159
meaning 3–5, 13, 16–18, 25–32, 37, 87–9
    internal/external distinction of 55
    of religious language 55
    vs. truth 107–8
meaningfulness 57–8, 62, 106, 130, 132, 159
meaninglessness 31, 56, 124, 155, 173
mentor 207–13
    roles of 212
metaphysical beliefs 63
method of correlation 120
method of projection 89–90
Middlemarch (Eliot) 204
Migliore, Daniel 69–70
models 43, 69, 71, 73, 92–3, 96, 126–7, 159–62, 168, 207–13
    role of 212
moral problems 33
Muriel, Lady 195

mystery 9, 18, 24–6, 37, 39–40, 43, 46, 48, 60, 68, 80, 85, 87, 94, 128, 156, 160, 181, 184–5
    conceptual 42
    of God 41
    natural 41

natural egoism 48, 149
natural propensity 6, 48, 70, 74–5, 146–8, 151–2
nature, quasi-epistemological in 46
Nava, Alexander 124
neighbor 6, 21, 28, 31, 138, 140, 142–5
    and acquaintances 204
    loving of 162
New Atheists 9
Nielsen, Kai 53, 55, 57–8, 60–1
    criticism of fideism 60
Nietzsche, Friedrich 8, 68–9
Noddings, Nel 137
non-anthropomorphic God 9
Nussbaum, Martha 167–8

objects 63, 107
    definition of 52–5
    dependent rules for counting 54
    language game 51, 54
    mereology of 107
O'Connor, Flannery 65–8
Oliver, Mary 137
ontological atheism 120–3
ontological domestication 28
ontological shock 121
Osteen, Joel 69
Otto, Rudolf 43–5

pain behavior 32, 110, 115–16
Parker, O.E. 65–7
paternalistic care 179
pattern of life 180
Pattison, George 122
Paul, Apostle 48, 70
Pensées (Engel) 83
Perez, Dionisia 192
Perry, John 148–50
personal transformation 70, 72
Phillips, D. Z. 21–2, 27, 39–40, 42, 53, 58, 61–2, 84, 88–9, 94–6, 106, 115–16, 119, 131

contemplative account of
    philosophy 99
  on criteria 118
  on meaningfulness 106-7
  meaning of religious belief 99
  philosophy of 33
  Problem of God and the Problem of Evil, The 81
  religious perspectives 21
  Wittgenstein and the Possibility of Discourse 58
physical objects 18, 61-2
physical well-being 192-3
pictures 5, 7, 35, 44, 66-7, 87-9, 126
  of God 96
  religious 4, 31, 89-92
  sacred 91
Placher, William 25-6
Plantinga, Alvin 13, 15
plurality 104, 118
  of perspectives 99
  of realities 101
  of truth 101
poverty 75, 143
practice
  belief and 76, 130
  grammatical description of 110
  religion 75
prayer of faith 70
Prince Andrey 133, 140
problem of evil 80-7
propositions/truth 5, 11, 15, 31, 35, 87-9
psychological adjustment 20
Pugh, Jeffery 22
purgatory 8
Putnam, Hilary 51, 54, 107

questions 5, 22, 27, 30-6, 45, 49, 52-3, 56-7, 61-3, 72, 76, 94, 99-100, 104, 107, 109, 112-13, 116, 118-22, 127-8, 136-7, 139, 150, 156, 162, 169, 178

radical agape 31
radical evil 146-7, 151
Radical Sacrifice (Eagleton) 154
Ramsey, Frank 104-5
Ramsey, Paul 140
Ransom, John Crowe 195

rationality 27, 53, 58-9, 191
reality 46-7, 88, 101, 126
  avoidance of 83-4
  believer places on 89
  meaning of 58
  nature of 43
  of physical objects 61
religion 9, 29, 31, 61-3. *See also* religious belief
  analytic philosophy of 26
  basic claims of 12
  of Christianity 22
  criticism of 59-60
  encroachment 59
  and fideism 49-51
  internal practice of 63-4
  language of 49-50
  Martin Buber's concept of 68
  philosophy of 15
  picture of 4
  practice of 22, 56-9
  truth of 50
religiosity 5, 35, 36, 62, 73, 95, 119
religious belief 9, 23, 29-32, 35-8, 48-53, 58-9, 63, 68-9, 74, 88-9, 129, 171, 219 n.50
  background of 8
  common and popular type of 4
  criteria for 119
  existential function of 32
  grammar of 29, 58
  groundlessness of 53
  in immortality 94-5
  justification for 119
  and language 132
  and practice 29, 36
  propositions of 88
  thinking of 88
  Whittaker on 129-30
  Wittgensteinian account of 58
religious community 91
religious context 80
religious conviction 130
religious doctrines 87-8
religious existence, challenges and rigors of 123-4
religious form of life 5, 19, 21, 23, 40, 50, 53, 55-7, 59-60, 62, 64, 132
religious idolatry 4, 9, 16, 19, 123

religious individual 22
religious language 3, 5, 18, 20, 28–32, 37, 42, 51, 56, 62, 87, 89–90, 111, 130–1, 135
    aspects of 32
    basis of 49
    meaning of 55
    and religiosity 35
    uses of 30, 57
religious life 18, 47–8, 50–1, 62, 133–5
    acceptance 155–6
    agapeic atheism 156–8
    anecdotal agape 144–6
    atheistic theism 162–3
    and care for other 135
    love without reason 158–62
    responsibility 142–4
    self at center 146–52
    sin, separation, and acceptance 153–5
    stories of love 135–42
    theistic-atheism 162–3
religious limiting questions 30–6, 49, 56, 63, 120
    nature of 34
    and theological answers 35
    variety of 35
religious pictures 4, 31, 89–92
religious practice 4, 42, 48–51, 58
    forms of 30
    idolatry and 17–19
    religious belief and 36
    truth of 50
religious seeker 19
religious symbols 67–9
    atonement and idolatry 69–70
    "cheap grace" as idolatry 71–4
    forgiveness and belief 70–1
    temporal immortality and idolatry 74–5
religious truth 119, 132
    formulations of 174–5
renunciation 61–2, 80, 89, 93, 157–8
resurrection, death and 181
Rhees, Rush 58, 78
Rollins, Peter 18–19, 26
Rozelle-Stone, Rebecca 83, 124
Ruth, Sarah 68

Sacks, Oliver 201–2
sacred pictures 91
Sagan, Carl 170–1
salvation 19–23, 28, 160
    flip-side of 20
    and spiritual materialism 19
Santayana, George 173
Saving God (Johnston) 10, 17
Saving the Appearances (Barfield) 29
Schnur, Susan 207
Schulz, Charles 198
Schweitzer, Albert 183
Scotus, John Duns 25
Secular Age, A (Taylor) 37–8
self-awareness 146–8, 151
self-centered attitudes 22
self-centeredness 48, 190
self-deception 50, 204
selfish/selfishness 6, 12, 19–23, 47, 77, 93, 96, 146–8, 152, 159
    anti-religious 77
    as basic principle 151–2
self-prescribed therapy 193
self-reassurance 219 n.49
self-sacrificial love 43, 159
self-seeking behavior 19–20
self-transcendence 47–8, 191
self-worship 19, 39
semantic atheism 126–9
semantic domestication of God 26
semantic fideism 55–7
semantic priority 106–8, 118–19
separateness 38, 47, 153
separation
    concept of 153
    from God 155
    from ground of being 155
    from others 153–4
    from ourselves 154–5
Shakespeare, William 184
Simone Weil and Theology (Rozelle-Stone) 124
Simon, Judy 207
sin 5, 11, 14, 16, 70–2, 124
    cause of 93
    defined 156
    forgiveness of 72, 75, 88
    theological account of 153
Singer, Peter 5, 141–5, 153
skepticism 117–18
skills, knowledge and 177–8
social conventions 111–14, 119
solidarity 92–3

Solzhenitsyn, Alexsandr 209
space and time 46, 80
spiritual health 33
spirituality 68, 173, 181, 185
spiritual language 3, 20
spiritual life 19, 183
spiritual materialism 19–23, 68, 85
    aspect of 19–20
    and idolatry 20, 42
    practice of 22–3
    salvation and 19
spiritual reality 60, 91, 94, 134
spiritual way of life 18, 134
Stenger, Victor 12–13
Strangeness of the Ordinary, The (Coburn) 21
Stroll, Avrum 127
substantial property 102
substitutionary atonement 69
suffering 8, 14, 16, 20, 23, 48, 56, 68–9, 80–8, 142, 145, 147, 154, 170, 174, 180, 183, 186, 201, 210, 212–13
    alleviation of 95
    of children 87
    human 82–3, 85
supernatural entities 30, 50–1
supernatural God 11–12, 119
supernaturalism 10–11, 30
supernatural theism 11–16, 38, 69, 81
    anthropomorphic God of 39, 84
    evil and 80–2
    God of 81
    idolatry and 23–8
    requirements of 13
    uses of 16
Surviving Death (Johnston) 135, 148
Swinburne, Richard 15, 82
Systematic Theology (Tillich) 120

Tarski, Alfred 104
tattoo 65–8
    of God 66–7
Taylor, Charles 37–8
Taylor, Richard 148, 153, 162–3
temporal immortality 79–80, 93–4
    and idolatry 74–5
theistic-atheism 162–3
theodicy 82–4, 86
theological discourse 35
theological language 32, 34, 120, 130
theological quietism 43
theology 5, 22, 24, 26, 32, 42–3, 62, 93, 134
    classical 122
    historical accounts of 57
    kenotic 159–60
    of religion 13
    systematic 122
    of Weil 93
This Is Water (Wallace) 48
Tillich, Paul 5, 41, 74–5, 120–1, 153–4, 226 n.64
    Courage to Be, The 121
    Dynamics of Faith, The 155
    theological method 121–2
time, and space 46, 80
Tolstoy, Leo 5, 9, 135–40, 142
    War and Peace 133
Tractatus 39, 45, 126–8, 228 n.93
transcendence 5, 17, 24, 27, 29–63, 159–60
    concept of 29, 36
    God 38–43
    importance of 128–9
    of nature 38, 43–7
    of self 37, 47–9
    senses of 36–8
    uses of 38
transformative faith, idolatry and 74
truth 5, 10, 27, 30, 37, 59, 104, 127, 132
    claims and criteria 115
    concept of 100, 106–7
    and criteria 109–13
    deflationary theory of 104
    domain of 102
    explanation of 103
    meaning *vs.* 107–8
    predicate 102–3
    religious 119, 132
    "transparency property" of 105
    univocal concept of 224 n.5
truth fideism 57, 60–2
truth pluralism 99–101
    belief and agape 129–32
    and criteria 109–18, 129–32
    ethical atheism 123–6
    ontological atheism 120–2
    and religious criteria 118–19
    semantic atheism 126–9
    semantic priority 106–8
truth predicate 102–8
Tuchman, Barbara 177

Turner, Denys 14, 39, 42
Twain, Mark 194

univocal being 26
univocal language 26
utter mystery 60, 80, 94

Valjean, Jean 157
Varieties of Religious Experience, The (James) 43
Veto, Miklos 139

Wallace, David Foster 45–6, 48, 147–9, 151
Walsh, Sylvia 161–2
War and Peace (Tolstoy) 133
Ware, Bishop Kallistos 43
Waskow, Arthur 175
Weil, Simone 5, 18, 28, 39, 75, 77–8, 123–6, 134, 139, 159, 163, 183
  on decreation 125
  on eternal life 79
  ethical atheism 126
  theological significance of 83
  theology of 93
Wettstein, Howard 85, 96
Whittaker, John 63, 129, 132
  on religious belief 129–30

Williams, Michal 113
Winch, Peter 106
witches 169–70
With Heart and Mind (Taylor) 162–3
Wittgenstein, Ludwig 3, 5, 33, 36, 39–40, 44, 49, 56, 62–3, 90, 104, 110, 112, 115
  approach to philosophy 99
  Blue and Brown Books 113–14
  On Certainty 63–4
  complex picture theory 127
  Culture and Value 36, 63
  fideism 55
  formulation 105
  Lectures and Conversations on Aesthetics, Psychology and Religious Belief 89
  temporal immortality 79–80
  Tractatus 127
Wittgenstein's Account of Truth (Ellenbogen) 109
worship/worshippers 10, 15, 17–22, 39, 61, 88–9, 123
  and community 18, 174
  of God 42
  life and actions 18
  object of 17–18

Zande, beliefs and practices 169–70